LEGAL HISTORY STUDIES
1972

PAPERS PRESENTED TO THE LEGAL HISTORY CONFERENCE
ABERYSTWYTH, 18-21 JULY 1972

EDITED BY
DAFYDD JENKINS

UNIVERSITY OF WALES PRESS
CARDIFF
1975

© University of Wales Press and the Contributors, 1975

ISBN 0 7083 0588 1

Printed in Wales by
CSP PRINTING, ST. FAGAN'S ROAD
FAIRWATER, CARDIFF

LEGAL HISTORY STUDIES 1972

Contents

Notes on Contributors

J. H. BAKER

University Lecturer in Law and Fellow of St. Catharine's College, Cambridge

J. L. BARTON

All Souls Reader in Roman Law and Fellow of Merton College, Oxford

J. S. BECKERMAN

Assistant Professor of History, Yale University

W. H. BRYSON

Assistant Professor of Law, University of Richmond, Virginia

W. H. DUNHAM, JR

George Burton Adams Professor Emeritus of History and formerly Master of Jonathan Edwards College, Yale University

J. A. GUY

Assistant Keeper of Public Records and formerly Fellow of Selwyn College, Cambridge

G. J. HAND

Professor of Legal and Constitutional History and Dean of the Faculty of Law, University College, Dublin.

ALAN HARDING

Lecturer in Medieval History, University of Edinburgh

E. W. IVES

Senior Lecturer in History, University of Birmingham

D. E. C. YALE

Reader in English Legal History and Fellow of Christ's College, Cambridge

Preface

THE papers here published represent the proceedings of the Legal History Conference held at the invitation of this College in July 1972. Details of the programme of the Conference are given below, and the Editor (who served as chairman of the organising committee) takes this opportunity of expressing appreciation of the initiative of Dr (now Professor) Edmund Fryde, Professor Hywel Moseley, and Sir Goronwy Daniel (Principal of the College), which led to the invitation, and of the enthusiastic help of his colleagues, Mr Hugh Beale and Miss Letitia Crabb, which made his chairmanship a happy sinecure. He must also record the organisers' joy in the excellent weather, which gave members of the Conference the pleasant memory of sunny walks along the sea-front between Alexandra Hall and the Old College, instead of the penance which wind and rain might have imposed on them.

This Conference seems to have been the first specialist legal history conference held in Britain since April 1913, when the Legal History Section of the International Congress of Historical Studies met in London under the presidency of Vinogradoff, deputising for the Lord Chief Justice, Lord Alverstone. We feel a certain pride in following in such distinguished footsteps, tempered by shame at having failed to follow our predecessors' example of prompt publication: the 1913 Conference proceedings, *Essays in Legal History*, bear the date of the same year, whereas the present volume will not appear until three years after the Conference. For this delay we apologise to readers and contributors: the blame for it does not lie with the contributors.

The Editor's work has been confined to a certain tidying of the contributors' scripts, of which the main feature is an endeavour (not wholly successful) to impose consistency on the references, with a generous use of abbreviated titles in an effort to banish *op. cit.* Non-lawyers should perhaps be warned that the lawyers' pattern for reference to law reports has been applied to periodicals: this means that an Arabic numeral placed before the name (or abbreviation) of the periodical indicates the volume, an Arabic numeral after it the page of the reference. A date in *square* brackets designates a volume known by its date-reference; dates in *round* brackets are given for information. For some Selden Society publications two dates are given: the first is that of the year (or years) *for* which the volume was issued, the second that of the year *in* which it appeared.

No attempt at uniformity in spelling or punctuation has been made; nor have the papers been cast into a uniform mould. Some are printed almost exactly as delivered; others have been fairly substantially revised; Professor Bryson's is represented by the summary circulated to members of the Conference, since an expanded version would unduly anticipate the substantial volume which he is to publish. Since neither chronology nor subject seemed to suggest a natural order in which the contributions should be arranged, they have been printed in alphabetical order of their authors' surnames, in the two series of longer papers and shorter communications.

The financial help of this College and of the Catherine and Lady Grace James Foundation towards the cost of publication is very gratefully acknowledged.

University College of Wales, Aberystwyth   D.J.
14 February 1975

THE CONFERENCE PROGRAMME

Tuesday, 18 July: 8.15 p.m., Mr Barton's paper (chairman, Professor J. A. Andrews).

Wednesday, 19 July: 9.30 a.m., Mr Harding's paper (chairman, Mr C. A. F. Meekings); shorter communications by Professor Hand and Dr Ives (chairman, Mr G. D. G. Hall). 5 p.m., Professor Dunham's paper (chairman, Professor J. C. Holt), followed by a reception by the Mayor of Aberystwyth and the Conference Dinner.

Thursday, 20 July: 9.30 a.m., Dr Baker's paper (chairman, Professor A. K. R. Kiralfy); shorter communications by Professor Beckerman and Professor Bryson (chairman, Professor Margaret Hastings). 5 p.m., Mr Yale's paper (chairman, Professor T. Hywel Moseley). 8.15 p.m., Mr Guy's communication (chairman, Dr E. B. Fryde).

Friday, 21 July: 9.30 a.m., concluding general session (chairman, Professor S. F. C. Milsom).

Accommodation and meals (including the Conference Dinner, at which the speakers were Sir Ben Bowen Thomas (President of the University College of Wales, Aberystwyth) and Mr G. D. G. Hall) were at Alexandra Hall. The two evening meetings and the final session were held there; the other sessions were held in the Council Chamber in the Old College. During the afternoons, materials for Legal History from the collections of the National Library of Wales were on display in the Library's Council Chamber, and were introduced by Mr Daniel Huws of the Department of Manuscripts. Current books and microphotographic reproductions of materials on Legal History were on exhibition in the Senior Common Room in the Old College.

The Dark Age of English Legal History, 1500-1700

J. H. Baker

IF anniversaries are anything to go by, 1972 is an appropriate year in which to hold this conference of legal historians. On 20 November we remember the accession to the Throne, seven hundred years ago, of our "English Justinian"—perhaps we should say our Welsh Justinian—whose legislative achievements are central to the historical study of English law. Three centuries later, in 1572, an equally important era commenced with the admission to the Inner Temple of Edward Coke and the call to the Bar of his future rival Thomas Egerton. Another journey of three centuries transports us to 1872 and the appearance at the head of the Moral Sciences Tripos list at Cambridge of a name too well-known to us to need mention; he was about to follow Coke's path to the Inns of Court, later to return to Cambridge and lay the foundations of our science.

These three anniversaries, besides reminding us of three particularly memorable men, suggest also a few thoughts about the study of legal history. Few would contend that English legal history should follow the Roman example by ending with its Justinian, and yet it is not a grave distortion to assert that much of what happened after his death, or at least after the death of his son Edward II, has been seriously neglected by historians of the law. One reason may be that we are still, in some ways, too near the Tudors and Stuarts to appreciate fully their distance. We use, almost without question, the anachronistic word "medieval" as denoting pre-Renaissance times; when, from the modern point of view, the Renaissance period has a much better claim to be regarded as a middle age.

We are told that the Renaissance gave man an awareness of his past, and if ever the history of English legal history comes to be written the story will begin in the first Elizabethan age—the age of William Lambard, John Dodderidge, Francis Tate and Roger Owen.[1] But those first legal antiquaries were preoccupied with dark and distant problems about the origins of the common law and its Englishness: problems which they had even less hope of solving than we have. Coke's devotion to things medieval, far from being crabbed pedantry, reflected this Renaissance spirit of enquiry. But he would have had difficulty in understanding why we have come together for this conference; his beloved "antiquities"[2] were a guide not to the past but to the present. The sense of continuity which they conveyed was of rhetorical and emotional and political, rather than historical, value.

The position was much the same when Hale wrote his *History of the Common Law*. Hale was doubtless a better historian than Coke, but history for him ended in a remote past. Hale's hero was Edward I. Of the later period he had little or nothing to say by way of history. The changes that had taken place in four centuries were not so much in the law, wrote Hale, as in the conditions of society;[3] and the Year Books and Tudor reports were still sources, not of history, but of living law.

Lawyers have always been bemused by the apparent continuity of their heritage into a way of thinking which inhibits historical understanding. "Pure" historians, on the other hand, have often fled in despair from the mysteries of the law which permeates their history. The first man to overcome both difficulties to the satisfaction of both disciplines remains an inspiration to us all. But Maitland left the impression that he did not care too much for the law of the sixteenth century.[4] Perhaps his youthful distaste for the antique features of the law he had read in chambers made the more recent legal history offensive to his palate: "Who shall interest us in contingent remainders, or the Statute of Uses, while Chinese metaphysics remain unexplored?"[5] Or it may be simply that he was compelled to begin at the beginning, and was not spared to proceed further than he did. He abandoned the idea (which Pollock favoured) of carrying the *History of English Law* beyond 1272, because the source material for the later period was not yet in proper shape. The Year Books, he wrote, needed a complete and tolerable new edition, and the plea rolls were "of so unwieldy a bulk that we can hardly hope that much will ever be known about them".[6] If it was too late for Maitland's contemporaries to be early English,[7] it was yet too early for them to be Perpendicular.

Historians since Maitland have gone far towards explaining the development of Tudor and Stuart legal institutions, but the study of legal thought and jurisprudence during the same period is still in its infancy. Most of our knowledge has been derived from printed sources, many of them miserably unable to bear the responsibility. Holdsworth, who wrote more (quantitatively) than any other writer on the subject, did not fully appreciate the value of manuscripts. He did not use the plea rolls as sources of legal history. Of the unpublished sixteenth-century reports he had little to say, save his comment on a list compiled as long ago as 1834, that "doubtless a systematic search would reveal other manuscripts".[8] He seems to have been unaware of the wealth of new material these manuscripts contained, perhaps thinking that most of the texts were substantially available in print. We should not be too hard on Holdsworth for failing to see what no one of his generation could see; there was more than enough material in print for a pioneer to work on. But so long as the sources were ignored it was inevitable that legends and misinterpretations should flourish.

The sixteenth century is surely one of the most interesting and vital periods in the history of the common law. If the twelfth and thirteenth centuries saw the birth of the common law, the sixteenth century witnessed its renaissance—or at least its reformation. To what extent the common law was influenced by *the* Renaissance is a question which, for the moment, must be laid aside.[9]

But that there were great changes is manifest.[10] The land law was changed almost beyond recognition by the resuscitation for fiscal purposes of the defunct feudal system, the perfection of the common recovery and the consequent challenge to conveyancers, the effects of the agrarian revolution, and the transformation of the use. Mercantile law assumed a new importance in an expanding world. The criminal law became more efficient with the abolition of abjuration, the severe restriction of sanctuary, the harnessing of benefit of clergy to secular policy, and the improvement of pre-trial procedure. The forms of action were virtually replaced by formless actions on the case, which would later divide into a new scheme of forms of action. Old courts acquired new functions and more business. New courts rose up, and a new profession. We cannot fully understand the later common law unless we first understand this Tudor legal revolution, but we still know little about its underlying causes. The deceptive proximity of the sixteenth century (compared with the so-called middle ages), and the professional tendency to confuse law and history, easily generated assumptions that what became law must have been "right": that it was the inevitable consequence of the relentless march of progress. It is always difficult to resist the temptation merely to set out how the story unfolded itself, as if it were all preordained. The losing arguments are soon forgotten, because in law they have been shown to be false. But the rightness of a legal argument is a matter of law, not of fact; and, although the law may have been settled for four centuries, the questions of historical fact remain open. In answering these questions, we find the legal sources more rather than less helpful. In an age less tied up in precedent, Tudor lawyers (like their predecessors) were as anxious to know how a case had been presented, and why it had proceeded in a particular way, as they were to know the outcome of the argument.

Two instances involving Coke may serve to illustrate the dangers of orthodoxy. It has generally been assumed that Coke was "wrong" in his quarrel with Ellesmere's Chancery, because Ellesmere and equity were held to prevail. The victory of the Chancery was necessary, wrote Maitland, if we were to have a Court of Equity at all.[11] But in fact the dispute did not turn on the relationship between law and equity in the abstract. It concerned the finality of a judgment at law where the unsuccessful party failed to seek equitable relief before judgment was given against him. On this narrower question, all the law and much of the equity were on Coke's side. He lost for political and personal reasons.[12] It may be questioned whether his defeat was constitutional, and whether (even in the seventeenth century) the King, acting on the advice of his counsel (not of his judges), could override a decision of the Exchequer Chamber. The matter was fully re-argued in 1670 in *R.* v. *Standish*. On this occasion, Twisden J. explained:

> Ellesmere had great power, and did much prevail in his time. And the reference in 14 Jac. was made to such persons as he that desired it would have, and they were all great practisers in the Chancery (at least except Sir John Walter [who] had not the spirit of infallibility). Beside, those persons were no court. The reason Ellesmere gave, that they would not undo the judgment but only examine the corrupt conscience of the party, is an eluding of the statute.

Kelyng C. J. took the same view, but hoped they could avoid the "stirr and heat there was in Lord Coke's time". In the event Hale C. J. persuaded his brethren that the statute of praemunire was intended to restrain eccles-iastical appeals only. Hale was, of course, correct in his interpretation of fourteenth-century history and of law. But Twisden's factual explanation of the events of 1616 is very persuasive, and is far easier to reconcile to the evidence than the Bacon-Ellesmere versions of the story.[13]

The other example is provided by *Slade's Case*, in which Coke's argument prevailed and was therefore treated by later lawyers as if it had been unanswerable. *Slade's Case* became, in the textbooks of law and history, the ultimate source of numerous principles of contract and quasi-contract. The professional tradition derived almost entirely from Coke's own report of the case, which, despite its brusque treatment of Bacon's arguments on the losing side, was the only full report to be printed. But in this case the law was against Coke; and justice was probably against him also, in that wager of law occasioned less perjury than jury trials in which the parties were not competent witnesses.[14] The "victory" in this case may simply have been the result of Morley's disinclination to bring error and so give the Common Pleas judges a stronger voice. The foremost judicial opponent of the new approach, Walmsley J., complained afterwards that

> Slade and Morlye was not resolved upon argument or reasons delivered [i.e. by the judges] but, the justices being assembled, it was asked of each of what opinion he was, and thus it was ruled by the majority opinion.[15]

This was an irregular way of proceeding, a manoeuvre by Popham C. J. which his successors were to rue. Vaughan C. J. attacked the "decision" as "an illegal resolution . . . grounded upon reasons not fit for a declamation, much less for a decision of law."[16] And Hale C. J. thought it was "hardly brought in (for it was by a capitulation and agreement among the judges)," and that it had "done more hurt than ever it did or will do good."[17] In 1671 he proclaimed actions on the case to be "one of the great grievances of the nation: for, two men cannot talk together but one fellow or other, who stands in a corner, swears a promise. . . ."[18] "It were well," he concluded, "if a law were made that no promise should bind, unless there were some signal ceremony, or that wager of law did ly upon a promise. For, the common law was a wise law, that men should wage their law in debt on a contract."[19] These observations escaped the press, but they were almost certainly among the principal motive forces behind the Statute of Frauds and Perjuries 1677, which for certain classes of debt required written evidence.

In both these instances the conventional view became unacceptable after a little delving into unfamiliar, unpublished legal sources. One cannot work for long on these sources without being almost helplessly conscious of the vast store of unworked material which has survived. It is impossible to spend an afternoon with a pile of manuscript law reports without finding something new, some detail perhaps which will not fit into the textbook stories, or which suggests a new and unforeseen story of its own. Before saying any more about this material, a little space may be devoted to the difficulties of research even in the printed books of the period.

THE PRINTED LAW BOOKS

THE first defect in our knowledge of the printed law books—and it is hardly a trifling defect—is that we know very little about the law printers and their work. The monopoly of printing common law books, first granted to Richard Tottell in 1556,[20] was the subject of almost continuous Chancery litigation with the London stationers for well over a century. The public records contain, in consequence, several bundles of papers from which the business practices of these printers may in part be reconstructed and valuable information unearthed concerning the mechanics of law publishing and the solus agreements by which the printers were financed after 1669.[21] Of the craftsmanship of these men we know far less than advances in bibliographical and typographical science have qualified us to discover, though Mr Howard J. Graham has made a useful start on the work of the earlier law printers. *Beale* has been a most useful work of reference, but it contains numerous errors and quite a few omissions, and the way is wide open for a new edition by professional bibliographers. For the period after 1600 we do not even have a *Beale*.

The second defect is that little work has been done to discover the extent and manner of the use of printed law books before, say, 1700. If, as will be suggested later, many printed law books are of slight value as evidence of the facts recorded in them, their principal value to the legal historian is that they show what lawyers read and may therefore reveal the source of certain ideas. But this kind of information is not fully within reach until research tells us about lawyers' libraries, their contents, and the use made of them. Very few lawyers' libraries of early date have been reconstructed, and some of those which have are exceptional in size or character.[22] After 1680 there are numerous printed catalogues of law libraries, drawn up by auctioneers;[23] before that date search must be made in wills and inventories and manuscript catalogues. The labour would probably be worth while. The sale catalogues are often marked with prices, and the fluctuation in price tells a great deal about the use made of law books. (Thus, the sale in 1797 of a *Statham* for four shillings and a set of *Term Reports* for seven guineas, in the same sale,[24] tells its own story about the decline in the study of Year Books and old abridgments.) Then there is the evidence of the books themselves, which contain much real evidence about their owners. Dr Knafla has pioneered the study of manuscript marginalia in printed law books in an examination of some of Egerton's books preserved in the Henry E. Huntington Library;[25] his results suggest there may be more to be learned from similar studies.

Textual Problems

(i) *Works prepared for the press by their authors*

It might be thought that works edited by their authors would present few, if any, textual difficulties, since what we read is presumably what the author wished us to read. But, while the text may be taken as a faithful representation of the author's personal opinions, and whether or not it was later accepted as an authoritative source of *law*, it is not necessarily to be relied on for any statements of *fact* it contains. The evidence may be hearsay. At least an effort should be made to ascertain the date, purpose, and method of composition, the sources drawn upon by the author, and the extent to which he was in a position to know the truth. It may be possible to find answers to such questions if the author left his notes or his manuscript sources behind. Coke's notebooks, for instance, enable some conclusions to be drawn concerning the sources of his *Reports* and the way in which they were compiled.[26] The solution is more difficult where the author did not leave such obvious clues, but hidden clues are often waiting to be uncovered. Thus, Mr Graham has shown how important facts relating to the composition of Fitzherbert's *Graunde Abridgement* could be deduced from a study of the almost contemporary *Tabula* and the *Liber Assisarum*.[27] Even if one accepts statements about authorship on trust from title-pages, the number of major law books prepared for the press by their authors before 1700 is small. We must exclude *Littleton's Tenures, Brooke's Abridgement*, and Coke's last three *Institutes*; all except possibly one Year Book;[28] and most of the later reports. Plowden's *Commentaries* are the only reports known to have been published in print by their author in the sixteenth century. And, apart from Coke, only three other reporters seem to have edited their own reports for publication before 1660: John Clayton, author of the almost forgotten small volume of cases decided at York (1651), Edward Bulstrode (1657–9), and William Style (1658).

(ii) *Works published posthumously*

When examining a work printed after its author's death there is obviously a need for more care in establishing the correctness of the text. In many cases the exemplar used will have been one which the author would not have wished to be published, and the printer will not normally have improved it. It will be remembered that the appearance in print (in 1585) of Dyer's notes, in their imperfect state, was an event which so alarmed Coke that it persuaded him to prepare his own reports for the press while he was alive.[29] Moreover, many of the collections ascribed to eminent men were either not their work at all or were crude notes collected in their youth or for transient purposes, and found among their papers after their death. *Rolle's Abridgment* was castigated by contemporaries as "nothing but a collection of year-books and little things noted when he made his common place book".[30] Vaughan C. J. said

> he wished it had never bin printed, for there are so many contradicting judgments in it that it makes the law ridiculous, and 'twas pitty there was not more paines taken with it before it was printed, to expung[e] those judgments which were not law, or to reconcile 'em to such as were law.[31]

Similar criticisms were made of many of the volumes of reports which appeared during the printing rush of the Interregnum, when the law printers' monopoly was in de facto abeyance. As early as 1653, in the preface to *Gouldsborough's Reports*, W. S[tyle?] alluded to the "trick, played by the subtle Gamesters of this serpentine age" of fathering spurious offspring upon dead men, and assured the reader that the present reports were under the author's hand and were such as "were he living he would not blush to own". Bulstrode and Grimstone spared no words in castigating the "flying reports" which had "surreptitiously crept forth",[32] and Style said the press had brought forth many births, but there was not a father alive to own many of them.[33] Francis North, later Chief Justice of the Common Pleas, said of this period:

> there was no copy so absurd but somebody would print it. Imperfect transcripts came out under great names that were a reproach to them; and some were so unskilfully printed that they could hardly be made use of.[34]

Some of these volumes were merely collections from other sources, or common-place books. Thus, *Noy's Reports* were identified by Twisden J. as a copy of an abridgment of the original reports of Noy made by Serjeant Evan Size (or Seys) when he was a student.[35] The practice of collecting cases explains why some cases verbally identical will be found in two or even three different books. One case, for example, appears three times in exactly the same words in Leonard's collections alone.[36] Typically the reports are greatly abridged, or are mere notes and scraps, and represent the lowest standard of this kind of material.

Rarely do we have the author's autograph copy for comparison. Dyer's own manuscript is said to have belonged to Coke,[37] but it is now lost. Croke's autograph notebooks of reports have survived in the Earl of Verulam's library, formerly at Gorhambury.[38] The judge's "small and close" hand justified their description by his son-in-law and editor Sir Harbottle Grimstone as "*folia sybillina*, as difficult as excellent."[39] There are other manuscripts which are said to collate exactly with parts of Croke, which invites the question whether Croke or his representatives lent out the notebooks to be copied, or whether Croke's collection is itself second-hand.

Since the printers often worked from inferior copies it is often possible to construct a better text from manuscripts. In the case of the more dubious texts, it is common to find different parts in different collections and apparently by different hands, thereby raising textual problems of frightening complexity. It seems to have been rare for the law printers of later times to engage professional help in editing the manuscripts, although during the Interregnum the necessity of having texts translated from law French into English at least compelled someone familiar with the law to consider what, if anything, the text meant. Perhaps we should be grateful that the texts were not corrupted still further by editors. But there were exceptions which warn us to be on our guard. A striking early example is afforded by Redman's masterpiece, his edition of the *Quadragesimus* or Year Book of 40 Edward III. This not only shows signs of textual comparison, but contains numerous and sometimes copious comments on the cases, in addition to mere cross-references.[40] That these interpolations belong to the sixteenth rather than the fourteenth century was overlooked even by Coke, who quoted one of them as an example of the mode of citing cases in the time of Edward III.[41] Redman's enterprising experiment is unique among the Year Books; perhaps it failed because readers preferred to make their own comments. Nevertheless, it shows how the printed word may deceive.

SAVE for a few works of outstanding merit and timeless fame, the only claim which the printed law books can make to our particular attention arises from the incidental distinction of their having been printed. Publication obviously increased their importance as sources of law in later ages. But it is not a very relevant factor in assessing their evidential value, and might be held against the bulk of them, were we to heed the unanimous opinion of those seventeenth-century lawyers who knew good from bad. The printed books cannot, in any case, lay claim to our exclusive attention. Compared with the mass of unpublished material which has been preserved in our older libraries, or sold to our wealthier neighbours, the printed matter is but a meagre and not very representative selection from the treasures which remain. These treasures cannot, like Tutankhamen's tomb, be laid open in a momentary flash of discovery; but, with so many of the doors still sealed, one can soon experience some of the excitement of the explorer at the prospect of what may be found in an unopened book. And, as Maitland said of the public records, the territory to be explored is "free to all, like the air and the sunlight".[42]

There are many more possibilities than it is feasible to indicate in a short space; only the three major classes of manuscript will therefore be discussed.

1. *Plea rolls*

We know something of the importance of the later common law records through the labours of Professors Kiralfy and Milsom.[43] They are the key to the development of the forms of action and to their replacement by the infinitely variable actions on the case, and to the forms of pleading. But our whetted appetite soon becomes nagging starvation when we contemplate the million or so membranes occupied by the records of the two principal common law courts between 1500 and 1650. How can anyone enter the Public Record Office with hope in his heart when to search the rolls of the Common Law courts for one year involves scanning up to 10,000 long skins of parchment, closely written on both sides? It would be profitable to know how Coke acquired his mastery of the forbidding rolls of Elizabeth and 1–14 James I, in spite of his admission that the judicial records (unlike the reports) were *thesauri absconditi*.[44] The one man who might have helped us, as he probably helped Coke, has long since passed away and taken his secrets with him. Richard Brownlow (d. 1638), prothonotary of the Common Pleas for forty-six years, knew more about these records than perhaps anyone ever will again; but the wise old man who looks down on us from his memorial in Belton Church is as silent as the Sphinx.

B

The collections of entries made by the prothonotaries and others provide some short-cuts, but they were not written for the ease of historians and they pose more questions than they resolve. A new collection, based on an original study of the plea rolls with the problems of legal history in mind, is an indispensable preliminary to a complete history of sixteenth-century law. It would demand the greater part of a man's academic career, assuming that is is within one man's competence at all. The earlier King's Bench rolls might be the easiest to start with, perhaps those of Henry VII and Henry VIII.[45] Until the latter part of Henry VIII's reign the bundles of rolls rarely contain more than a hundred membranes and so they are relatively simple to peruse. This was the period of greatest innovation, and the King's Bench is thought to have led the way. The results of such a study, however, would be inconclusive until they could be compared with the results of a parallel review of the cumbersome *De Banco* rolls.[46]

2. *Readings and Moots*

Professor Thorne's study of the fifteenth-century readings[47] has taught us all what valuable sources of information they are. There is reason to think that the later readings are no less valuable, although they have been almost totally overlooked by modern scholars.[48] Coke, it is true, decried the later readings as "liker rather to riddles than lectures, which when they are opened they vanish away like smoake".[49] No doubt his strictures are applicable to some of the weaker perfomances, but they could not fairly be used to describe his own readings, or those of comparable merit. Of the thousand or more readings given between 1500 and 1700,[50] if only one quarter merited our notice there would be enough material for countless books and theses. Of course, not all have survived, and we may be fortunate if we can salvage more than one-fifth of the total. Yet, in the nature of things, many of those which have survived are those which someone thought to be worth preserving.

The readings of Henry VII's and Henry VIII's time provide us, *inter alia*, with vital information relating to the history of criminal law and procedure; they desperately need publication. The later readings were normally delivered on the "modern" statutes: that is, the statutes passed after the time of Edward I. Many were given on the legislation of Henry VIII. The most obviously interesting are the lectures on uses, among which may be noticed those of Edmund Knightley (1523) and Thomas Audley (1526) on the statute of Henry VII, and of John Brograve (1576), Richard Shuttleworth (1583), Francis Bacon (1588), Edward Coke (1592), Thomas Richardson (1613), Edward Estcourt (1618), Robert Tanfield (1623), and Arthur Tourneur (1633). Of similar interest are the lectures on wills, which include those of James Dyer (1552), Ambrose Gilbert (1556), Robert Nowell

(1561), John Popham (1568), Robert Gardiner (1575), Henry Blanchard (1581), John Shurley (1588), Hugh Hare (1591), Augustine Nicholls (1602), and Henry Sherfield (1623). Another popular statute was the 32 Hen.VIII, c.28, of leases, which was chosen by William Symmonds (1549), John Kitchin (1562), Edward Fenner (1576), Thomas Egerton (1582), Thomas Wentworth (1611), Richard Reynell (1614), John Hutchins (1634), and William le Hunt (1667). That is a very random selection of lectures on but three statutes; but it indicates the wealth of almost unknown[51] legal literature which awaits investigation.

The reports of moots are valuable not as legal decisions but as an indication of the educational background of a Tudor lawyer. Many of the points argued are not to be found answered in Littleton or the Year Books, because the academic coverage was necessarily more comprehensive than that provided by the accidents of litigation and more modern than that provided by the old books. Yet all this learning, some of which may have been almost axiomatic to anyone who had been through the course, is hidden away in unpublished (and virtually unread) notebooks. None of these moots have been printed since 1602.[52] The material is less plentiful than the readings, and it dies out rather earlier. Most of the material for Henry VIII's reign is of Gray's Inn provenance.[53]

3. *Reports of cases*

More important even than the two preceding classes of manuscript are the unprinted reports. Much of their importance is simply a matter of quantity. For every printed volume of cases there are perhaps half a dozen or a dozen unpublished volumes which provide reports of cases—sometimes of whole terms—not in print, and of otherwise unknown speeches and observations in cases which were printed from inferior texts.

(i) *1500–1590*

The greater part of the sixteenth century is poorly served by printed reports. Only seven years of Henry VIII were printed as "Year Books", to which "Keilwey" added another ten; without counting missing terms in these seventeen years, this leaves more than half the years of Henry VIII's reign without reports in Year Book form. A few more cases are to be found in Dyer, which begins in earnest in 28 Hen.VIII. To these must be added a group of about fifty notes in abridged form which are usually associated with the name of Serjeant Bendlowes, a few of which have also strayed into *Anderson* and *Moore*.

There is, strangely enough, only one known manuscript corresponding to any of the printed Year Books of Henry VIII, and it is probably misleading to apply the term "Year Books" to any of the other sixteenth-century manuscripts.[54] Neither is there any trace of the original Keilwey manuscript from which John Croke published the reports of 1–3, 5–10, 21 Henry VIII in 1602.[55] Mr Simpson has identified the collection from which these reports were taken as that known in the sixteenth century as "Carrell's Reports".[56] Carrell's collection certainly contained much that is not in the 1602 volume;[57] and it continued until at least 27 Hen.VIII,[58] by which time Serjeant Carrell was dead. Some of the later reports seem to be by the serjeant's son, John Carrell, Attorney of the Duchy of Lancaster;[59] but it is possible that the serjeant wrote the earlier part.[60] Fortunately there are some surviving copies of extracts from Carrell's collection;[61] these ought to be published without delay to supplement the printed reports. A few of the Henry VII cases were printed in the Year Books of that reign.

These reports are, however, by no means the only reports of Henry VIII's reign. At least four other series were used in compiling a volume which formerly belonged to Sir Christopher Yelverton and is now MS.Hargrave 388 in the British Museum. The principal source has been identified both from internal and external[62] evidence as the reports of Sir John Spelman, justice of the King's Bench. Spelman's autograph book was handed down in the family at least until the time of Sir Clement Spelman (d.1679),[63] and it was known to Bishop Burnet; but its subsequent fate is unknown. Study of the Yelverton copy shows that the original text must have been arranged alphabetically and not chronologically, though the copyist made things difficult for later generations by rearranging part of the material (presumably so much as Spelman had dated) in chronological order to give the series a more conventional appearance. It is not impossible to reconstruct a substantial part of the original work from this mangled and inaccurate version. The importance of the collection has been demonstrated by Mr Simpson,[64] and it merits publication.[65]

The scribe of MS.Harg.388 also inserted in his collection a few cases (14–26 Henry VIII) from a source identified as "Pollarde", reports possibly by the John Pollard who became a serjeant in 1547. They cannot be the work of Sir Lewis Pollard, the judge, who died in 1526. They are poorer in quality than Spelman's but were arranged in similar fashion.

A third collection used by the same scribe contains Somerset and Gray's Inn material, and may be identified as the work of Serjeant Roger Yorke. Three other copies of these reports are known.[66] They seem to be neither chronologically nor alphabetically arranged, but the cases are grouped under random subject headings.

There is yet a fourth collection copied into the Yelverton manuscript, of which other copies are known; as yet it is not possible to identify the author.[67]

Perhaps of the same type was the volume sold in Umfreville's sale of 1758 as "Judge Elliot's common place, temp.Hen.VIII."[68]

One example of the new method found its way into print: the new cases added by Robert Brooke in his *Graunde Abridgment*. The intention, apparently, was that new case law should be recorded in such a way as to augment the abridgments rather than the Year Books, and these alphabetical collections indicate a brief triumph of the abridgment over the chronological register as the most convenient way of storing law. The new method did not survive, however, and before the end of the century lawyers had gone to the trouble of rearranging *Spelman* and *Pollarde*, just as some lawyers distilled cases from the printed abridgments to produce Year Books in miniature.

The next batch of reports carries us from the end of Henry VIII's reign through the much shorter reigns of Edward VI and Philip and Mary, into the reign of Elizabeth. This period is well served by *Plowden* and *Dyer*, but the former was limited to exceptionally full reports of a few select leading cases argued upon demurrer or special verdict, and does not present a typical picture of litigation during this period. The unpublished store does not compare well in quantity with these two great works, since it is characterised by the note form. These reports, which usually begin "*Nota que* . . .", make no pretence of recording legal arguments; they simply note resolutions or dicta in summary form. Two series, however, deserve special mention and ought to be considered for publication. One contains, apparently, the residue of Dyer's collections which were not printed; it will be recalled that Dyer did not himself select the cases for the press, and therefore it is arguable that everything he left deserves attention. (Some limited use of them was made by Mr Vaillant in his edition of *Dyer*.) Certainly the contents of the surviving copies make rewarding reading, part of them providing a unique record of the work of a mid-sixteenth-century circuit judge.[69]

The other important collections for the middle of the century are those attributed to William Dalison, justice of the Queen's Bench for three years from 1556 to 1559. One of these collections seems to have survived in only one copy, which was made by William Lambard in 1569.[70] It contains good reports of cases from 6 Edw.VI to the end of Philip and Mary, including some most useful Serjeants' Inn discussions on criminal law. Lambard occasionally cited these reports in his own printed works, and his identification is entitled to some weight since he was related by marriage to the Dalisons.[71] The second series circulated far more widely, and its attribution to Dalison is less certain. The many variant copies are distinguishable by the fact that they all begin in Michaelmas Term 38 Hen.VIII (1546), the last term of that King. Some versions are associated with Dalison's name, others with the name of Richard Harpur, Justice of the Queen's Bench 1567–1576/77; and several continue beyond the lifetime of both. Dr Abbott has tentatively suggested that Harpur was the author, and that the association with Dalison is false.[72] Although it may be rash to challenge this thesis before it has been fully developed in print, the opposite conclusion seems at least tenable. The confusion is all a result of the practice of "collecting" cases as a preliminary to beginning a new series of reports. Many of the early Elizabethan reports began with a selection of abridged cases from the collection which starts in 38 Hen.VIII; these abridged or selected cases must be further from the original reports than the fuller versions. Three copies of fuller versions have been inspected. They are far from being identical; but one of them is bound as *Dalison's Reports*,[73] and another is stated to have been copied in 1583 from the reports of Justice Dalison.[74] Of the multitude of abridged and paraphrased versions, some are attributed to Dalison;[75] some to Harpur;[76] and some to others.[77] There are even abridged versions of Harpur.[78] Since Dalison died in 1559, and Harpur not until 1577, it is more likely that the latter abridged the former than vice versa. There is, of course, the difficulty that the Lambard text overlaps in date with this series and has a different content, and so it may be wrong to associate Dalison with the second series at all. Whatever the answer may be, these series are well worth publication even if they are not up to the standard of Dyer and Plowden.

By the time of Elizabeth I many, if not most, of the judges were keeping reports of some kind. No doubt most of them were intended for private reference only, and it is only fair to give the authors due allowance for this; but it is also wholly proper that we should delve into them and concern ourselves with what judges put into their private notes. Most of the notes are lost; we know of the former existence of reports by Wray C. J., Peryam C. B., Wyndham J., Manwood C. B., and others. Of the survivors, some were printed in the following century (for instance, *Anderson*), and some were never printed (for instance, *Harpur* and *Clench*). It is impossible in a short compass to begin to describe all the other series written by serjeants, readers, barristers, and young students.

(ii) *1590–1640*

In the fascinating half-century between 1590 and the Civil War, when litigation reached a peak and the finishing touches were made to the new jurisprudence, law reporting became a routine occupation for keen young lawyers and part of the way of life of some of their elders. There are too many series to describe or evaluate here, but it might be helpful to attempt to identify the main characteristics of the different kinds of report which may be encountered.

(a) *Notes and brief reports*

A majority, or at least a substantial minority, of the reporters in this period continued the tradition of taking what are better described as notes of cases than reports. This was probably all that the average student desired to have or was prepared to produce. The notes were sometimes derived from a wide variety of sources, but only rarely does the writer oblige us by specifying them. It would be incorrect to assume that such notes were necessarily scribbled down by someone sitting in court. Undoubtedly there were facilities for writing,[79] but most of the crowd of lawyers at the bar were unable to sit down, let alone write continuously, and would have had to carry away a general impression of what had happened for entry into their notebooks later in the day. We ought not even to assume that the writer was an eyewitness. Often he was noting what a friend had told him, or what was going round the inns, or was simply copying or abridging what somebody else had written down (sometimes years before the copy was made). For all their imperfections, these notes are still useful provided they are not used in isolation. They show what ordinary lawyers felt to be the kernel of a case—what they regarded as worth using again—and they may occasionally supply the best evidence of something quite significant which the loss of better texts has otherwise obscured. It would be pointless to try to draw a line between a note and a report, though most of the printed "reports" of this period (including *Croke*) could best be classified as notes. Obviously notebooks kept by judges or senior practitioners, such as Coke, Croke, Hyde, and Fleming, command particular notice; and these better writers often expand into the style of a reporter when the need arises. Coke's extensive notebooks provide perfect examples of the whole range of reports from brief notes, some attributable to hearsay, to fully minuted discussions.

(b) *Minute record of arguments*

At least two extant series of King's Bench reports preserve a uniformly detailed and minute account of what must have been virtually all the business of moment transacted at the bar of the King's Bench during the period covered. Neither of them were published, perhaps because they were too bulky, and they are both anonymous.

The first extends from Michaelmas Term 1598 to Hilary Term 1604. In the most complete copy, which belonged to St. John C. J. in the seventeenth century,[80] these five years occupy 1,390 neat and closely written pages. This seems to be a professional copy by a law stationer, and other partial copies are known to exist.[81] It gives by far the fullest and most obviously reliable accounts of the cases during this period, including *Slade's Case* and the *Case of Monopolies*, and the reports are preferable to Coke's as factual records of what was spoken in court.[82]

The second series extends from Easter Term 1629 to Easter Term 1638. Two full copies have been seen. In the Cambridge University Library copy the series fills two large volumes containing between them 2,392 pages.[83] They are written in a large scrivener's hand, and have a full index. The other full copy, in the Hardwicke collection, is closely written and covers 968 pages.[84] Other partial copies are known.[85] The quality is similar to the earlier series, though sometimes the note form is resorted to. Occasionally the writer acknowledged that reports were based on hearsay; his chief informants being "Mr Heath" (probably Edward Heath, of the Inner Temple), "Mr Ellis" (probably William Ellis of Gray's Inn), and "T.H." or "Thomas Hard[re]s" (of Gray's Inn). These relate to courts which the writer did not attend, and the fact that he notes the source suggests that they are exceptional. The Exchequer reports related by Hardres show that this reporter had attended in that court (if only briefly) well before his printed series begins.[86]

The style of these two series is reminiscent of the Year Books, in so far as the arguments are treated as being instructive in themselves and worth recording in verbatim form even where they were not followed immediately by judgment. The wealth of detail shows that the reporter must have taken full notes in court; no one could have committed so much material, complete with references, to memory. The author of the second collection indicates as much when he says of a case heard in 1635, that he would make a summary report (although the case was well argued) because *"ieo ne la poy escrier pur le malvesity de mon penne"*.[87] This circumstance poses two or three questions.

Firstly, one would like to know whether either of these reporters had recourse to the novel art of stenography. The art had been popularised by John Willis, whose manual had apparently passed through ten editions between 1602 and 1632.[88] Similar techniques had been available even at the date of the earlier series, for in 1588 Dr Timothy Bright had published his rare treatise on *Characterie* to enable his readers to "write orations of publike actions of speech . . . verbatim." This had been followed in 1590 by Peter Bales' textbook, in which he wrote that "Brachygraphy, or the art of writing as fast as a man speaketh tractably . . . is in effect very easy."[89] It is not yet possible to demonstrate that any of these systems were used by lawyers before the Restoration period, but the possibility cannot be dismissed. Whether or not this was so, the text which remains cannot be verbatim because it is in law French, and the actual words have probably been redrawn in the traditional phraseology of the reports. By 1700 over twenty authors had written manuals of short-writing and the technique was widely practised;[90] Sir George Treby wrote stenographical memoranda in his reports, and other legal notes in such form are known.[91]

The second question is whether the writers enjoyed any special privilege of sitting within the bar of the King's Bench, so that they could write at the table. There were no seats outside the bar, though it may have been possible to write in the gallery. If the writers did have special privileges, they were either clerks or officers of the court, or persons recognised and encouraged by the court as reporters. This brings us to the more important question whether any of the reports in this period were in any sense official.

(c) *The official reporters*

The two series just mentioned might be thought to provide in themselves a good prima facie case for supposing the existence of official reporters in the King's Bench. Whether or not the reporter had publication in mind, the reports certainly were widely circulated within a short time of their publication. Is there any evidence to corroborate such a supposition?

It is well-known that Bacon persuaded James I in 1617 to appoint two official law reporters at a stipend of £100.[92] The writs of appointment provided, most significantly, that the reporters should be allocated convenient seats in court. Turner discovered that the two first appointees, Edward Writington and Thomas Hetley of Gray's Inn, actually began work sitting in Chancery at the feet of Lord Keeper Bacon, and were still in receipt of their salaries in 1619.[93] Moreover, in one of the accounts of the general call of serjeants which was held in October 1623, Mr Serjeant-elect Hetley is described as "*un des reporters del ley*",[94] which suggests that he had continued in that capacity until 1623 at least. The fruits of his labour, however, are lost. There is, of course, a series of reports from 3–7 Charles I which was printed in 1657 with Serjeant Hetley's name on the title-page and the statement that he was appointed by the King and the Judges for one of the Reporters of the Law. But there are no known reports from 1617 to 1623 bearing Hetley's name. Even the printed series is probably not by Hetley, but by Humphrey Mackworth;[95] the statements on the title-page were bookseller's puffs. Some of the same reports are also to be found in "*Littleton*", which seem to be no more the work of the future Lord Keeper than of the official reporter.[96] No reports known to be by Writington have survived either.[97]

It is perfectly clear that neither Hetley nor Writington was responsible for the series from 1629 to 1638 with which this discussion began. Hetley died in 1637, and the anonymous author revealed himself as a member of the Inner Temple when he recorded the elevation of "*Mr Gardiner de nostre meason*" to the Recordership of London.[98] The only further obvious clues to authorship which this reporter left are that his father died in or immediately before Michaelmas Term 1635,[99] and that he regarded Viscount Savage (d.1635) as his "treshonorable amie".[100] Whether he was in any way Hetley's successor can only be proved if some unknown record comes to light; but there are no known texts bearing the judicial fiat contemplated by the Baconian scheme.

(d) *Verbatim drafts of speeches*

The fourth type of "report" does not belong to the same class as those just described and is perhaps not properly so described. A few examples may be found of copies of single speeches, written (and often signed) by the counsel who delivered them, in English, either to assist themselves in court or to preserve their wit and learning for future reference. The phenomenon seems to have been confined to the later years of Elizabeth I and the reign of James I. Coke's report of *Shelley's Case*, in its original state before the publication of the first part of the *Reports* in 1600, was in this form. It was primarily a polished account of Coke's own speech, with a signed dedication to Lord Buckhurst, and was copied and distributed widely in the profession.[101] Other examples of the same species are Dodderidge's argument in *Slade's Case* (1598),[102] Bacon's argument in *Lord Zouch's Case* (1603),[103] Fuller's argument in the *Case of Monopolies* (1602),[104] Yelverton's argument in *Zangis* v. *Whiskeard*,[105] and Davenport's argument in *Shuttleworth* v. *Bolton*.[106]

These oddities show us precisely how lawyers phrased their arguments in the vernacular. The actual performances may not have been equal to the eloquence of these written drafts; indeed, some maintained that nothing in Coke's report of his argument in *Shelley's Case* had been spoken in open court.[107] Perhaps they indicated what the speaker had wanted to say, rather than what he did say, in the manner of those ancient historians who reported not what great men said but what they ought to have said, or might have said if they had been better prepared. Nevertheless, we derive from these texts a clearer notion of what a legal argument sounded like than we can guess from the convenient stereotyped and inanimate law-French phrases of the conventional reporter.

(iii) *1640–1700*

The last division of the period under review has been better served by modern scholarship in so far as a collection of reports from this period has been published this century. Mr D. E. C. Yale's edition of Lord Nottingham's *Case Book*[108] is the only volume of reports between the Year Books and 1700 to have been edited and published in the present century. For the last edition of a collection of seventeenth-century common law reports, we have to go back as far as 1823, when Saxe Bannister published a selection of the judgments of Sir Orlando Bridgman. Needless to say, the manuscript material has not yet been exhausted.

The decade of the Civil War is poorly served by reports, probably because the work of the courts dwindled and the Inns of Court all but closed down. March's *New Reports* end in Trinity Term 1642, and *Style* and *Aleyn* both begin again in 1646. It is doubtful whether much of the gap can be filled from unprinted sources. Rolle reported cases from the 1640s and inserted them in his *Abridgment*. Another good source is Hargrave MS. 42, described by Umfreville (a former owner) as "very judiciously and carefully taken"; it extends from 1639 to 1652, with a gap between Trinity Term 1642 and Hilary Term 1646. The reporter noted the trial and execution of Charles I without comment, but betrayed royalist (or at least conservative) sentiments by continuing to date his reports by the regnal years of Charles II. The author may be identified with reasonable confidence as Thomas Twisden of the Inner Temple, later a judge.[109]

During the Interregnum there are several good series of reports to supplement *Style*, *Aleyn* and *Hardres*. Thomas Cory, Chief Prothonotary of the Common Pleas, filled a substantial volume with reports written in a peculiar crabbed hand which only a prothonotary could have developed, and which requires immense patience to decipher.[110] Francis North also took reports during this period,[111] according to a system of censorship which Roger North disclosed in the original draft of his *Life of Lord Keeper Guildford*, but which he evidently thought it politic to omit from the printed version:

> I have heard him say, that if the most stupid judge, such as Archer, said anything that closed with his reason, he noted it, and if the most accute judge said what he in his own reason did not approve, he took no notice of it. And if a serjeant or other councel said that was notable and new to him, he set it down.[112]

The quality of reporting in the Restoration period was not generally good, but nevertheless the best reports are still unpublished. Two series deserve special mention, as they were written in some detail by future chief justices and are full of interesting memoranda about events in the legal world. One is the work of George Treby between 1667 and 1672, which fills two folio volumes of 782 pages, now in the Middle Temple Library. Treby is mainly remembered for his learned annotations to *Dyer*—including the famous "brickbat" case—which betoken a close study of manuscript reports and readings, and which contain the only printed specimens of several forgotten collections. His own reports, which have been referred to once or twice above, add greatly to his credit. The other noteworthy series is the work of Edward Ward, and is in two parts. The first part consists of two volumes of reports from 1660 to 1678, and the second of five notebooks of cases from 1673 to 1697. They are all in Lincoln's Inn Library.[113] In the same collection is a third set of notebooks

(1674–1714), some of which contain Ward's judicial notes as Chief Baron of the Exchequer.[114] These are amongst the earliest examples of a class of record which seems never to have been used by legal historians: the judge's notebook. Several have been preserved from the period 1700–1875. Although they might be regarded as having a semi-official character, since they supplement the record with notes of evidence and arguments, they were never regarded as public records and they remained in private ownership. Amongst the examples noticed (though outside our period) may be mentioned those of Dudley Ryder,[115] Nathaniel Gundry,[116] Thomas Burnet,[117] Lord Hardwicke,[118] Thomas Denison,[119] Martin Wright,[120] Lord Denman,[121] Sir Cresswell Cresswell,[122] J. F. Pollock,[123] T. N. Talfourd,[124] Samuel Martin,[125] and J. S. Keating.[126]

There would be little point in merely listing all the unprinted reports from the period 1660–1700, and this brief selection may be brought to an end with a note on Lord Raymond. The reports published under his name mark the transition from the generally poor seventeenth-century reports to the modern methods of reporting which were perfected in the eighteenth century. The reports were not printed until 1743, and the title was "Reports of Cases taken *and collected* by Lord Raymond." It is not generally realised that even such an authoritative series as this is of dubious authorship. The first volume is full of reports communicated by others: *ex relatione* Place, Nott, Mather, Daly, Salkeld, Jacob, Shelley, Northey, Lutwyche, Cheshyre, Thornhill, Peere Williams, Bury and Pengelly.[127] Many of these were reporters in their own right, and the cases in Lord Raymond really come from these other series. Worse still, surviving manuscripts suggest that quite a number of the better reports, including *Ashby* v. *White* itself, were written not by Lord Raymond (whose contributions are marked "R.R.") but by Serjeant (later Chief Baron) Pengelly.[128]

THE STUDY OF LEGAL MANUSCRIPTS

IT is easier to extol the wonders of our manuscript heritage than it is to begin to indicate how one can go about rescuing it from oblivion. The task certainly requires more trained scholars than are at present engaged upon it. Yet the potential recruit is easily discouraged. He has virtually no bibliographies, glossaries, or palaeographical guides to help him find and read his material. He must learn the language and palaeography himself by slow and painful perseverance. The challenge of deciphering texts written in an unfamiliar tongue, abbreviated almost beyond recognition, and disguised in hands not illustrated in any of the textbooks on Tudor or Stuart handwriting—and often not intended to be read by anyone but the writer— is more likely to deter than to stimulate those to whom it is presented.

The first requirement, if further work in this field is to be undertaken on anything like an encouraging scale, is a book or booklet devoted to the problems of reading later legal texts. Students of the public records are well catered for; Latin abbreviations and the set hands of the courts and official departments are comparatively easy to conquer with the printed aids. What is now urgently needed is a glossary of later law-French, with some guidance as to the ways in which it was contracted in writing, and a collection of facsimiles of specimen private law-hands of the later period.

The second requirement is a union catalogue of legal manuscripts, or at least further work towards adequately listing and cataloguing all collections of such material. The old catalogues of the collections in the British Museum, the university and college libraries, and Lincoln's Inn library, will not suffice for this purpose. In the Harleian Catalogue, for instance, a Year Book may be missed under a description such as "Adversaria Juridica", or Sir Edward Coke's autograph notebook passed over as "precedents and cases in law." Some collections are not catalogued in print at all: for instance the immensely important Ellesmere collection in the Henry E. Huntington Library, San Marino.[129] This conference brought to the writer's attention an interesting small collection of legal manuscripts in the Wynnstay MSS. at the National Library of Wales. The publication (since this paper was delivered) of a detailed catalogue of the manuscripts in the Inner Temple Library, compiled by the late Dr Conway Davies, is most encouraging. It is much to be wished that other institutions will be spurred to follow this example.

A third difficulty arises from the scattering of the material. Originally most of it was in London, but then it was not generally accessible because it belonged to numerous private owners. The great collectors of the seventeenth to the nineteenth centuries deserve our eternal gratitude for accumulating many of these smaller collections at a time when their contents were little valued. The libraries of Maynard, Hale, Glynne, Bishop Moore, Hardwicke, and Hargrave, are still the nucleus of all the legal manuscripts in public collections in England. Unfortunately, other large collections have themselves been dispersed. Francis Tate (d.1616), one of the earliest collectors, owned a library which rivalled that of his friend Robert Cotton (now in the British Museum). It was mainly composed, as far as we can tell, of medieval legal manuscripts—including the unique copy of the *Mirror of Justices* and the famous *Liber Luffield*. This library was dispersed in the seventeenth century, and only about a dozen legal items can now be traced in Cambridge, Oxford, and London. Edward Umfreville (d.1758) not only built up an enormous collection of post-medieval legal manuscripts in the eighteenth century, but actually read them and made notes and indices throughout his collection. But he made insufficient financial provision for his issue, and therefore his manuscripts were dispersed at auction (in 1758 and 1792). Fortunately, about half of them have found their way into the British Museum *via* Lord Lansdowne and Francis Hargrave; the other half are almost all lost. The vast and important collection of Lord Somers was divided between Sir Joseph Jekyll and the Yorkes; the former portion was dispersed in 1739, and the latter destroyed by a fire in Lincoln's Inn on 27 June 1752.[130] Only a few odd volumes can now be traced. The largest collection of all was that formed in the last century by Sir Thomas Phillipps, whose library of over 40,000 manuscripts included at least 600 of interest to legal historians. Most of these were sold at auction sales between 1893 and the present, and over half have disappeared once more.[131] One consequence of the Phillipps sales, and other large-scale auction sales at the end of the last and in the present century, is that a considerable share of the material has crossed the Atlantic at the behest of librarians with more foresight or (latterly) more funds than their English counterparts.[132] It is also safe to assume that material still lurks in old country houses: the best known, if under-explored, example being Serjeant Thynne's collection at Longleat.

The wide dispersal of the material makes study extremely difficult. The nature of legal research necessitates the use of a multitude of texts, since it is nearly always desirable to read as far as possible all the literature and case law on a given subject in a given period. At present such work cannot, for most practical purposes, be done with any degree of thoroughness; and the Englishman is at a particular disadvantage because of the expense of getting to and staying in the United States and the lack of any research funds. One answer to these problems would be to film as much of the material as possible, and make it available to scholars and librarians in microfiche. A project is already under discussion to publish manuscript Year Books, readings, and reports in microfiche, and to produce a cumulative listing as the work proceeds. If this project is successful, many of the above difficulties will disappear, and also editors might be relieved of the need to print original texts alongside their translations—thus freeing more badly needed space for the publication of edited material.

One final suggestion concerns the manuscripts which have been lost. These probably represent the greater part, at least in quantitative terms, of all that once existed. Mention has already been made of the loss of Lord Somers' collection. Other libraries are known to have been destroyed in their entirety. For instance, Sir John Vaughan lost all his books and manuscripts in the Great Fire of 1666, which swept through the north-eastern corner of the Inner Temple.[133] Sir William Jones lost three volumes of his reports while crossing to Ireland.[134] Probably far more volumes were simply thrown away by ignorant descendants, who did not realise that (generally speaking) the less legible a manuscript, the more likely it is to be of historical importance. It is not impossible to reconstruct some of these libraries, and it is by no means a futile exercise to try to calculate what has gone missing; and there is always the slight hope that research of this kind may now and then lead to the discovery of something which has survived.

The study of this Dark Age of English legal history has only just begun, and the prospect, though challenging, is not entirely hopeful. There are far more questions than answers, and many more questions than we have yet learned to ask. There are few volunteers coming forward who can add some feeling for the common law to their expertise in history. The sources remain in an appalling state of intellectual, if not physical, neglect. But some day a history of the law of Renaissance England will be written from the material which is now coming to our notice. It may well read very differently from our present textbooks, and it may contain a few surprises. For anyone who will contribute to this work, there is a lifetime of rewarding study ahead.

NOTES

[1] See R. J. Shoeck, "The Elizabethan Society of Antiquaries and the Lawyers" (1954) 199 *Notes and Queries* 417.

[2] Co.Litt. 244v. His unpublished notebooks are crammed with historical matter. For Coke's contribution to the "Norman yoke" controversy, see his *Reading on Fines* (1592) and the prefaces to Parts 3, 6, and 8 of the *Reports*.

[3] Preface to H. Rolle, *Abridgment des Plusieurs Cases* (1668) sig. a2.

[4] Cf. *Letters of F. W. Maitland* (ed. C. H. S. Fifoot, Cambridge, 1965) 1 SSSS no. 233.

[5] CP i.190.

[6] PM Introduction and ii.673.

[7] *Township and Borough* (Cambridge, 1898) 21, alluding to *Patience* by W. S. Gilbert.

[8] HEL v.369.

[9] Meanwhile, see F. W. Maitland, *English Law and the Renaissance* (Cambridge, 1901; reprinted in AALH i.168–203 and, with few of the many notes, in *Selected Historical Essays* (ed. Helen M. Cam, Cambridge, 1958) 135–51); Holdsworth, HEL iv.252–93; H. D. Hazeltine "The Renaissance and the Laws of Europe" in *Cambridge Legal Essays* (ed. P. H. Winfield and A. D. McNair, Cambridge, 1926) 165–9; T. F. T. Plucknett, "The Legal Profession in the History of English Law" (1932) 48 LQR 328; H. E. Bell, *Maitland* (London, 1965) 130–37; S. E. Thorne, "English Law and the Renaissance" in *La Storia del Diritto nel quadro delle scienze storiche* (Florence, 1966) 437–45; E. W. Ives, "The Common Lawyers in pre-Reformation England" (1968) 18 TRHS/V 145; G. R. Elton, "Reform by Statute: Thomas Starkey's *Dialogue* and Thomas Cromwell's Policy" (1968) 54 PBA 165, esp. at 176–80 (reprint, *Studies in Tudor and Stuart Politics and Government* (Cambridge, 1974) ii.236, 246–50).

[10] See S. E. Thorne, "Tudor Social Transformation and Legal Change" (1951) 26 *New York University Law Review* 10.

[11] *Constitutional History of England* (Cambridge, 1908) 270.

[12] See "The Common Lawyers and the Chancery: 1616" (1970) 4 IJNS 368.

[13] The best report (the source of the quotations above) is in Treby's MS. Reports, Middle Temple Library, 458–61, 602–3. See also 1 Mod. 59, 94; 2 Keb. 661, 787; 1 Lev. 241; 1 Sid. 463.

[14] See "New Light on Slade's Case" [1971] CLJ 213.

[15] BM Hargrave MS. 29, f.94.

[16] Vaughan 89, 101; cf. 1 Mod. 163 (1673).

[17] *Anon.* (1672) Treby's MS. Reports 747.

[18] *Buckridge v. Shirley, ibid.* 651.

[19] *Anon.* (1672) *ibid.* 747; cf. *Anon.* (1672) *ibid.* 775.

[20] Pat. 2 & 3 Ph. & Mar., pt 1, m.28, renewed in 1559 for life. The earlier patent of 1553 (Pat. 7 Ed. 6, pt 3, m.29) conferred copyright privileges but not a monopoly.

[21] I hope to publish a summary of this story in the near future, in an account of the printing of the Year Books.

[22] E.g. the immense library at Holkham: W. O. Hassall (ed.), *A Catalogue of the Library of Sir Edward Coke* (New Haven, 1950). See also E. W. Ives "A Lawyer's Library in 1500" (1969) 85 LQR 104 (Serjeant Keble, 1500). For an inventory of William Rastell's library, seized in 1562, see (1844) 31 *Law Magazine* 57–8 (24 law books and 17 others). There is an inventory of 1572 (William Dalison, jun.) in Kent Archives Office MS. U.552.E.1/2, mm.8–9. See further R. J. Shoeck, "The Libraries of Common Lawyers in Renaissance England" (1962) 6 *Manuscripta* 155.

[23] The best collection is in the British Museum.

[24] Sir Henry Gould sale, lots 917, 1152.

[25] L. A. Knafla, "The Law Studies of an Elizabethan Student" (1969) 32 *Huntington Library Quarterly* 221. Other collections which merit study are those of Sir Edward Coke (deposited by the Earl of Leicester in the Inner Temple) and Sir John Popham (at Littlecote House).

[26] See "Coke's Notebooks and the Sources of his Reports" [1972A] CLJ 59.

[27] "The Book that 'made' the Common Law: the first Printing of Fitzherbert's *La Graunde Abridgement, 1514–1516*" (1958) 51 *Law Library Journal* 100.

[28] Pynson's undated edition of 14 H.8 (STC 9945, Beale R.418) is the only nearly contemporary printed Year Book. Pynson died in 1530, and Pollard and Redgrave assign a date as early as c. 1525, a mere three years after the reports were taken. The only copy known is Rastell's, in Lincoln's Inn.

[29] This is the inference to be drawn from 8 Rep. preface xxxii–xxxiii, 10 Rep. preface xxxiv.

[30] Treby's MS. Reports 514, per Twisden J. (1670).

[31] *Anon.* (1673) Roger North's MS. Reports, BM Add. MS. 32527, f.29.

[32] E. Bulstrode, *Reports* (1657), epistle dedicatory to Part I; H. Grimstone, Part I of *Croke's Reports* (1657), preface.

[33] *Narrationes Modernae or Modern Reports* (1658), epistle dedicatory.

[34] Speech in the case concerning the privilege of the law printers (1669): BM Add. MS. 32519, f.211v.

[35] Treby's MS. Reports 433; same point, 2 Keb. 652, 1 Vent. 81.

[36] *Anon.* (1566) 3 Leo. 13, 4 Leo. 167, 224. It should be observed that even the publisher did not pretend that any of these reports were *by* Leonard.

[37] See [1972A] CLJ 69 n.57.

[38] Hertfordshire Record Office, Verulam MSS. XXII.A.6, C–E, and XII.A.14.

[39] Part I of *Croke's Reports* (1657), preface sig. a3.

[40] See the *Telos* in Redman's edition, STC 9587. Bolland noticed this, but thought only references had been added: *Manual of Year Book Studies* (Cambridge, 1925) 69. Turner wrongly attributed the additions to Tottell: *Year Book 4 Edward II* (1911/1914) 26 SS xvi. See also T. Ellis Lewis, 46 LQR 343–4, who was misled by the 1679 edition.

[41] 10 Rep. preface xxi, referring to STC 9587, f.[xvi], misprinted as "xiii". Holdsworth attached some weight to the passage: HEL v.373.

[42] CP i.496.

[43] E.g. A. K. R. Kiralfy, *The Action on the Case* (London, 1951); Milsom, *Foundations* 271–352.

[44] 10 Rep. 75. See also *Reports of Judgments delivered by Sir Orlando Bridgman* (ed. S. Bannister, London, 1823) 349: "In the time of Sir Edward Coke, and before him, there was not the freedom of access to records which there has been since." The judges probably had access to the records without fee.

[45] Since the delivery of the lecture, the writer has been through the King's Bench rolls KB 27/980 to 1120 (1506–41). The results of this investigation will appear in the introduction to *The Reports of Sir John Spelman*.

[46] Dr Sue S. Walker's valuable *Checklist of Research in British Legal Manuscripts* (1974), the outcome of a conference on plea roll studies in Chicago on 13–14 April 1973, does not reveal much interest in the legal content of the later common-law plea rolls.

[47] *Readings and Moots at the Inns of Court* i (1952/1954) 71 SS. See also his edition of Robert Constable's reading on *Prerogativa Regis* (New Haven and London, 1949) with notes from other readings.

[48] Cf. W. R. Prest, *The Inns of Court under Elizabeth I and the earlier Stuarts* (London, 1972) 119–30.

[49] Co. Litt. 280. Thorne, *Readings*, 71 SS xvii, seems to accept Coke's criticism.

[50] Two were delivered each year in four inns. (This excludes readings in Chancery, fewer of which were reported.) Towards 1700 many readers defaulted.

[51] For a modern study of a later reading see Gareth H. Jones, *History of the Law of Charity 1532–1827* (Cambridge, 1969) 22–101, 229–50 (Francis Moore on charitable uses).

[52] Professor Thorne is said to be editing a volume of moots for the Selden Society. The 1602 collection is Keil. 102v–137, which was probably printed unwittingly because Serjeant Croke did not appreciate its nature.

[53] See Bodl. Lib. Rawl. MS. C.705; BM Add. MS. 35939; Harvard Law School MS. 125(1); BM Harl. MS. 5103 (by William Coke), Harg. MS. 253 (perhaps by William Yelverton). For Middle Temple moots in this reign see Bodl. Lib. Rawl. MS. C.707; Harvard Law School MS. 125(2). For the Inner Temple: BM Harl. MS. 1691. Nothing is known to survive from Lincoln's Inn.

[54] Cf. J. Nicholson, *Register of Manuscripts of Year Books extant* (London, Historical Manuscripts Commission for Selden Society, 1956) 26–8. The one Year Book MS. is not listed by Nicholson; it is the Gell MS. in the Library of Congress.

[55] *Relationes quorundam Casuum selectorum ex Libris Robert Keilwey*, STC 14901. The earliest, and best, manuscript text is in the Huntington Library, MS. EL.6108–6138. Cf. note 61, below.

[56] "Keilwey's Reports" (1957) 73 LQR 89. Keilwey himself in 1558 reported to counsel a case "*in son liuer de Reports de Serieant Carell*": Dyer 174v.

57 See e.g. Arthur Tourneur's Reports, BM Harg. MS.30, f.71: "Cest ieo ad de veiell reportes. Mr Carrell ad reporte en son lyuer de Reportes que il fuit cite in anno 22 H.8 que un Wise fuit indite de felony . . ."

58 In BM Lansd. MS. 1084, f.3, is a case abridged as "27 H.8 lib. Carell". See also a case of 26 Hen. VIII cited from "un liuer report per Carrill" in Inner Temple Petyt MS. 511/13, f.58.

59 See BM Harl. MS. 1691, f.98: "Hec habui ex libro Magistri Johannis Caryll Attornati ducatis Lancastriae viri valde pii ac docti ac interioris templi socii."

60 See Dyer 174v (note 56 above) and Lansd. MS. 1084, f.3, "per Frowike et Grauntham de libro de reportes de seriant Carell". (Presumably a collection of Inner Temple moot cases similar to that printed in Keil. 102v–137.) Both Carrells were of the Inner Temple.

61 Cambridge UL MS. Gg.iii.26, ff.97–108 ("cases in temps H. septimi ex libro Roberti Kiloway", including some which are in print); BM Harl. MS. 1691, ff.67–90 (4–11 H.7), ff.98–107 (H.8), ff.111–112 (moot cases "de libro alio Magistri Carell"); Harl. MS. 1624, ff.1–33 (4–6 H.7), 33v–55r (1–11 H.8).

62 See note 64 below. The author refers to himself by name on f.57v, where he records his appointment as a judge. There is much material relating to Spelman's part of Norfolk, and to Gray's Inn. The Spelman portion of Harg. MS. 388 seems to end at f.154. The brief selection in Cambridge UL MS. Gg.ii.5, f.29 (which is in alphabetical order) is headed "Certaine cases in temps H.8 Reporte per Spilman". Other citations of Spelman by Coke and others correspond with passages in Harg. MS. 388.

63 See the note cited in W. Dugdale, *Origines Juridiciales* (1680 ed.) 137, which shows that the MS. belonged to Clement Spelman in 1663. Spelman B. cited the MS. in 1676: 73 SS 414, Kelyng 56.

64 "The Reports of John Spelman" (1956) 72 LQR 334–8. The spelling of the judge's name varies.

65 The writer has begun to prepare an edition for the Selden Society.

66 BM Harg. MS. 388, ff.155–216; Harg. MS. 3, ff.1–21; Lansd. MS. 1072, ff 4–35 (lacks first 14 cases); Gonville and Caius College, Cambridge, MS. 601 (titled "De abrig' Rogeri Yorke seruientis ad legem"). The identification is confirmed by two notes in the first person.

67 It is headed "En temps H.8", and the last case begins "Nota per Baron Hales . . .": Harg. MS. 388, ff.217–239v; Lansd. MS. 1072, ff.35–48. It is followed in both MSS. by cases "En temps Phillip et Mary", which also occur in Harg. MS. 3, ff.24–32. In all three MSS. this collection is found next to Yorke's, though it cannot be his since he died in 1536.

68 *A Catalogue of a Genuine Collection of Law Manuscripts* 42, lot 89.

69 Inner Temple Petyt MS. 511/13, ff.34–48 ("certaine cases which are probablie thought to be of the Lord Diers collection in his circuite" from Mary to 23 Eliz. I); *ibid.* ff.49–70 ("Here followe certaine cases of the Lord Diers collection which for some private reasons hee thought not fitt to make them vulgarr"); BM Harg. MS. 26, ff.166v–174. See also [1972A] CLJ 69.

70 Harl. MS. 5141, ff.1–45. At f.14v (after Edw. VI) is the colophon "Gulielmus Lamberdus transcripsit 1569" and at f.45 the final colophon "Huiusque ex libro Willelmi Dallison conscript' Willelmus Lambert Examinavit 1569."

71 He married Sylvestria, widow of the judge's son.

72 In "Lawyers and Law Reporting in the Sixteenth Century", London Ph.D. thesis, 1969. This was published by the Athlone Press in 1973, as *Law Reporting in England 1485–1585*. On pp.123–6 is a useful list of Harpur MSS.

73 Bodl. Lib. Rawl. MS. C.112.

74 BM Add. MS. 24845. The date 5 December 1583 appears at the end of 1 Mary. Both the Edw. VI and the Marian sections end "finis secundum Dalison Justice del Banck le Roy."

75 E.g. the printed "Dalison" and BM Add. MS. 35941, ff.261v–268v ("Ascuns cases hors del reports del Dalison Justice del bank le Roy").

76 See BM Harg. MSS. 6, 8, 10 (note by Umfreville), 374 (note by Hargrave); Lansd. MSS. 1060, 1072, 1121; Lincoln's Inn Misc. MS. 791. The true limits of Harpur's reports are probably 2–19 Eliz.I.

77 In the Verulam collection (Hertfordshire Record Office) is a small selection by William Lewis. A different series of abridged cases is BM Add. 35940.

78 E.g. Verulam MS. XII.A.6A, f.74, "Cases ex libro Harp[er]" abridged by George Croke.

79 Below, p. 16. A drawing in the Print Room of the British Museum shows the Court of King's Bench in about 1600, and there is a wooden gallery on poles at the side of the court, in which (presumably) students could sit to make notes. The curious frontispiece to G. Billinghurst, *Arcana Clericalia or the Misteries of Clerkshipp* (1674), shows six reporters wearing cloaks and *standing* on either side of the bench, with their long reporters' notebooks in their left hands and pens in their right hands.

80 BM Add. MS. 25203.

81 BM Stowe MS. 398 (part of Mich. 1598 only); Harg. MS. 13 (Mich. 1600–Trin.1601); Lincoln's Inn Misc. MS. 492 (1600–1604); Exeter College, Oxford, MS. 144 (Pasch. 1598–Pasch. 1599); Harvard Law School MS. 2076 (Mich. 1600–Mich. 1602); Yale Law School MS. G.R.29/12 (Trin. 1598–Pasch. 1599).

82 See "New Light on Slade's Case" [1971] CLJ 51, *passim*.

83 MS. Gg.ii.19, 20.

84 BM Add. MS. 35958.

85 BM Add. MS. 35968, 35969 (Serjeant Waller's copy, lacks first five years and last term); Harl. MS. 4811 (Robert Paynell's copy, lacks first five years).

86 The printed series begins in 1655. In the MS. are some Exchequer cases of Michaelmas Term 1637 related by "T.H." Hardres was called to the bar of Gray's Inn in 1636.

87 *Allen* v. *Nash*, BM Add. MS. 35958, f.317v. The case is even more briefly reported in W. Jones 393.

88 *Art of Stenographie*, STC 25744–7 (some of the editions not recorded).

89 T. Bright, *Characterie, an arte of shorte, swifte and secrete writing by Character* (London, 1588) STC 3742 (reprinted in 1888); P. Bales, *The writing schoolemaster* (London, 1590) STC 1312.

C

90 See I. Pitman, *History of Shorthand* (4th ed., London, 1918) 9–40. The methods were variously known as charactery, brachygraphy, tachygraphy, semigraphy, stenography, cryptography, thoography, and short-writing.

91 MS. in Middle Temple, *passim*. Sir Dudley Ryder's notebooks (1717–55) are in shorthand; they have been deposited in Lincoln's Inn (Misc. MSS. 861–78) by Lord Harrowby. The writer's copy of Savile's *Reports* (1688) has some shorthand notes in the index. A small volume at present in the possession of Winifred A. Myers Ltd contains some reports of James I's time in shorthand; but it seems to have been written later, and was probably transcribed in this way from a longhand exemplar.

92 The writ of privy seal was enrolled as a patent: C.66/2147, no.2 (printed in 26 SS xxii–xxiii and as *Ordinatio qua constituuntur lez Reporters de lege* in Rymer's *Foedera* xvii.27 (Reprint vii, pt iii, 19). See also J. W. Wallace, *The Reporters* (4th ed., Boston, Mass., 1882) 270–71.

93 See 26 SS xix–xxiii.

94 Cambridge UL MS. Gg.v.6, f.216v.

95 Thus in three copies, some of the terms are headed "Ex relacione Humphridi Mackworth": BM Add. MS. 35957, ff.126–239; Add. MS. 35962, ff.2–470; Harg. MS. 362, ff.97v–217 (ends Hil. 1629). Many other copies are known: e.g. BM Lansd. MS. 1085; Cambridge UL MS. Mm.vi.67, ff.182, continuing in MS.Dd.iii.46; MS. Ii.v.35; MS. Mm.vi.12 (ends Pasch. 1628); Inner Temple Barrington MSS. 8, 12; Harvard Law School MSS. 1125, 1178, 1195.

96 Umfreville was probably correct when he observed (in a note in Harg. MS. 362, f.3v) that "many of these cases from P.3 C.1 are printed most incorrectly in the Book falsely called Hetley's Reports and Winch and Littleton. The Book called Winch's Reports is no more than a Bad abbreviated impression of the Reports of Allestree tempore Jacobi as Hetley and parts of Littleton are of him and Mackworth in C.B. tempore Caroli, but neither of the three are genuine." See also Umfreville's note in Lansd. MS. 1091. Sylvester Douglas wrote of "Hetley": "Whether it was he or the Lord Keeper Littleton, who was really the author of those reports (many of them being exact duplicates of those ascribed to Littleton), they are so far from bearing any marks of peculiar skill, information, or authenticity": *Reports of Cases in the King's Bench* (2nd ed., London, 1786) preface xi. Cambridge UL MS. Ii.v.22 is attributed to Littleton; for reports attributed to Winch, see BM Add. MS. 25197, Lansd. MS. 1091, Cambridge UL MS. Ii.v.34, Yale Law School MS. G.R.29/22.

97 Turner attempts to father on him some of Widdrington's Reports, but he is not convincing: 26 SS xix–xx. For Widdrington's work, see BM Harg. MSS.38, 39, Lansd. MSS. 1083, 1092.

98 BM Add. MS. 35958, f.314; Harl. MS. 4811, f.125.

99 "Nota jeo fuit absent grand part de cest terme [M.11 Car.1] per encheson del mort mon beau pere": Add. MS. 35958, f.297; Add. MS. 35968, f.568; Harl. MS. 4811, f.119.

100 "Nota en ceo terme [M.11 Car.1] mon treshonourable amie le seigniour [Viscount] Savage chancellor al Roigne mor[ust]": Add. MS. 35958, f.314; Harl. MS. 4811, f.125 (slightly corrupt). Thomas, Viscount Savage of Rock-Savage, Cheshire, was buried at Maxfield in the same county. The word *amie* may denote patronage, but it is rather vague.

101 See [1972A] CLJ 71.

102 BM Harl. MS. 6809, ff.45–46v, parts of which are printed in [1971] CLJ 51–67 (text "G").

103 Printed by Henry Owen in (1901) 14 *Y Cymmrodor* 33–41, from BM Harl. MS. 141.

104 Noy 172–85. Cf. Inner Temple Petyt MS. 516/5, ff.347–362v. Another copy in Phillipps MS. 11125(1), now in Leeds Public Library (MS. SRF.942.06.c.685).

105 BM Harg. MS. 29, ff.116–25.

106 Cambridge UL MS. Ee.iii.45, ff.74v–83.

107 1 And. 71.

108 (1954/1957) 73 SS and (1961–2/1961) 79 SS.

109 Cf. BM Add. MS. 10169, called *Twisden's Reports*, which is an alphabetical abridgment of Year Books and later cases, some of them identifiable in Harg. MS. 42. At Harg. MS. 42, f.104v, the reporter says "*I* moved in arest de judgment . . ."; the same case is reported in Sty. 175, where Twisden is the counsel who moves in arrest of judgment. The existence of reports by Twisden is alluded to in DNB.
    The history of Twisden's extensive law library is still obscure. Some of his manuscripts were dispersed in 1924, when the Harvard Law School purchased five of them: MSS. 1165–6, 1171 (Hutton), 1195 ("Hetley"), 1207 (Lane, Rolle). The last volume was removed from Bradbourne, Kent, the Twisden seat, on the death of Sir John Twisden, the last baronet, by T. L. Hodges (d. 1857).

110 BM Harg. MS. 23. There is a copy by Prothonotary Moyle, if anything even less legible, in Lincoln's Inn Misc. MS 586.

111 Lincoln's Inn Hill MS. 82 (1658); later reports lost, some copied by Roger North in BM Add. MS. 32521 ("An extract out of his Lordship's court books of divers cases which came afore him as Judge"). See also Add. MS. 32523, f.33.

112 BM Add. MS. 32508, f.59. John Archer (d. 1682) became a judge in 1659 and was reconstituted by Charles II in 1663.

113 Misc. MSS. 499–500, 555–9.

114 Misc. MSS. 510–40 (1674–1714). One of the cases is printed in J. Rayner, *Cases concerning Tithes* (1783), i, "Authorities", p. xxxiv; ii.361.

115 (1717–56), Lincoln's Inn Misc. MSS. 861–80, deposited by Lord Harrowby. The notebooks relate mostly to the period before Ryder became Chief Justice in 1754.

116 (1722–42), Lincoln's Inn Misc. MSS. 31–45.

117 (1730–51), Lincoln's Inn Hill MSS. 37–48. Burnet became a judge in 1741.

118 (1733–56), BM Add. MSS. 36028–69. Sir Philip Yorke became Chief Justice of the Common Pleas in 1733 and Lord Chancellor in 1737.

119 (c.1736–1758), Harvard Law School, uncatalogued. Some of them are more like reports.

120 (1740–54), Inner Temple Petyt MS. 509.

121 (1832–49), Lincoln's Inn Misc. MSS. 609–703.

122 (1842–57), deposited in the Inner Temple.

123 (1848–58), divided between the Middle Temple, the Squire Law Library (Cambridge), and BM Add. MS. 43839, 43840.

124 (1849–53), Reading Public Library.

125 (1850), BM Add. MS. 43646.

126 (1859–75), Squire Law Library, Cambridge.

127 See Wallace, *Reporters* 402.

128 See BM Add. MS. 35987 and Harg. MS. 66.

129 There is a microfilm copy of the old Bridgewater shelf-list in the University Library, Cambridge. Since the delivery of the paper, I was able to visit the Harvard Law School and Yale University. The collection at Harvard is far more extensive than De Ricci's *Census* indicates; whilst Yale has an important collection of Hale MSS., purchased from the Hale family in recent times, and including over twenty volumes of reports (nowhere described in print).

130 See C. E. Wright (ed.) *Fontes Harleiani* (1972) 308–9. The catalogue in Harl. MS. 7191 indicates the richness of Somers' collection. Several volumes survive, presumably from the Jekyll portion.

131 The writer is indebted to Dr A. N. L. Munby, Librarian of King's College, Cambridge, for permitting him to study his annotated set of Phillipps catalogues. Some of the Year Books are now in the British Museum. The largest collection of Phillipps' legal manuscripts is in the Harvard Law School.

132 Before the last War, legal manuscripts on paper tended to sell for shillings rather than pounds. No attempt was made to buy them for the principal English libraries.

133 See Lincoln's Inn Misc. MS. 499, f.435, *per* Vaughan C.J. at his installation: "[Vaughan] diʌable luy mesme pur cy grand liew per reason del discontinuance de son study occasion'd partment per les guerres en les darrain temps et le seizing de son study et sequestring de son estate, et partment per le grand losse que il sustayne en le darrain few en Londres en quel son study et ses liures et papers que il ad retrieve a sequestracion fueront ure." Cf. the obituary by Serjeant Waller in BM Add. MS. 36076 f.301v: "[Vaughan] fuit en tresgrand rationall parts et bien studdye en le veiell ley et yeare bookes mes nemy mult verse in les novell reports ayant este sequester in les times pur son loyaltie al roy et plunder de mults . . . et ayant mults de son livres et manuscripts burnt in le inner Temple per fire que happen la."

134 BM Add. MS. 35958, f.233, *per* Jones J.: "iav null authority in point car en mon passage en Ireland ieo perde 3 report-books MS."

Nullity of Marriage and Illegitimacy in the England of the Middle Ages*

J. L. Barton

I SHOULD perhaps warn my auditors that the object of this paper is to suggest questions rather than to answer them. The matrimonial law of medieval England is not easily stated, for the claims of ecclesiastical and secular authority were not wholly reconcilable, and the degree of deference which was shown to the law of Holy Church varied from one period to another, and even from one judge to another. The actual working of that law cannot be adequately investigated from the printed sources. I shall be more than satisfied if I have succeeded in indicating some of the problems involved, and perhaps in encouraging some of you to investigate certain of them further.

In the law of the Church, any parties who had reached the legal age of puberty—fourteen for the man, and twelve for the woman—might contract a valid marriage by bare consent. It was their duty, however, to contract it publicly in the face of the Church, and those who married secretly might be put to penance and required to go through a public ceremony.[1] A marriage which had been publicly celebrated and duly consummated was a good marriage in possession. If it were alleged to be invalid, the burden of proof would be upon the party who attacked it, and if one of the spouses alleged that the marriage was invalid, and left the other on that ground, the deserted spouse would be restored to possession until the question of right had been tried. There was only one substantial exception to this rule. For the prevention of sin, a spouse who alleged that the marriage was within the prohibited degrees, and was ready to litigate the question at once, would not be restored *quoad torum*.[2] There is no text which expressly states that a clandestine marriage could not be a good marriage in possession, but such a situation, even if theoretically possible, would be very unusual. If parties who had not been through a public ceremony of marriage lived together, this raised a presumption of fornication, unless a marriage were actually proved,[3] and if the marriage established were an irregular one, one consequence of proving it would be that the parties would be admonished to celebrate it publicly.[4] Thus, at best, an irregular marriage would ordinarily be good in possession only during the short interval between the sentence of the ecclesiastical court which established it and the public celebration. The importance of this fact will be appreciated when we come to consider the attitude of the common law courts to questions of the validity of marriage.

A marriage, whether regularly or irregularly celebrated, might be invalid by reason of some impediment. Impediments were usually, though perhaps not wholly accurately, said either to arise from the defect of the party or to be intended for the prevention of sin. Error, coercion, or the sexual incapacity of one of the parties were impediments of the former type. Consanguinity, affinity, or a previous subsisting marriage fell into the latter category. A marriage invalid because of an impediment of the latter kind might be annulled at the suit of third parties, or of the Ordinary proceeding *ex officio*. If, on the other hand, the impediment arose from the defect of the party, no third person had any *locus standi* to take proceedings, and if the parties themselves saw fit to ratify the marriage it would be valid for all purposes.[5] This general principle must be taken subject to two qualifications. Whether the ratification of an invalid marriage would involve sin was to be decided at the moment when the question of ratification arose. Thus, the party who married in good faith a spouse whom he did not know to be married already would be free to ratify if, at the moment when he discovered the truth, the previous wife or husband of his spouse had died.[6] In the second place, a marriage which had not been and could not be consummated could never be so ratified by the parties as to render it a complete marriage in the sight of God. If the potent spouse had ratified the marriage after discovering the impediment, he would be refused a decree of nullity, but if he remarried without one his second marriage was valid,[7] and the most that the Church could do was to insist that he provide adequate maintenance for his former wife.[8]

Since cohabitation outside marriage was a sin, proceedings to establish that parties holding themselves out as married were not married in truth were, in principle, penal.[9] Penal proceedings are not ordinarily competent after the death of the guilty parties. If this principle were to be rigorously applied, it would follow that if an invalid marriage had been regularly celebrated, and the parties had contrived to escape the attentions of the Ordinary during their lives, their deaths would put the validity of their marriage beyond dispute.[10] This was a conclusion which the Church declined to draw if the parties had been in bad faith.[11] If, in consequence, the Church might be obliged to determine whether sin had been committed after the sinners were dead, it could be argued that there was civilian authority that a pecuniary interest was enough to make a litigant a good party to a cause of status, or even in some cases to found criminal proceedings after the death of the criminal, and that there was such a pecuniary interest here, for the legitimacy of the issue depended on the validity of the marriage, and their rights of inheritance depended on their legitimacy.[12] The principle that a marriage contracted in good faith could not be attacked after the spouses were dead was replaced by the wider doctrine of putative marriage: the children of an invalid marriage would be legitimate if one of the spouses had been unaware of the impediment, whether the parents were dead or alive and whether or not the marriage had been annulled in their lifetimes. This privilege, however, was limited to the issue of parents who had been publicly married in face of the Church.[13] Those who married in secret were suspected of taking precautions to avoid discovering what they did not wish to know.

It is perhaps a little unfortunate that Bracton is the earliest author to whom we can look for detailed information about the English law on this subject, for he wrote at a time when there was a violent dispute in progress between the secular and the ecclesiastical authorities over legitimation by subsequent marriage, and his account of it, as has been pointed out long ago, is not altogether accurate. Whether, as Maitland charitably thought,[14] his deviations from the strict truth are due to *bona fide* error, or whether he speaks as a royal judge arguing an anti-clerical case, I confess that I should not like to say. There had been an ordinance made in 1234, that when in future cases the legitimacy of a party born before the marriage of his parents should come in issue in the King's court, the court should not ask the Ordinary to certify whether he were legitimate, but whether he were born before the marriage of his parents, and the Ordinary should answer the question put to him in this form. It was said that the prelates had agreed to this ordinance, and it is possible that they were thought to have done so, but if they had they soon had second thoughts. In the Parliament at Merton they made their celebrated protest that their consciences would not permit them to answer this question if it were referred to them, and the baronage returned their equally celebrated answer that they were not prepared to change the law to accommodate the consciences of the prelates. There, for the moment, the matter rested. Bracton reverses the order of events, and represents the ordinance to have been made as a result of the protest at Merton, and in order to provide the Bishop with a question which he could conscientiously answer in accordance with the law. It would be easier to regard this as merely a mistake if the rest of his account were less anti-clerical. He declines to admit that there is any such thing known to the law as a plea of general bastardy. The party who pleads that his opponent is bastard must always say how he is bastard, so that the court may determine whether the question be a proper one for the Ordinary, or whether it be one which can be determined in the King's

court. Thus, if it be alleged that A is bastard because he is issue of a bigamous marriage, or because his parents were never married at all, this puts
the rights of espousals in issue, and should be tried by the Ordinary. If it
be alleged that A is bastard because he was born before the marriage of
his parents, it is no usurpation on the spiritual power to try this issue in
the King's court, since it is only the date of A's birth that comes in
question. However—a surprising and somewhat lame conclusion after this
preface—though the King's court might legitimately try this issue, the
King's court does not ordinarily do so. The proper course is to write to
the Ordinary in the form envisaged by the ordinance of 1234, though the
King's court will inquire or at least may inquire if the Ordinary refuse to
certify, or certify in equivocal terms.[15]

It had indeed been decided at one stage that the issue of birth before or
after marriage should be determined in the King's court. We know this
much from a writ of 1236, which also tells us that it remains to be settled
whether the trial shall be by the country or in some other manner.[16]
Apparently nothing was done. The result we may see from *Brevia
Placitata*.[17] The tenant in a writ of right *de rationabili parte* pleads that
the demandant is a bastard, because he was born before espousals. The
court sends the question to the Ordinary. The Ordinary certifies evasively
that the parents of the demandant and the tenant were lawfully married.
The demandant is told that this is not a certificate upon which the court
can proceed to judgment. The tenant shall therefore continue to hold as
he holds now, and the demandant may sue to the Ordinary for a more
explicit certificate, if so advised. The Ordinary will not answer the question
referred to him. The King's court is not prepared to try it. The result is
that possession is not nine, but all ten points of the law. If the party born
before the marriage of his parents be tenant in possession, he cannot be
dislodged, for he will not be certified bastard. If he be out of possession,
he cannot recover, for the Ordinary will not certify him legitimate in terms
which will satisfy the King's court. Little more than half a century after
Bracton's death, the court has ceased to go through the form of writing to
the Ordinary, and we have a new rule of pleading. In an ancestral action,
the demandant cannot allege that the tenant was born before the marriage
of his parents, but is obliged to plead general bastardy.[18]

Once the rule was established as a rule of pleading, rather than a
necessary consequence of certain procedural difficulties, there was no
longer any very obvious reason for distinguishing between demandant
and tenant, or indeed between an ancestral action and any other. Bracton's
principle that a party who pleads bastardy must state the cause of bastardy
was no longer law, if it ever had been. If the cause be in fact alleged, it
will not be entered on the roll. The allegation of bastardy is the material

part of the plea, and the cause merely evidence or argument.[19] The rule
that birth before espousals may not be pleaded against a tenant looks
very like a particular application of this principle, and if this be the case,
to plead the same allegation against a demandant is equally objectionable.
Counsel do in fact argue, repeatedly and strenuously, that the law recog-
nises no distinction between demandant and tenant. The point seems to
have been considered a very difficult one,[20] though I have not encountered
any reported case in which a demandant who had been born out of
espousals actually recovered against the legitimate issue in possession.
The distinction between ancestral actions and novel disseisin at first caused
less difficulty. In novel disseisin it was possible to try even general bastardy
by the country, and if it were thought desirable to spare ecclesiastical
susceptibilities, the assize could always be taken at large. This was the
course adopted by Inge J. in 1313.[21] The tenant made title by descent.
The plaintiff replied that the tenant had been born before the marriage of
his parents. Inge, who was a cleric, held that this replication was so close
to bastardy that he ought not to put it to the assize for the estate of Holy
Church. He therefore took the assize at large and carefully refrained from
directing them upon the point, but when they found that the tenant was
in truth born before the marriage of his parents, he gave judgment for the
plaintiff. The distinction could be reconciled with principle by holding that
the plea that a party was born before the marriage of his parents is a
possessory plea, and therefore appropriate in a possessory action.[22]
However, the respite was a temporary one. In the earlier part of the
fourteenth century, it was becoming progressively more usual to employ
novel disseisin as a substitute for ancestral actions. The party claiming
would enter, and bring assize if the tenant refused to surrender possession.
If it be law that a plea which is in the right requires an answer which is
equally high up in the right, then it can fairly be argued that even in novel
disseisin, if the tenant expressly plead a title by descent, a replication that
the tenant was born out of espousals is bad, for the bar is in the right,
and the replication merely in the personalty.[23] Had this opinion been
accepted, the result would have been that the son born before marriage
who could contrive to get possession of the inheritance could be evicted
by his legitimate younger brother only if his pleader were so incompetent
as to allow the assize to be taken against his client at large instead of
pleading specially in bar, and the theoretically better right of the legitimate
son would have been of little more force than a parole condition.[24]

In fact the rule, at least in its original form, disappeared. In 1343, the
tenant in a writ of cosinage attempted to abate the writ by pleading that
the heir of the ancestor upon whose seisin the demandant had counted had
entered after the ancestor's death and been seised. The demandant replied

that the party alleged to have entered as son and heir had been born before espousals, and the court accepted the replication, despite the tenant's objection that this might have been a good replication against a demandant, but was not admissible against a tenant. Counsel for the demandant was prepared to grant that he could not have alleged that the tenant had been born before espousals. The position was different where third parties were concerned. Hillary J., however took a very much more radical view. He could see no reason to take any distinction between demandant and tenant, and he had known birth before espousals to be pleaded in a writ of right. Shardelow, who was against admitting the issue, said that this was indeed true, and that Bereford had been blamed by Hengham for allowing it, and when the replication was finally accepted by the court, we are told that Shardelow murmured, which the editor translates as "Shardelow dissented".[25] The plea here, however, was in abatement, and the party who was alleged to have been illegitimate was no party to the writ, so that Hillary could offer as an additional reason for his decision the much less heroic argument that the question would be tried by the country in any event, and therefore the court would not be trespassing upon the jurisdiction of the Church by allowing the plaintiff to plead specially rather than generally. In the following year, however, a tenant in assize made title by descent, the plaintiff replied that the tenant had been born out of espousals, the tenant objected that this was no answer to a tenant in possession, and the parties were adjourned to Westminster, where judgment passed for the plaintiff. This case was complicated by the fact that during the adjournment the tenant had contrived to get himself certified legitimate in an action of formedon. The court refused to allow him to plead the certificate, since judgment had not yet been given upon it, but held *obiter* that even if judgment had been given, the certificate would have been no answer to an averment of birth before espousals.[26] This was assize. Two years later, in another writ of cosinage, the question was squarely raised whether the same principle was applicable in an ancestral action. The tenant made title as heir. The demandant replied that the tenant was born before the espousals between his parents. According to the reporter, the tenant offered to demur to the replication. From the roll, it appears that he ingloriously abandoned his valiant stand and took the issue tendered.[27]

We hear no more of this particular principle of pleading, but it, or the memory of it, may have had some influence upon the subsequent development of the privileges of the party born before the marriage of his parents. If we are to consider this question, however, we must for a moment return to Bracton's day, in order to trace the decline of an even more remarkable principle, which has not so far been mentioned. For Bracton, the plea of bastardy is one which can be advanced only against a living person: a dead man cannot answer the exception. Nevertheless, though a dead man cannot be bastardised, it is permissible to inquire by the country whether he were a bastard or not, just as we may inquire whether a dead man held freely or in villeinage, though it be not permissible to inquire of the status of such a person after his death.[28] The point could have been more clearly put, but the reference to *mutatio status defuncti* gives us a clue to the sense. The civil law did not encourage attempts to attack the status of the dead. For the canonists, this was a serious difficulty in the way of anyone who wished to contend that spouses now dead who had been publicly married were not husband and wife in the eye of the law.[29] The common lawyers may very well have adopted the rule from the civilians. At least, it was still possible to bastardise the dead at the end of the twelfth century. There are two decretals in the Gregorian collection addressed by Alexander III to English prelates who have been required by the King's court to determine the legitimacy of persons now deceased. In the second, the Pope actually says that the bishop may feel that this is a rather singular form of proceeding, but he ought nevertheless to obey the mandate addressed to him.[30] However, we must bear in mind the limits of the principle. Bracton is not being muddle-headed when he tells us that a dead man may not be bastardised, but we may inquire by the country whether he was a bastard. From the mediaeval standpoint, a status is something which can be possessed as easily as an acre of land. To contend that a man was not entitled to the status in which he died is an attempt to change his status, and is not allowable. To inquire in what status he died is merely to attempt to determine what his status in fact was, and to that there is no objection.

So far as legitimacy is concerned, when we reach the period of the early Year Books the principle that one may not dispute the status of the dead is a rule as much of property as of status. It does not apply unless the party who is alleged to have been a bastard has actually died seised of the tenements in demand. Thus in 1313 a writ of cosinage is brought against an abbot, who pleads in abatement the last seisin of one Ralph, who entered as son and heir after the death of the ancestor on whose seisin the demandant has counted. The demandant replies that Ralph was a bastard. The tenant rejoins that Ralph was brought up as the son of his reputed father and known as such all his life, and had entered upon his father's inheritance and held in peace until he enfeoffed the tenant's predecessor. Inge J. observes that the parties are at issue. The tenant has confessed that Ralph did not die in seisin of the tenements. Therefore the only answer he can give to the demandant's replication is that Ralph was legitimate.[31] By 1343, it is being argued that the principle is based upon the laches of the legitimate heir, who allowed the bastard to die in seisin when he might have entered upon him. It would therefore be only logical to hold that it does not apply against issue in tail, for it is elementary learning that the laches of tenant in tail does not prejudice his issue.[32] From this, it is no more than a step to arguing that the rule does not apply if the legitimate heir were an infant at the date of the bastard's death: laches cannot be imputed to an infant.[33] This argument, however, was rejected. By the latter part of the fifteenth century, the old doctrine of possessory legitimacy has been transformed into the classical rule of *bastard eigne* and *mulier puisne*. If the son born before marriage enters as heir and dies seised, his heir has a title good against the legitimate younger son and his issue. The principle is no wider than this. Indeed, it is arguable that this statement of it is too wide. According to Littleton, there are those who hold that it applies only where the elder and the younger brother are both issue of the same parents. This is Littleton's own opinion.[34] We have certainly come a very long way since the brave days of the thirteenth century, when an attempt to bastardise a man after his death could be compared to an attempt to convict him of felony after his death.[35] To retrace the route followed is a hazardous enterprise, for we have little but conjecture to guide us, but perhaps I may be permitted an attempt.

Even at the beginning of the fourteenth century, the doctrine of *possessio filiationis* was still a good deal more than a rule of the law of legitimacy. It gave a limited legal effect to what was, in substance, adoption. If A had been brought up in B's household as the son of B, a collateral relation would not be allowed to aver after B's death that A was not B's son, and it was quite immaterial whether he were attempting to bastardise A, or whether his contention were that A was the legitimate son of a third party.[36] It is probably for this reason that at the same period it seems to be felt that the principle that an heir who has been taken as legitimate in his life cannot be bastardised after death applies against collaterals and strangers, but does not apply between those who claim by descent from the same ancestor. Thus in 1302, the demandant in a writ of right *de rationabili parte* claimed a moiety of the land as heir to a sister of the great-grandfather of a tenant who had died without issue, against the tenant, whom he alleged to be heir of the other sister. The tenant pleaded that the demandant had made his resort through a bastard. Counsel for the demandant asked whether he pleaded this as privy or as stranger. Counsel for the tenant answered that he pleaded as stranger. Counsel for the demandant prayed that this admission might be entered upon the roll, and only then replied that Sidoine, the alleged bastard, was taken for the legitimate daughter of her father all her life.[37] The exception is natural enough, if the rule be regarded as a particular application of the principle of *possessio filiationis*. It is one thing to allow a landowner to disappoint his collaterals, another to permit him to disinherit his issue by introducing strangers into his household. The exception was finally repudiated in 1360,[38] at a time when the wider doctrine of *possessio filiationis* seems to have been abandoned. At least, we hear no more of it.

Now a bastard is no man's son. So strictly is this rule applied that if I bring a writ against "A son of B" I must discontinue and purchase another writ if I propose to allege that A is a bastard.[39] Suppose that in a real action in which my opponent claims through a bastard who entered as son and heir and died in seisin I avoid the dangerous word bastard, and instead plead that A was not the son of B? There is one situation in which this will cause my opponent no difficulty at all. If B were at any time married to A's mother, he will plead the marriage, and that A was born after the espousals. To that I can answer only that A was born before espousals, and that will reveal my real case. If, on the other hand, B were never married to A's mother, and if it be no longer law that a reputed son is deemed a son as against strangers, A's counsel will be hard put to it to find a reason for refusing the issue tendered, and if he takes it he will lose his case.[40] This, it is submitted, is the most probable explanation of how it came about that the rule that the heir who dies in seisin cannot be bastardised after his death came to be restricted in the later middle ages to the bastard born before the marriage of his parents.

At this point, however, we have another rule to reckon with, a rule which, unlike the doctrine of *possessio filiationis*, applies between rival heirs claiming under the same ancestor, the rule that, in certain cases at least, the heir who is "out" cannot plead birth before espousals against the heir who is "in". As we have seen, this rule in its original form seems to have disappeared at about the same time as the wider doctrine of *possessio filiationis*. The most probable reason, it is submitted, is that once the principle that an heir cannot be bastardised after his death has become a privilege of the heir born before the marriage of his parents, the distinction between the privilege to which the *bastard eigne* was entitled as against his uncle and the privilege to which he was entitled as against his brother the *mulier puisne* would not have been easy to maintain even had there been any desire to maintain it, and it may well have appeared irrational. The two were assimilated, and the doctrine of *bastard eigne* and *mulier puisne* took its classical form.

The progressive abandonment by the common lawyers of their scruples about a too minute investigation of the status of the dead meant a progressive increase in the number of cases in which a jury of the country might be required to find not merely whether a man had been reputed a bastard in his life, but whether he had in truth been legitimate. Nor was it only the legitimacy of the dead which might be submitted to a jury. As

the court would not write to the Ordinary to certify the legitimacy of a
dead man, since the dead could take no part in the proceedings, so the
court would take the verdict of a jury if it were necessary to determine the
legitimacy of someone who was no party to the writ.[41] It was also arguable
that since trial by the Ordinary was the highest form of trial of legitimacy
known to the law, it was not appropriate in possessory actions. Quite how
seriously this argument was taken in practice is not an easy question. As
late as 1306 we may find a plea of general bastardy challenged (though
unsuccessfully) in a writ of cosinage, on the ground that it is higher up
in the right than the nature of the action allows,[42] but Bracton gives a form
for the writ to the Ordinary where bastardy has been pleaded in *mort
d'ancestor*, which was a more possessory action than cosinage.[43] The real
difficulty arose in novel disseisin. According to what we may call the
classical doctrine, the question depends upon the manner in which the
assize is taken. If it be taken at large, the recognitors may find bastardy,
as they may find any other fact material to the title, and the court will
act on their finding. If the tenant in the assize sets up a title by descent,
and the plaintiff replies that the tenant cannot be heir because he is bastard,
the issue will go to the Ordinary. As early as 1313 we find the punctilious
Inge J. taking an assize at large in order not to blemish the estate of Holy
Church by asking the recognitors for their verdict on an issue which was
"close to bastardy",[44] but at this period it was by no means clear that even
a direct issue of bastardy would have gone to the Ordinary. William of
Denham, a serjeant who was more or less contemporary with Inge J., told
a student that bastardy in assize was normally tried by the country, but
he thought that within ten years it would be sent to the Ordinary, as it was
in every other action.[45] In 1335, it is asserted that if bastardy be pleaded
in bar, the Ordinary must try it,[46] but even thirty years later, it can still
be said that to write to the Ordinary in assize is a novelty, and whether it
be a desirable novelty, and how far the court has a discretion, are questions
upon which different opinions are held.[47] The real motive of the change
was probably the transformation of novel disseisin into an action for the
trial of titles. If titles are to be tried in any action, it is well that they
should be tried finally. This argument certainly influenced the practice
in trespass. In 1412 we find Thirning observing that it was not customary
in the past to write to the Ordinary in actions of trespass, but that there
was much to be said for trying titles at Westminster in trespass now that
there was such great maintenance in the country in assize,[48] and in the
latter part of the century it was certainly the practice to write to the
Ordinary in trespass.[49]

A much more serious complication in the later middle ages was that the
doctrine of legitimacy which had been developed by the common lawyers

in these cases where bastardy was tried by the country diverged steadily further from the law of the Church. First, the common law could not try the right of espousals. As Belknap put it in 1374, if the banns be cried and the marriage celebrated in face of the Church, the common law cannot determine whether it were celebrated lawfully or unlawfully.[50] A man might marry his sister, and he would still be a married man in the eye of the law until his marriage had been declared invalid by a tribunal which had jurisdiction to determine the question.[51] It is not absolutely clear whether we can argue *a contrario sensu*, that if a marriage celebrated regularly is a good marriage in possession which the common law must accept until it has been annulled by sentence,[52] a marriage not regularly celebrated is a marriage in right only, which the common law must ignore until it has been established by sentence. There seems to be no case in the books in which an irregular marriage was pleaded. The Common Pleas in 1374 was prepared to accept that a death-bed marriage to a pregnant mistress might legitimate the issue.[53] However, this was almost certainly a marriage celebrated by a priest—it was said to have been celebrated to ease the husband's conscience—and had it been celebrated by licence it would have been regular in every respect,[54] though in the thirteenth century such a marriage did not entitle the widow to dower.[55] For what it may be worth Swinburne, writing in the sixteenth century, tells us that the common lawyers hold the children of irregular marriages illegitimate,[56] and when at a much later period Lord Hardwicke's Marriage Act provided that no suit should lie to compel the celebration in face of the Church of any contract *per verba de praesenti*, it was held to have invalidated such marriages altogether. The learning on what constitutes a good irregular marriage is so complex, and the distinctions are so many and so nice[57] that it is hard to believe that a common law court which was asked to determine whether parties had been validly though irregularly married would not have come to the conclusion that it was being asked to try the right of spousals.

As the common lawyers were obliged to hold that a marriage regularly celebrated was valid and the issue legitimate unless the marriage were annulled by sentence, so they were obliged to accept that a marriage which had been annulled was no marriage at all. The effect of annulment on the issue was a more difficult question. The earlier opinion was that a divorce for precontract would bastardise the issue had before, but a divorce for consanguinity or affinity would not.[58] On this latter point, however, there seem to have been doubts. As early as 1317 a litigant who has sued out his writ in a form which makes it impossible for him to bastardise his opponent has himself nonsuited, and we are told that he has done this *per bonum consilium*. His opponent's parents were divorced for consanguinity, and when he brings his new writ in a better form he will be able to plead bastardy.[59] There is a decision of 1366 in which it seems to be assumed that a party who has proved that the parents were divorced for consanguinity has bastardised the issue, but the point did not require to be decided.[60] Our first definite information that the law has changed comes from a note at the bottom of the last page of the Year Book of 47 Ed. 3. The various causes of divorce *a vinculo* are set out, and we are told that all of them bastardise the issue, with the exception of divorce *causa professionis*. The exception remained good law. Indeed, it was reaffirmed by a decision of all the judges assembled in the Exchequer Chamber in 1504.[61] There was rather more hesitation about the rule.

In the canon law, as we have seen, the issue of an invalid marriage publicly contracted would be legitimate if either parent were in good faith. This principle was never adopted by the common lawyers, but at the same time it was never repudiated firmly enough to put it beyond argument that it was no part of the law. In 1317 the demandant in a writ of aiel, whose grandfather had been divorced for precontract, argued that the doctrine of putative marriage had preserved his father's legitimacy. Bereford would have none of this argument,[62] but as late as 1479 the son of parents who had been divorced for consanguinity deliberately pleaded his pedigree in a manner which put the effect of the divorce upon his legitimacy in issue, and his counsel urged the doctrine of putative marriage on the court.[63] The court again rejected it, and Brian observed that it did not invariably apply even in the canon law. If a married man took a second wife while his first was living, the issue of the second marriage would be bastards in the canon law, for the second espousals were void. Apparently the common lawyers thought that the distinction which they had abandoned must have been founded on the canon law, for we find the same observation made by Catesby J. in 1481,[64] though he was at once corrected by the canonists present. Catesby, indeed, was apparently prepared to hold that the doctrine of putative marriage was recognised, within the limits which he stated, by the common law, but his observations on the point were *obiter*.

The bigamous marriage, indeed, was particularly well calculated to put a severe strain on the principle that the common law was concerned not with the right of marriage, but merely with the fact of espousals. One of the reasons for which the doctrine of putative marriage was rejected in the fifteenth century was that a divorce *a vinculo* set the parties free to marry again, and if the children of the first marriage were to be held legitimate it would be necessary to hold the children of any second marriage bastards. Whatever the logical difficulties which this situation might involve, they were as nothing to the problems presented by the husband who had one wife in possession in one county, and another wife in possession in another county—yet it had to be admitted that such a case was perfectly possible.[65] The law was long controversial. As late as 1440, we may find Paston J. stoutly defending the strict doctrine of possessory marriage from the bench. The tenant in *scire facias* had made his title by descent through a certain lady. The demandant alleged that the lady in question had married a man who had a previous wife alive, and that her husband's first wife outlived her. Paston's reaction was to suggest that the demandant had pleaded himself clean out of court. He had confessed in pleading that the second marriage had been regularly celebrated in face of the Church, which was enough for the common law. He had attempted to avoid the effect of this confession by pleading matter to show that the marriage was invalid. This was not an averment which a court of common law was entitled to consider. Then one of the parties died, the proceedings abated, and a disappointed reporter ends his account of the case with *ideo quaere legem.*[66] It is worth noticing, however, that the argument that a bigamous marriage is none the less a good marriage in possession came from the bench rather than the bar. Counsel who supported the tenant's demurrer preferred to rely upon the ingenious but rather desperate argument that the demandant had stated that the husband of the lady in the case was already married, but had refrained from stating that the lady herself was not already married. If she had been a bigamist too, any children born after the date of the second ceremony would have been accounted in law the legitimate issue of her first husband. This is an argument which clearly assumes that the second marriage is to be disregarded for all purposes, and that a bigamous union is to be treated in the same manner as adulterous cohabitation. This was not a new suggestion. As early as 1406, in a *scire facias* to execute a remainder limited to the heirs of a certain lady, the tenant made title as heir, and the demandant attempted to plead that the tenant claimed through the issue of a bigamous marriage. Rickhill cited, so far as I have discovered for the first time, the celebrated legal adage "whoso bulleth the cow, the calf is yours", and informed the demandant that if his replication were true, the tenant's ancestor would be the legitimate son of the lady's first husband, provided that the husband were within the four seas.[67] The question seems to have been settled by 1457. The plaintiff as heir in tail brought an action of detinue for a charter by which land had been given in special tail to A and B his wife. The defendant pleaded that long before A had married B he had married X, and the espousals between them continued all their lives. The plaintiff demurred, but on the ground that this was an argumentative plea of general bastardy, and it is clear from the argument that the question was regarded as one of form. The defendant contended that his special plea was more appropriate, for if issue were taken upon it the issue would be tried by an inquest of the visne where the first espousals were alleged to have taken place, and such an inquest would be better informed of the facts than would a jury of the county where the action was brought.[68] No judgment is reported, but for us the significant point is that it is no longer thought worth while even to argue that the issue of a bigamous marriage which has not been anulled may be reckoned legitimate.

In the later middle ages, it is generally said that another distinction between the common and the canon law is that in the canon law the child of a married woman may be bastardised, but this is impossible in the common law, if his mother's husband be within the four seas. Upon this subject, opinion seems to have fluctuated. On one occasion in 1369, a common law court actually allowed issue to be taken on the paternity of the child of a married woman. In a *scire facias* the tenant prayed aid of one A, as son and heir of H, of whose lease the tenant held. The demandant counterpleaded that A's mother was married to H by the covin of the tenant when H lay sick on his death-bed during the late pestilence, that A's mother was then heavily pregnant of A by one J, and that H was *non compos mentis* at the time and died two days afterwards. The tenant replied that A's mother was pregnant by H whose mistress she had been, that he married her out of conscience, and that the espousals between them continued for fifteen days. At the suggestion of the court, the parties finally took issue on the question whether A's mother were pregnant by H or by J.[69] So far as I have been able to discover, there was no precedent for this decision. Many years previously Bereford had made it clear that in his opinion birth after the espousals, no matter how promptly, would settle the paternity of the child in the eye of the law,[70] and this principle was emphatically reaffirmed in 1422, in a case which arose out of the adventures of one of those enterprising medieval ladies who contributed so much to the elucidation of the trickier points of the law of legitimacy. Again, the case arose on a *scire facias*. The demandant claimed as son and heir male of the body of his mother K, and counted that K had married F and had had issue him. The tenant pleaded that when K had married F she was heavily pregnant with the demandant by one T, and that she then eloped from F and lived in adultery with a third man, in whose house the demandant was born. The court made short work of this plea. If the tenant were attempting to allege that the demandant was not the son of F, he would have to show that K had had a previous husband whose son the demandant might have been.[71] It is tempting to suspect that in the case of 1369 the judges allowed a particularly hard case

D

to make bad law, but there seems also at this period to have been some hesitation over the question whether it were possible to bastardise the child of a married woman who was living in adultery at the time of his birth. Thus in 1366 the tenant in an assize taken before Shardelow rejoined to a replication of bastardy that he had been born within espousals. Shardelow held this no answer, since he might have been born while his mother was living with an adulterer, and took the assize at large. The reporter regrets that nothing was entered save *nil dicit*, so that no writ of error could be brought.[72] However, the stricter view eventually prevailed. We have already seen it applied with extreme rigour in 1406, and it does not seem to have been challenged thereafter. The only exception well supported by authority is that the child of a married woman may be bastardised if his mother's husband were clearly too young to be capable of begetting issue. The decisions deal with child marriages,[73] but in 1422 the minimum age for procreation in the male was put as high as fourteen.[74]

Thus in the middle ages, whether a man were legitimate or bastard might well depend upon the tribunal which decided the question, and this in turn would depend upon the proceedings in which the question arose. Suppose that A and B, who are within the prohibited degrees, marry and have a child, C. If the marriage be annulled, C is a bastard in the eye of the common law, but before the Ordinary he will be legitimate if either of his parents were unaware of the impediment. If he bring an action as heir, and bastardy be pleaded against him, the case will go to the Ordinary, who will certify him legitimate, and he will be legitimate for good and all thereafter. If he do not sue as heir during his life, and die leaving a child, D, D is the child of a bastard, for if he should claim as heir to his grandfather the legitimacy of his father will be tried by the country. Suppose that the marriage is not annulled, and C's parents die, the position is reversed. So far as the common law is concerned, C's legitimacy is now beyond attack. The Church might be prepared to entertain proceedings to bastardise the children of an invalid marriage, but in England the Ordinary has no business to try legitimacy unless the question be referred to him by the King's writ, and a prohibition will go if he attempts to do so.[75] Nor will he be permitted to do indirectly what he is not allowed to do directly. A sentence of divorce pronounced after the death of the parties will be disregarded. It cannot be a divorce, since a divorce is merely *pro peccatis*, and whatever it may be, the only purpose for which posthumous divorce proceedings can have been taken is to bastardise the issue of the marriage.[76] A prohibition will even go against an heir who takes proceedings for defamation against a lady who claims to have been married to his father. The assertion is defamatory of the heir only because it implies that he is illegitimate, and that the Ordinary is not entitled to investigate until he is asked to do so by the proper authority.[77] Thus C's legitimacy will be open to attack only if it be referred to the Ordinary by the King's writ, when the Ordinary will certify him bastard if his parents were in bad faith.

The situation is rather different where the impediment to the marriage of A and B was a previous regular marriage. If A were married to X when he married B, C is a bastard at common law, though he may be able to rely on the doctrine of putative marriage before the Ordinary. If B were married to Y when she married A, it is quite possible that C may be the legitimate son of A in the eye of the Church, and the legitimate son of Y at common law.

If the marriage between A and B were valid, but B eloped after C's birth and lived with a paramour by whom she had further issue, these children would be A's children at common law, and bastards in the ecclesiastical court. Suppose that C is a daughter, and that B has male issue by her paramour. If the title to A's inheritance comes in question between C and B's son, C may hope to have the issue of legitimacy sent to the Ordinary, and she will then recover as heir of A. Suppose, however, that A outlives B's son, who dies leaving issue. The issue of the son is the nearer heir, and since the legitimacy of his father will be tried by the country, he will recover against C.

For the party who was bastard by one law but legitimate by the other, the question was naturally how he might best insure that his legitimacy was tried by the law most favourable to him. If the canon law were in his favour, he might hope to take advantage of the rule that the court would only write to the Ordinary once, and that the certificate once given was conclusive between all persons and in all causes. The court would not defer giving judgment on the Ordinary's certificate merely because some third party attempted to intervene to allege that the action had been brought collusively to deprive him of his rights,[78] and though Bracton had held that it was allowable to aver against a certificate that it had been obtained in a collusive action[79] judicial attitudes appear to have changed. In 1429 an assize had been adjourned to Westminster on bastardy pleaded, and on the day *in banc* the party alleged to be a bastard pleaded that since the last continuance he had been certified legitimate in a replevin brought against his bailiff, who had made cognisance for rent arrear under a lease granted by his ancestor and had prayed him in aid as heir, and that judgment had been given on the certificate. Paston, for the other side, at once offered to aver that there was no such lease ever granted, but the only comfort he received from the court was an assurance that they would be happy to seal a bill of exceptions if he cared to tender one.[80] We should perhaps add that the reporter seems to have been rather shocked at the decision. It is only fair to say that the judges seem to have taken a less benevolent view of those who were attempting to bastardise their opponents rather than to establish their own legitimacy. Thus in 1464 we find the Common Pleas deferring judgment. One of the plaintiffs in an action of trespass had been certified bastard by the Ordinary. However, nobody had seen this particular plaintiff in court. Nobody knew, or at least, nobody was prepared to say, who had appeared and pleaded on his behalf. Finally, he lived at a very considerable distance from the land in which the trespass was alleged. The court clearly suspected that the action had been brought in his name by someone who wished to have the question of his legitimacy determined without interference from him, and had the plaintiff called. When he did not appear, they adjourned to consider whether they should not enter a nonsuit.[81]

The precise effect of the rule that the court would not write to the Ordinary more than once is a more difficult question. On what may be called the anti-clerical view, if a certificate be pleaded as an estoppel against an allegation of bastardy, it will prevent the other party from raising any issue which would have to be sent to the Ordinary for trial, for that would be to require the court to write to the Ordinary a second time. It will not, on the other hand, prevent the court from receiving any averment which is triable by the country.[82] In 1354, in assize, the King's Bench actually held that since in assize general bastardy may be tried by the country, it is allowable in assize to plead general bastardy against a party who has been certified legitimate in formedon.[83] No other case goes quite so far as this, and in the fifteenth century the rule is stated in more moderate terms. If the Ordinary should certify a party bastard this is conclusive, for a bastard by one law is bastard by the other. If he certify the party legitimate, an averment may be admitted against the certificate, for there are cases in which a man is legitimate by the spiritual law but a bastard by the law of the realm.[84] As we have seen, it is not entirely true that anyone who was bastard by the spiritual law was a bastard by the law of the realm, and it is rather doubtful whether in practice the court would have been very willing to admit any averment against a certificate except birth before espousals, which is the averment most commonly offered in the reported cases.

The problem for a party who had the common law in his favour and the spiritual law against him, was how far he could by careful pleading withdraw the question from the Ordinary and send it to the country. Upon this, it is not very easy to express a definite opinion—for a number of reasons. Counsel would ordinarily be reluctant to hazard his case upon a demurrer unless he were very sure of his ground, or very sure that if the issue to which he objected were admitted the case was lost in any

event. Thus a party may accept an averment which he would not have
been bound to accept, and if an objection be abandoned when the other
side proves obstinate, it does not necessarily follow that the objection
was a bad one. Again, judicial attitudes varied. We may cite an exchange
between Hankford and Norton in 1410. Hankford observes in the course
of discussion that the issue of a marriage within the degrees are bastards.
Norton asks how they are bastards. Hankford answers that the court will
write to the Ordinary, who will certify them bastards. Norton replies that
this may be true in novel disseisin brought by the issue, but should the
issue die and his heir bring a writ of entry *sur disseisin* on the same ouster,
the court will try the question by the country and the issue will be held
legitimate.[85] Neither judge is wrong. The question is, if we state simply
that A is bastard, which law is to be regarded as setting the standard of
what constitutes bastardy, and which law merely engrafts certain exceptions upon the general rule? There were certainly some judges who were
not at all distressed by the reflection that the Ordinary might very well
arrive at a conclusion which a court of common law would not have
reached upon the same facts. Thus in 1365 the tenant in assize made title
be descent, the plaintiff replied that the tenant was bastard, the tenant
rejoined that his father had married his mother in Aldgate and that he
was born within the espousals, and the plaintiff surrejoined that the tenant
was born at Lambeth out of any espousals. The question was, whether
this were an issue for the country or for the Ordinary. One of the reasons
which the court gave for sending it to the Ordinary was that there were
grounds of legitimacy which might be considered in Court Christian, but
of which a court of common law could not take notice.[86] So again, in
1370 the tenant in assize claimed that the parents of the plaintiff had been
divorced, and the issue of legitimacy was sent to Court Christian. The
Ordinary certified in rather careful terms that the plaintiff's parents had
been lawfully married, and the court refused to hold the certificate insufficient. Since a divorce could only be granted on the ground that the
marriage was unlawful, if the plaintiff's parents had been lawfully married,
it necessarily followed that they could not have been divorced.[87] However,
it should be observed that it seems to be assumed that if the court had
been placed in a position in which it was bound to take judicial notice
that the plaintiff's parents had been divorced, it would have been bound
to apply the common law. The same assumption underlies the reasoning
in an even more remarkable case upon a certificate, which had been decided
some years earlier. The tenant in assize pleaded that J was seised and
married A, and had issue the tenant, a son, and the plaintiff, a daughter.
The plaintiff replied that the tenant was a bastard, and despite the tenant's
protest that the plaintiff ought to answer the allegation of birth within

espousals, the issue was sent to the Ordinary. The Ordinary certified that the tenant had been born after his mother had eloped from her husband, and when she was living in sin with an immoral cleric, and he was therefore bastard. The tenant petitioned everyone who was available to be petitioned. There was a hearing in Parliament. There were consultations with the Chancellor. There was a hearing before the Council, of whose views the King's Bench declined to take any notice, since the Council had no power to reverse their judgments. Finally it was decided that the only material part of the certificate was the conclusion, that the tenant was a bastard. If reasons were given, they were surplusage, and if they were contrary to law they would not vitiate the certificate, but would be rejected.[88] If, as the Year Book report would have it, the plaintiff had actually disclosed that she was proposing to bastardise the tenant on the ground that he was born in adultery before the tenant was forced protesting to the Ordinary, the case is an even more striking example of judicial nescience, and such a high standard was not very easy to maintain. There was no doubt that if it were admitted upon the record that a party's parents had been married, he could be bastardised only by special pleading.[89] It could fairly be argued that in these circumstances it was not entirely logical to hold that if he pleaded that his parents were married, the other side was not bound to answer the allegation, but might allege bastardy generally. Thus, in another assize reported in the same year as the notable case of the over-specific certificate, the tenant made title by descent and gave colour to the plaintiff as bastard. The plaintiff replied that his father had espoused his mother at a named Church and that he was born after the espousals, and prayed the assize. The case was adjourned to Westminster, and the court seemed very definitely to incline to the opinion that the tenant ought to answer the replication, since there were cases in which one born within espousals was legitimate by the common law and a bastard by the spiritual law. The tenant's counsel thought it more prudent to do so, and lost the case as a result. He attempted to aver that the plaintiff's parents had been divorced for spiritual affinity by the Ordinary in his visitation, but was not prepared to allege that sentence was given during their lives.[90] The reporter of the *Liber Assisarum* thought that he would have done better to demur. Once the marriage was confessed, and he had nothing better than a posthumous "divorce" to allege against it, the case was at an end. On demurrer, his case would at least have been arguable. The position was still uncertain in the following century. In 1432, in a writ of entry in nature of an assize, Candish pleaded that A was seised, and married B, by whom he had issue C, whose estate the tenant had. The demandant replied that C was a bastard. Candish protested, but finally took the issue tendered. Paston then asked him why he had not demurred. Martin, who was given to emphatic language, declared that he would have demurred in Candish's place if the land had been worth twenty pounds a year. However, Strange thought that a demurrer would have failed, and Cottesmore said that there were precedents both ways.[91] The last pre-Reformation case in which this question arose directly is perhaps rather special. In trespass *de bonis asportatis* the defendant pleaded that the plaintiff was his villein. The plaintiff replied that he was a bastard. The defendant rejoined that the plaintiff was born within espousals. The rejoinder was held insufficient, since the plaintiff might have been born when his mother's husband was beyond the four seas.[92] The actual decision was probably influenced by the *favor libertatis*, but it is noteworthy that the court was not prepared to go so far as to hold that the only admissible answer to an allegation of bastardy is an equally general allegation of legitimacy. The pleadings in the case of 1479, which is generally and not unreasonably taken as marking the final rejection by the common lawyers of the doctrine of putative marriage, are also of some interest. The action was trespass. The defendant pleaded that A was seised, and married B, and had issue him. The plaintiff replied that A and B were divorced for consanguinity, and to this replication the defendant demurred.[93] If we are to judge the defendant's pleading by the standards of a century earlier, it was imprudent, to use no harsher term. For a party obliged to rely on the doctrine of putative marriage, the sensible course was to claim as son and heir of A, and, if the other side then attempted to allege that he was issue of a marriage which had ended in divorce, to argue that this was bastardy and should be so pleaded—and sent to the Ordinary. It is a little difficult to believe that the defendant's pleader would have offered the plaintiff an opportunity of putting the divorce in issue unless this were an issue to which, as the law then stood, he could have been forced in any event. Once it has become settled that the rules of the common law must be applied where the facts which make them applicable appear, the relationship between civil and ecclesiastical jurisdiction is necessarily a delicate and somewhat unstable one, and the encroachments of the common lawyers did not necessarily begin with Sir Edward Coke.

NOTES

* At the time when this paper was written, I was no acquainted with the article "Bastardy Litigation in Medieval England" published in volume 13 of the *American Journal of Legal History* by R. B. Helmholz, who was present at the conference and who subsequently favoured me with an offprint. Much of this paper deals with questions which he had already covered, and from a wider range of sources. I have thought it more candid to print the substance of my own paper as it was delivered, but the reader who wishes to inform himself about the subject would do well to consult Helmholz's article.

1 X. 4.3.2 (For an explanation of the mode of citation, and a list of the editions of the texts used, see p. 49).

2 X. 4.19.3; 2.13.8 (juncta gl. *legitime*); 2.13.10; 2.13.13.

3 c.1, 30 q.5.

4 Johannes Andreae at X. 4.17.5 (who points out that the presumption against marriage does not apply with the same force if the parties are dead).

[5] Durandus, *Speculum*, Lib. IV, Partic. III, Qui Matrimonium Accusare possunt; Hostiensis, *Summa Aurea*, Lib. IV, Quis Admittatur ad Accusationem Matrimonii.

[6] X. 4.7.1.

[7] Hostiensis, at X. 4.15.4.

[8] Innocentius, *ibid.*

[9] gl. *separari*, X. 4.19.3.

[10] X. 4.17.11.

[11] X. 4.17.10.

[12] gl. *incongruum*, X. 4.17.7, and compare gl. *quod autem*, 24 q.2, in princ.

[13] X. 4.17.14.

[14] BNB i.104ff.

[15] Bracton f.416ff.

[16] BNB i.104ff.

[17] 66 SS 7.

[18] YB 5 Ed.2, Trin. pl.10, f.171 (33 SS 161); 7 Ed.2, Mich, pl.14, f.208 (36 SS 158).

[19] YB 7 Ed.2, 208 (36 SS 159).

[20] YB 12 Ed. 2, Pasch. pl.14 (70 SS) 133.

[21] YB 6 Ed.2, Hil. pl.35 (43 SS) 72, 74.

[22] YB 5 Ed.2, Trin. pl.10, f.171 (33 SS 161 . 163).

[23] YB 8 Ed.3, Mich. pl.43, f.14; 8 Ass. p.5.

[24] On the position of the feoffor who has delivered seisin on condition but has no deed to show, see Littleton, ss.365–9.

[25] YB 17 Ed.3, Trin. pl.20, f.41 (RS 546–7).

[26] YB 18 Ed.3, Mich. pl.12, f.33 (18 & 19 Ed.3 RS 33).

[17] YB 20 Ed.3, Trin. pl.31, 1 RS 563.

[28] Bracton f.420b.

[29] Gl. *incongruum*, X. 4.17.7.

[30] X. 4.17.5, 7.

[31] YB 6 Ed.2, Trin. pl.11, f.200 (36 SS 31, 32).

[32] YB 17 Ed.3, Mich. pl.43, f.57, pl.93, f.68 (17 & 18 Ed.3 RS 239, 386).

[33] H. 33 Ed.3, Verdict 48.

[34] Littleton ss. 399–401.

[35] 11 Ed.1, Bastardy 27.

[36] YB 2 Ed.2, Trin. pl.99A, f.43 (17 SS 184).

[37] YB 30 & 31 Ed.1 (RS) 287 (in Eyre).

[38] H. 33 Ed.3, Verdict 48.

[39] YB 11 Ed.2, Mich. pl.21, f.328 (61 SS 74).

[40] See, on this form of pleading, YBB 5 Ed.2, Trin. pl.14, f.171 (33 SS 186); 11 H.4, Pasch. pl.4, f.56, Trin. pl.15, f.74; 13 H.4, Mich. pl.8, f.14. It was a controversial question whether it were not necessary to give A another father, but this would not be a serious difficulty in practice. If once the question of A's paternity could be got before a jury, it would be for him to establish that he was the son of B.

[41] YBB 32 & 33 Ed.1 (RS) 143; 3 & 4 Ed.2, Mich. pl.3 (32 SS) 30; 11 Ed.2, Mich. pl.18, f.327 (61 SS 63); and contrast 9 Ed.3, Trin. pl.4, f.19.

[42] YB 33–35 Ed.1 (RS) 119.

[43] Bracton f.419.

[44] YB 6 Ed.2 (43 SS) 72 (above, n.21).

[45] 42 SS xxxvi (Introduction to YB 4 Ed.2, from MS. *Y*).

[46] YB 8 Ed.3, Mich. pl.43, f.14; 8 Ass. pl.5.

[47] YBB 38 Ed.3, f.26; 39 Ed. 3, 31; cf. 26 Ass. pl.64.

[48] YB 14 H.4, Hil. pl.12, at f.36.

[49] YB 3 Ed.4, 11.

[50] YB 49 Ed.3, Pasch. pl.11 at f.18.

[51] YB 39 Ed.3, f.31 (*per* Thirning); 11 H.4 at f.38.

[52] *Catesby's Case*, YB 49 Ed.3, Pasch. pl.11, f.17, 50 Ed.3, Trin. pl.13, f.19; 49 Ass. pl.7, S.C.

[53] YB 44 Ed.3, Pasch. pl.21, f.12; 45 Ed. 3, Trin. pl.45, f.28, S.C.

[54] Lyndwood, Lib. IV, tit. III, c. quia, *circa finem.*

[55] H. 10 H.3, Dower 201. This decision somewhat perturbed the author of the *New Natura Brevium*, since in his time women of a certain social position were ordinarily married by special licence in private chapels. See F.N.B. 150N.

[56] *Swinburne on Spousals* at p.15.

[57] *Swinburne on Spousals* provides a reasonably full account in English.

[58] *Casus Placitorum* (ed. W. H. Dunham) (1950/1952) 69 SS lxxvi, 8; YB 11 Ed.2 (61 SS) 262; YB 11 & 12 Ed.3 (RS) 481.

[59] YB 11 Ed.2, Mich. pl.21, f.328 (61 SS 75).

[60] YB 39 Ed.3, Mich. f 31.

[61] YB 21 H.7, Mich. pl.53, f.39.
[62] YB 11 Ed.2, Hil. pl.39 (61 SS) 262.
[63] YB 18 Ed.4, 29.
[64] H. 22 Ed.4, Consultacion 5.
[65] YB 39 Ed.3, Mich f.32, at 33, *per* Knivet.
[66] YB 18 H.6, 30.
[67] YB 7 H.4, Hil. pl.13, f.9. Cf. *ibid.*, Mich. pl.2, f.22.
[68] YB 35 H.6, 9.
[69] Note 53 *above.*
[70] YB 2 Ed.2, Mich. pl.129 (19 SS) 53.
[71] YB 1 H.6, 3.
[72] 33 Ass. pl.8.
[73] 29 Ass. pl.54. Cf. 38 Ass. pl.24.
[74] YB 1 H.6, 3.
[75] Bracton f.405.
[76] YB 39 Ed.3, Mich. f.31; 39 Ass. pl.10. In the *Liber Assisarum* it is Kirkham who appears for the tenant.
[77] H. 22 Ed.4, Consultacion 5.
[78] YB 30 Ed.3, Trin. f.8.
[79] Bracton f.419b.
[80] YB 7 H.6, 37.
[81] YB 3 Ed.4, 11.
[82] YB 11 Ed.3 Mich. (RS) 223, at 231–5.
[83] 26 Ass. pl.64, YB 27 Ed.3, 6, S.C.
[84] YB 11 H.4, Trin. pl.32, f.8 ; 33 H.6 at f.50, *per* Prisot.
[85] YB 11 H.4, Trin. pl.18 at f.78.
[86] YB 38 Ed.3, Mich. f.26, 38 Ass. pl.30, S.C.
[87] 43 Ass. pl.43.
[88] 38 Ass. pl.14, YB 39 Ed.3, Trin. f.14, Bastardy 8. The reports vary.
[89] YB 40 Ed.3, Pasch. pl.6, f.16.
[90] 39 Ed.3, 31; 39 Ass. pl.10.
[91] YB 10 H.6, 23.
[92] YB 19 H.6, 17.
[93] YB 18 Ed.4, 29.

MODE OF CITATION

In the *Decretum*, the first part is cited by the number of the Distinction, and of the canon, thus: 76 dist., c..2 The second part is cited by the number of the canon, of the *causa*, and of the *quaestio*, thus: c.2, 25 q.5, save for the *Tractatus de Poenitentia*, which is cited as *De Poen.*, with the number of the distinction and of the canon. The third part, the *Tractatus de Consecratione*, is cited as *De Cons.*, again with the number of the distinction and of the canon.

The Decretals are nowadays indicated by the letter X., followed by the number of the book, the title, and the chapter. The Sext and the Clementines are cited in the same manner, with the addition of Lib.6 or Cle.

Glosses are cited by the word to which they are appended, and the text in which the word occurs, thus: gl. *legitime*, X.2.13.8.

EDITIONS USED

Andreae, Johannes *Novellae.* Venice, 1523.
Durandus, Gulielmus (Nimatensis Episcopus) *Speculum Juris.* Venice, 1585.
Hostiensis (Cardinalis, Henricus de Segusio) *Summa Aurea.* Basel, 1673. *In Quartum Decretalium Librum Commentaria.* Venice, 1581.
Innocentius (IV, Papa) *Apparatus super Quinque Libris Decretalium.* Lyons, 1525.
Lyndwood (Guilelmus) *Provinciale.* Oxford, 1679.

A Transatlantic View of the British Constitution, 1760-76

William Huse Dunham, Jr

> What do we mean by the Revolution? The war? That was no part of the Revolution; it was only an effect and consequence of it. The Revolution was in the minds of the people, and this was effected, from 1760 to 1775, . . . before a drop of blood was shed at Lexington . . . the public opinion was enlightened and informed concerning the authority of parliament over the colonies.
>
> *John Adams to Thomas Jefferson, 1815.*[1]

KING George III's subjects living overseas, who called themselves British Americans, held the British constitution in high esteem and often applauded its excellence. James Otis in 1764 wrote of "the grandeur of the British constitution", and other colonials constantly praised its virtues and considered it the prototype of their own forms of government. In addition, the Americans included within the constitution the subjects' rights and liberties as expressly stated in the 1689 Bill of Rights and as inferred from England's history since the days of Magna Carta. These men had learned their English history, Whiggish in tone, from writers like Bulstrode Whitelock, Gilbert Burnet, and Paul de Rapin; and their knowledge of the common law came from Coke and Hale, and more recently from Blackstone. Nearly 2,500 copies of his *Commentaries* had reached the Atlantic seaboard before 1776. Many British Americans had for long accepted the British constitution as a thing fixed, settled, static, and, of course, sacred. They continued to laud, as did Samuel Langdon, the president of Harvard in 1775, "that constitution of government which has so long been the glory and strength of the English nation". And even after Independence, Alexander Hamilton in 1787 proclaimed the British system of government to be "the best model the world ever produced".[2]

However, most Americans' understanding of the British constitution after 1760 led them to believe that King George III's ministers and his parliaments, in their dealings with the colonists, were acting unconstitutionally. This belief produced a sense of moral outrage and self-righteousness that drove the continental colonists to a military solution, the War of Independence. During the 1760s, the British Americans' view of the constitution was conservative, and only in the 1770s did they contemplate innovation. Their point of view gradually changed from a retrospective one to a prospective and progressive outlook—as did that of many Britons in the 1780s. In contrast, ministerial policy and parliamentary legislation seemed to follow the dictates of logic more than those of creative imagination. Harmsworth explained it all to the House of Commons on 29 March 1928:

> If we are to rule the country and make the constitution on the grounds of logic and abstract theory, we shall have to scrap most of the British constitution and most of the time-honoured traditions of the House. . . . Only on one occasion in our history have we acted on grounds of logic, and on that occasion we lost the United States of America.[3]

Following the 1763 Peace of Paris, however, logical solutions to administrative problems—how to make the American colonies pay their way and how to make the British Americans pay up—produced a period of transatlantic conflict. The economic urge led to political quarrels in several colonies, and these in turn the colonists translated into constitutional issues. The laws, orders, and commands of George III's ministers and of his parliaments put the British Americans into a defensive posture. They took the British constitution's existence for granted, they believed that the British government was violating its principles, and these they cited to justify their position. From their belief in the British constitution followed naturally the idea that unwanted words and disliked deeds were contrary to the accustomed rules of public law and might be called unconstitutional. The stand that the Americans took was at first conservative and was based on the old shibboleths, Magna Carta, the 1628 Petition of Right, 1689 Bill of Rights, and the Revolution Settlement. Consequently, they denounced the innovative practices of the British ministers and certain acts of the Westminster parliament as unconstitutional.

Paradoxically, the British Americans' conception of the unconstitutional worked to determine their view of the constitution, one that was for the year 1760 historically sound and traditional. The colonists had not yet comprehended, let alone accepted, those non-constitutional novelties, prime minister and cabinet, party and formed opposition, as authorised parts of the British frame of government. Nor did they wholly accept parliament's legislative competence throughout the British Empire. At Westminster the transatlantic "people" were represented only "virtually", and the political ineptitude of six different ministries compelled the colonists to adopt a constitutional position like the one that Abel Boyer, a pamphleteer, described in January 1731:

> The people or their representatives the parliament, may impeach the king's advisers, but never can impeach himself. Indeed if the king pretend to defend his ministers by arms, the representatives in parliament may take arms against such advisers, and in

defense of our constitution: Or if the king in any manner prevent the peoples having representatives in parliament, the collective body of the people may then take arms, and thereby punish the evil counsellors of the king, but cannot touch his sacred person.[4]

The practice of attacking evil counsellors, as old as Edward II, was useless to the British Americans since they had no spokesmen from America in parliament. The colonists could not criticize effectively those ministers, let alone oppose or impeach them, whose conduct, words, and policies, whose orders-in-council and acts of parliament seemed to Americans unconstitutional. And so their concept of the British constitution, of the lawful way to govern, made the Americans, not rebels, but conservators of the ancient forms and principles of constitutional governance. Their formula was, until 1775, reformation by conservation, in contrast to the British government's reformation by innovation. John Adams attacked the British as "innovators": "When so many innovations are introduced, to the injury of our constitution of civil government," Adams proclaimed in 1771, "it is not surprising that the great securities of the people, should be invaded, and their fundamental rights drawn into question." The next spring, 1772, Adams asked the citizens of Braintree: "What is the tendency of the late innovation?" "Is not the natural and necessary tendency of these innovations, to introduce dark intrigues, insincerity, simulation, bribery and perjury, among customs officers, merchants, masters, mariners and their servants?"[5]

The British American assumptions of what was constitutional and what unconstitutional were the familiar ones that Britons themselves took for granted. They relied upon past precedent, the established rules of public law, and upon England's history, too, and this may explain their excessive legalism and their moral self-righteousness. However, the constitutional reasons that impelled the British Americans to deny their allegiance to the crown and to declare the thirteen colonies free and independent states, just as Henry VIII had declared England's independence in 1533, are simple and clear. They refused, after a trying decade of constitutional conflicts, to be taxed without the consent of their representatives; they objected to the British parliament's claim to an imperial sovereignty and to its making their laws; and they did not like to have their disputes and litigation adjudicated in courts manned by judges whom the king of Great Britain and his ministers appointed and over whom, and over their salaries, the colonists had no control. In short, the British Americans believed that George III's ministers and his parliaments, from 1763 to 1775, were violating fundamental principles of public law and governance.

The political events that produced these constitutional issues sprang directly or indirectly from Acts of Parliament. The British Americans' evasion of the customs duties imposed by the 1733 Molasses Act provoked the collectors in 1761 to seek writs of assistance such as the British exchequer granted. These were like the general warrants for search and seizure that Lord Camden condemned in the Wilkes case in 1763. The 1764 Sugar Act assumed that parliament had a right to tax the Americans. The 1765 Stamp Act, to tax legal documents and newspapers, again raised the issue of taxation without the consent of the taxed, or of their representatives. The Declaratory Act that repealed the Stamp Act in 1766 was entitled, tactlessly, "an act for the better securing the dependency of his majesty's dominions in America upon the crown and parliament of Great Britain;" and it declared, impoliticly, that the "colonies . . . in America have been, are, and of right ought to be subordinate unto and dependent upon the imperial crown and parliament".[6] This statute, some Americans felt, broke the original contract between the colony and the king as expressed in its royal charter or compact. Townshend's Revenue Act, 1767, evaded the constitutional issue and simply declared it expedient to raise money in the king's American colonies; but to do so ran contrary to precedents that the consent of the subjects, or of their representatives, was given when they granted gifts and taxes to the king. This law also affirmed a colonial court's right to issue writs of assistance and thereby asserted the validity in America of Acts of Parliament and, implicitly, of the Westminster parliament's sovereignty overseas.

The year before, in June 1766, New Yorkers had refused, in accordance with the spirit of the 1628 Petition of Right, to quarter British troops as the 1765 Quartering Act prescribed. So in June 1767 parliament passed a bill that suspended the New York assembly. The next January, the Massachusetts general court sent letters of protest against the Townshend Acts to Lords Shelburne, Rockingham, Chatham, and Camden. Samuel Adams drafted these documents, and they expressed the assembly's belief that "there are, my lord, fundamental rules of the constitution, which it is humbly presumed, neither the supreme legislative nor the supreme executive can alter. In all free states, the constitution is fixed." Then they asked, "if the remotest subjects are bound by the ties of allegiance, . . . are they not by the rules of equity, intitled to all rights of that constitution, which ascertains and limits both sovereignty and allegiance?" The men of Massachusetts believed that the sanctity of property and the principle of consent were "ingrafted into the British constitution as a fundamental law". In October 1768 British troops arrived in Boston to pursue a military solution to these administrative problems. Thereafter, the constitutional position deteriorated. The Boston Massacre occurred in 1770, and in 1773 the Boston Tea Party demonstrated against the still retained tax on tea. Parliament followed in 1774 with "an Act for the better regulating the government of" Massachusetts, a statute that seemed to revoke the colony's charter—what was to the colonists a mini-constitution.[7] On 19 April 1775 the skirmishes, as they are euphemistically called, at Lexington and Concord produced a body count, as we say today, of 49 Americans and 173 British; and two months later, 17 June, the Battle of Bunker's Hill took the lives of 140 Americans and 226 Britons. A war, an undeclared one, was on, and thus ended the first stage in the Americans' intellectual and constitutional revolution.

All this time the British Americans had been contemplating their relation to the kingdom and the crown and the empire under the British constitution. Men took for granted the existence of that constitution. The word now meant more than a frame or structure of government, and more than a monarchy, whether mixed, limited, or balanced. Bolingbroke had defined the word, about 1735, as "that assemblage of laws, institutions, and customs, derived from certain fixed principles of reason . . . that compose the general system, according to which the community hath agreed to be governed". And David Hume called the constitution, just as vaguely, "the established practice of the age". Others, however, preferred Obadiah Hulme's more precise definition (one printed in London in 1771 and in Pennsylvania in 1776): "a set of fundamental rules by which even the supreme power of the state shall be governed". British Americans had recognized in 1765 that the British constitution possessed both "principles and spirit", and in 1769 the Reverend J. J. Zubly of Savannah held that "all the British subjects everywhere have a right to be ruled by the known principles of their common constitution". Then the First Continental Congress declared in 1774 that the North American colonists enjoyed their rights "by the immutable law of nature, the principles of the English constitution, and their several charters or compacts". When deeds and words ran counter to such basic, organic rules of governance and principles of public law, men called such offences anti-constitutional ("opposed to the constitution"). In New York in 1728 Governor Burnet was accused of fostering "an anti-constitutional project"; and in Britain Bolingbroke wrote of the "anti-constitutional dependency of the two houses of parliament on the crown". The idea of unconstitutionality was enriched when the *Maryland Gazette* in 1748 asked "whether a parliament (or in America an assembly . . .) has a power, i.e. a right, to enact anything contrary to a fundamental part of the British constitution".[8]

The word *unconstitutional* (meaning "at variance with the recognized principles of the state") first appeared, perhaps naturally, in North America. *The Committee on Grievances of the Pennsylvania Assembly* in February 1757 charged the proprietors with having "abridged and restricted . . . [the] governor's discretion in matters of legislation, by their illegal, impracticable, and unconstitutional instructions and prohibitions". The idea of unconstitutionality was implied in James Otis's remark of 1761 that a statute "against the constitution is void". The Stamp Act and the Declaratory Act brought the words *constitutional* and *unconstitutional* into play, and they passed to and fro across the Atlantic in each packet. Benjamin Franklin, in London in 1766, referred to internal taxes as "unconstitutional and unjust"; while in Philadelphia the next year John Dickinson declared an "act of parliament . . . to be unconstitutional". The Abington town meeting in 1768 was quite confident that Boston's non-importation agreement would "frustrate the schemes of the enemies of the constitution and . . . render ineffectual the said unconstitutional and unrighteous acts" of the Westminster parliament. Bolingbroke had put parliament beneath the constitution when he wrote in 1733: "Great Britain, according to our present constitution, cannot be undone by parliaments; for there is something, which a parliament cannot do. A parliament cannot annul the constitution." Three dissentient peers in 1763 became "seriously alarmed at a stretch of power so wide, so unnecessary, and so unconstitutional"; and Blackstone used the word in 1765 when he wrote of "the unconstitutional oppressions, even of the sovereign power". In 1770 dissentient lords called a bill "highly repugnant to every essential principle of the constitution", and Chatham proclaimed in parliament, "the constitution at this moment stands violated".[9]

British Americans, too, believed that parliament could violate the constitution. The First Continental Congress resolved in 1774 that several Acts of Parliament were "impolitic, unjust, and cruel, as well as unconstitutional"; and this same year Robert Carter Nicholas, at Williamsburg, Virginia, carried the concept of unconstitutionality towards a logical conclusion: "no obedience is due to arbitrary, unconstitutional edicts calculated to enslave a free people". At Westminster in February 1775, eighteen lords, including Rockingham and Camden, condemned parliament's refusal to accept the petitions of American merchants, and these peers denounced "the disgrace and mischief which must attend this unconstitutional, indecent, and improvident proceeding". By 1775 the transatlantic crisis had made men on both sides of the ocean well aware and mindful of the unconstitutional; and twenty years later the foremost founding father, George Washington, coined the abstract word *unconstitutionality*.[10] Long before this, the idea of the unconstitutional had begun to perform its inherent function: to define the negative aspects of the presumed British constitution, and to set a limit to legitimate governance.

The British Americans' concept of the constitution contained three strains of thought. First, there were fundamental rules that ministers, committees, the Board of Trade, and some statutes had laid down to control the actual governance of a colony. Then there were the two great myths, or theories, of mixed government and a balanced constitution, and these circulated up and down the Atlantic seaboard. Most significant of all, however, was the colonists' belief in the fundamental constitutional principles transmitted from England's medieval past: contract and consent, responsibility and representation, majority rule with its corollaries criticism and dissent, and the rule of law through the duly recognized processes of legislation, administration, and adjudication. The instructions given to each new governor at his departure overseas contained the rules and principles that were to guide his conduct. Those that Benjamin Fletcher took with him to New York in 1692 describe a replica of the English frame of government. The governor was the king's viceroy, "our captain general and governor-in-chief", who was to call together the "council for that province". He might seek the council's advice, and he was to administer to the councillors the oath of office prescribed in the 1689 Bill of Rights. He might instruct them as he saw fit and convenient, but he was to allow the council "freedom of debate and vote in all things to be debated of in council." The appointment of "the principal officers, judges, assistants, justices, and sheriffs," was the governor's duty, and the appointees were to be "men of estate and ability, and not necessitous people or much in debt;" and they were to "be persons well affected to our government". The council with the assembly might enact laws, ordinances, and statutes, and grants of money to the king were to be made "according to the style of acts of parliament in England". Here, then, was New York's authority to legislate and raise revenue, and the governor was not to issue or dispose of "any public money" except "by and with the advice and consent of the council".[11]

The colonists ardently believed that the British government was both mixed and balanced, and this affected their understanding of the British constitution. The idea of mixed monarchy had begun to wane in Britain, but it lingered on to 1861 when Lord Brougham expounded its history and its theory. A century earlier, the notion puzzled and plagued Americans who confounded mixed government with a balanced constitution. For mixture, many Britons had substituted balance as the operative principle, whereas many Americans still believed the constitution a mixed one. They accepted the apparent identity of the king, lords, and commons assembled in parliament with the three estates of the realm and, simultaneously, with the Aristotelian trilogy, monarchy, aristocracy, and democracy. Then to maintain unity and consistency, they balanced king, lords, and commons against one another; and they counterpoised the governmental functions, executive, legislative, and judicial. To make their confusion worse confounded, they put into an equipoise the three estates—

the lords spiritual, the lords temporal, and the commons, or the king, the lords, and the commons. British Americans tried valiantly to make sense out of this welter of inherited constitutional ideas and to conceive of a balanced British constitution, one that had begun as a metaphorical description but was rapidly becoming a prescriptive principle. In the spring of 1776, John Adams' book, *Thoughts on Government*, advocated a government that would balance the functions, legislative, executive, and judicial, on the basis of a separation of their respective powers and authority.

Concern over a balance of power among the parts of government had appeared early in the century when Americans compared their colonial governments to the British. In 1728, the royal governor, William Burnet, had told the Massachusetts House that the British parliament was "a pattern to the Assemblies in the plantations," and he pointed out how "the three distinct branches of the legislature, preserved in due balance, form the excellency of the *British* constitution." And Burnet concluded, "I need not draw the parallel at length; it speaks for itself." Fatal words that fell on an all too fertile soil. In 1766 Franklin told the House of Commons committee that the colonists had "assemblies of their own, which are their parliaments." Already in 1749, Dr William Douglas of Boston had combined mixed and balanced government when he compared the American and British forms. The colonial governments,

> in conformity to our legislature in Great Britain . . . consist of three separate negatives; thus, by the governor, representing the king, the colonies are monarchical; by the council, they are aristocratical; by a house of representatives or delegates from the people, they are democratical; . . . the several negatives being checks upon one another. The concurrence of these three forms of government seems to be the highest perfection that human civil government can attain to in times of peace . . .: if it did not sound too profane by making too free with the mystical expressions of our religion, I should call it *a trinity in unity*.

However neat and symmetrical this verisimilitude to the British constitution might appear, it was not one that held up in practice. The governor was not the king, nor could he be identified as yet with the prime minister; and the council, whether elected by the assembly or appointed by the governor, was neither an English privy council nor a house of lords. Down south, men were aware of this discrepancy, and in Maryland they asserted, "the upper house is no part of our constitution". In South Carolina, its *Gazette* of 1756 had contrasted, rather than equated, the colony's government with Britain's. "Since there is no nobility . . . one estate or part of the British constitution" was lacking. A council appointed only during the king's pleasure could not act as a second chamber and, as the *Gazette* said, "must necessarily destroy the balance and be contrary to the usage of our mother country".[12]

E

Other Americans detected other fallacies in the apparent resemblance between the British and the colonial constitutions. During the 1760s they came to realize that the British constitution, which they so much admired, did not describe the actual form of their own colonial establishments. Richard Henry Lee noted in 1766 that Virginia's constitution had been modelled on the British; but

> unhappily for us, my brother, it is an exterior semblance only; . . . essential variations appear between it and the happily poised English constitution. . . . That security therefore which the constitution derives in Britain from the house of lords is here entirely wanting, and the just equilibrium totally destroyed.

A destruction of the balance, an imbalance, or an absence of balance would seem, from the British Americans' point of view, to nullify the basic principle of any constitution. James Otis waxed lyrical in 1764 over a highly romanticized British constitution. He mistook the ideal for the real and set forth the doctrine of checks and balances. When an error in government occurred, such as a bad Act of Parliament, and became "evident and palpable," then, Otis proclaimed,

> the judges of the executive courts have declared the act "of a whole parliament void". See here the grandeur of the British constitution! See the wisdom of our ancestors! The supreme legislative, and the supreme executive, are a perpetual check and balance to each other. If the supreme executive errs, it is informed by the supreme legislative in parliament: if the supreme legislative errs, it is informed by the supreme executive in the king's courts of law. Here the king appears, as represented by his judges, in the highest lustre and majesty, as supreme executor of the commonwealth; and he never shines brighter, but on his throne, at the head of the supreme legislative. This is government! This is a constitution![13]

So complete a confusion of mixed and balanced government anticipated both the United States Constitution of 1787 and Walter Bagehot's *English Constitution*.

When Bostonians in 1772 drew up a list of violations of their rights, the whole constitutional vocabulary exploded like shrapnel. They put together into an illogical conglomerate the concept of a mixed constitution with that of a balanced. They combined the separation of powers with a connection of parts, the idea of an equilibrium with that of a greater confidence in the crown, and they joined government by contract with the constitutional principles. First they declared that "fleets and armies have been introduced to support these unconstitutional officers in collecting and managing this unconstitutional revenue", a "revenue arising from this tax unconstitutionally laid". Then they laid down the fundamental proposition:

> It is absolutely necessary in a mixt government like that of this province, that a due proportion or balance of power should be established among the several branches of legislative. Our ancestors received from King William and Queen Mary a charter

by which it was understood by both parties in the contract, that such a proportion or balance was fixed; and therefore everything which renders any one branch of the legislative more independent of the other two than it was originally designed, is an alteration of the constitution as settled by the charter.

The Boston Town Meeting condemned His Majesty's action in paying the governor of Massachusetts £1,500 annually out of the American revenue, "independent of the assembly". This was why "the ancient connection between him [the king] and this people is weakened, the confidence in the governor lessened and the equilibrium destroyed, and the constitution essentially altered". Governor Burnet's father's *History* of the Glorious Revolution had taught Bostonians all too well. By the 1770s British Americans were well aware that instructions to the royal governors, practices of their officers, orders-in-council, and Acts of Parliament no longer jibed with the basic principles that they believed to belong to the estimable English constitution. Their roseate view of that constitution made it easier for them to detect the unconstitutionality of many words and deeds that flowed from London. Samuel Seabury, a Tory and America's first Bishop, reported in 1774 that his fellow countrymen thought "the British government—the *king, lords*, and *commons*—have laid a regular plan to enslave America, and that they are now deliberately putting it in execution".[14] This conspiracy they attributed to the king's ministers who had gained control over parliament itself by influence, management, and corruption and so had perverted the British constitution.

All that America's friends, like Chatham, Burke, and Camden, had to offer were new names—imperial constitution and imperial parliament—for the same old things, the British constitution and the Westminster parliament. Burke argued that this parliament had a dual capacity, but the idea that a different title could convert the national legislature of the United Kingdom into an imperial one for the crown's dominions overseas seemed unreal, if not downright false. When parliament's committee asked Franklin in 1766 how "did the people of America use to consider the parliament of Great Britain," he answered:

They considered the parliament as the great bulwark and security of their liberties and privileges, and always spoke of it with the utmost respect and veneration. Arbitrary ministers, they thought, might possibly, at times, attempt to oppress them; but they relied on it, that the parliament, on application, would always give redress.

This faith in parliament, this parliament worship, explains in part the British Americans' disillusionment with the Acts it passed after 1763 and their utter disbelief in the fiction of its imperial character. Among Franklin's notes is the question: "Do your lordships mean to call the parliament *imperial*?"[15]

Worse still was the myth of an imperial constitution which was but another label slapped on to the same, undefined, and impalpable British constitution. In the house of commons on 19 April 1774 Burke made his speech on reconciliation, one chuck full of emotion—"my voice fails me . . . Well, sir, I have recovered a little"—a speech that has rung down the corridors of schoolboy oratory. In it he described his "idea of the constitution of the British empire, as distinguished from the constitution of Britain"; but it was only an ignis fatuus, for Burke also believed that "subordination and liberty may be sufficiently reconciled through the whole". Therewith, America's good friend rejected a policy of co-ordination. Instead, he proclaimed the British parliament's supremacy and accorded each colony an inferior constitutional position. Burke even conjured up an imperial war to which the colonies "would cheerfully furnish whatever is demanded"; but should one or two hold back, he added, "surely it is proper that some authority might legally say—'Tax yourselves for the common supply, or parliament will do it for you.' "[16] These Georgian statesmen did not have Disraeli's romantic genius that made Victoria an empress. No one, not even a colonist, had the wit to turn King George III into a Holy British Emperor with a proper imperial diet.

Through the crown, however, many Americans hoped for a constitutional settlement against a presumptuous parliament. Franklin had constantly worked for what he called "a closer connection with the crown". When several dissentient peers protested against the Americans' "contempt of the sovereignty of the British Legislature", he answered incisively, "The sovereignty of the crown I understand. The sovereignty of the British legislature out of Britain, I do not understand." The American vision of an empire under the crown imperial reached out beyond the horizons of Whitehall and Westminster. The Reverend J. J. Zubly, for example, pointed out in 1769 that the word *empire* was more "extensive" than was *kingdom*. For him, the British Empire included "England, Scotland, Ireland, the Islands of Man, Jersey, Guernsey, Gibraltar, and Minorca, etc., in the Mediterranean; Senegal, etc. in Africa; Bombay, etc. in the East Indies; and the islands and colonies in North America, etc." For such an empire, John Adams' *Novanglus*, published in January 1775, proposed "a new constitution . . . to be formed for the whole British dominions, and a supreme legislature coextensive with it". He denied that the continental colonies were incorporated into the United Kingdom, and he argued, a bit pedantically:

> The question should be, whether we are a part of the kingdom of Great Britain. This is the only language known in English laws. We are not, then, a part of the British kingdom, realm, or state; and therefore the supreme power of the

kingdom, realm, or state is not, upon these principles, the supreme power of us. That "supreme power over America is vested in the estates in parliament", is an affront to us; for there is not an acre of American land represented there; there are no American estates in parliament.

Adams then went on to urge numerical representation, and since America had three million inhabitants to Britain's six, she should send 250 members to Westminster. Moreover, Adams' logic led him to propose, perhaps a little tactlessly, that "instead of holding parliaments always at Westminster, the haughty members for Great Britain must humble themselves, one session in four, to cross the Atlantic, and hold the parliament in America."[17] But would Adams himself have gone to Bombay or Senegal? To create a truly imperial legislature and an imperial constitution under the imperial crown needed both the telephone and the airplane.

John Adams, like Franklin and other Americans brought up in the tradition of British constitutional governance, recognized the principles, contract and consent, representation and responsibility, and the rule of law as the cornerstones on which the constitution's balance depended. He reminded his readers that the Glorious Revolution had taken place in New England, too. On that occasion, "we, as well as the people of England, made an original, express contract with King William". From this somewhat marginal fact, Adams drew the happy conclusion: "if it follows from thence, that [the king] appears 'King of Massachusetts, King of Rhode Island, King of Connecticut, etc.,' this is no absurdity at all." Nor would it have seemed so had George III's ministers in 1775 been half as imaginative as John Adams, or as Mr Gordon Walker was to be on 3 March 1953 when he set forth in the House of Commons "the idea that the queen is equally queen of each of her realms, and that she acts only on the advice of her ministers in each of the realms, and that in a certain sense there are seven queens and not one queen, or, at any rate seven crowns and not one crown."[18] But in 1775, the old, medieval, hierarchical mentality clogged the minds of the men at Whitehall and Westminster. They failed to devise a viable form of imperial government under an imperial constitution. This failure the British Americans attributed to ministerial influence, management, and corruption—and even to a conspiracy to "enslave" the colonists.

Men of reason, like Harvard's president, Samuel Langdon, gave way to deep emotion. In an election sermon preached on 31 May 1775, he declared that the Americans' "submission to the tyranny of hundreds of imperious masters [the Members of Parliament] . . . united in the same cruel design of . . . making their own will our law . . . is the vilest slavery, and worse than death." Conspiracy and corruption also stirred the radical writer, Tom Paine. He believed that he had seen through the false facade

of the British system—mixed government and the balanced constitution—
to its actualities. His sharp mind penetrated the formal parts of government and reached the functional; and he exposed fallacies about the
British constitution that had bemused men in Britain, Europe, and
America. In *Common Sense*, 1776, Paine anatomized the English constitution with sweeping generalities. First, he granted "that it was noble
for the dark and slavish times in which it was erected;" but then with
barely a modicum of common sense, and still less of reason, he used
quick and slick logic to reduce the monarchy to "something exceedingly
ridiculous." He wrote syllogistically in Bagehotian prose, "the state of a
king shuts him from the world, yet the business of a king requires him
to know it thoroughly; wherefore the different parts, by unnaturally
opposing and destroying each other, prove the whole character to be
absurd and useless". Paine, with a flippant dialectic, effectively reduced
mixed monarchy and checks and balances to "a mere absurdity". Since
the monarchial and aristocratic parts of the constitution were hereditary
and "independent of the people," they contributed nothing "in a *constitutional sense*" "towards the freedom of the state". Then with a grandiloquent
flourish, Paine swept the whole thing away: "to say that the constitution
of England is an *union* of three powers, reciprocally *checking* each other,
is farcical; either the words have no meaning, or they are flat contra-
dictions".[19]

More generous than Paine was President Langdon, and his sermon,
entitled, *Government Corrupted by Vice, and recovered by Righteousness*,
was downright English, in fact Pan-British. He extolled "the constitution
of government which has so long been the glory and strength of the
English nation". He lauded "the noblest and most faithful friends of the
British constitution, who have powerfully plead our cause in parliament;"
but he condemned the British government for vice, corruption, and a
conspiracy to install in America arbitrary rule by "artifices to stretch the
prerogatives of the crown beyond all constitutional bounds, and make
the king an absolute monarch". Already, the Boston Town Meeting in
1770 had warned the Massachusetts assembly that "the august and once
revered fortress of English freedom—the admirable work of ages—the
BRITISH CONSTITUTION seems fast tottering into fatal and inevitable
ruin. The dreadful catastrophe threatens universal havoc." With an
unswerving selfrighteousness, men like Langdon and Adams went on to
condemn vice and corruption and to expound what they understood to
be the principles of the British constitution, one that they alone, with
the help of God, might save from "hastening to its final period of
dissolution". Langdon's text for this election sermon was Isaiah i.26:
And I will restore thy judges as at the first, and the counsellors as at the

beginning: afterward thou shalt be called, the City of Righteousness, the faithful City." Revolution by restoration of the traditional, historical, and fundamental principles was the keynote of Langdon's address. The colonists stood on the principle of contract, as embodied in royal charters; and in Massachusetts they began to raise money by "a taxation which depended on general consent". Like Locke, Langdon claimed the subjects' right to dissolve one government and to create a new one. "When one form is found, by the majority, not to answer the grand purpose in any tolerable degree," he declared, "they may by common consent put an end to it, and set up another."[20]

In the end, the president of Harvard jumbled up constitutional principles and rules of public law with theology, morality, and history. He appealed to high heaven and England's past to save the world-wide subjects of King George III. "Have our statesmen always acted with integrity? And every judge with impartiality, in the fear of God? In short, have all ranks of men showed regard to the divine commands, and joined to promote the Redeemer's kingdom, and the public welfare?" "But alas!" Langdon declaimed, "have not the sins of America, and of New England in particular, had a hand in bringing down upon us the righteous judgements of heaven?" Then Langdon turned to Britain's golden age, one as romanticized as was the transatlantic view of the constitution:

> "in former times the great departments of state, and the various places of trust and authority, were filled with men of wisdom, honesty, and religion, who employed all their powers, and were ready to risk their fortunes, and their lives for the public good. They were faithful counsellors to kings . . . They were fathers of the people, and sought the welfare and prosperity of the whole body . . . and justice was administered with impartiality."

Instead, both British and Americans had rebelled against God and had lost the true spirit of Christianity—and, perhaps, the spirit of that "august and once revered fortress of English freedom—the admirable work of ages—the BRITISH CONSTITUTION".[21]

NOTES

[1] Quoted by Bernard Bailyn, *The Ideological Origins of the American Revolution* (Cambridge, Mass., 1967) 1.

[2] Samuel Eliot Morison (ed.), *Sources and Documents illustra·ing the American Revolution, 1764–1788, and the formation of the Federal Constitution* (New York, 1965) 7, 259; F. W. Maitland, *English Law and the Renaissance* (Cambridge, 1901) 32 (AALH i.204, SHE 147); Edmund S. Morgan (ed.), *Puritan Political Ideas* (New York, 1965) 352–3.

[3] (1928) 215 Hansard (Commons)/V 1409.

[4] Abel Boyer, *Political State of Britain*, xli (London, 1731) 89.

[5] Quoted by Timothy H. Breen, "John Adams' Fight against Innovation in the New England Constitution: 1776", 40 *New England Quarterly* 501, 506.

[6] 6 Geo. 3, c.12; Henry S. Commager (ed.), *Documents of American History* (New York, 1934) 60–61, no.41.

[7] 14 Geo. 3, c.45; Commager, *Documents* 65, 72.

[8] Henry St John, Viscount Bolingbroke, *A Dissertation upon Parties* (second edition, London, 1735) 108 (Letter X), 157 (Letter XIII), 227 (Letter XIX); Hulme is quoted in Bailyn, *Revolution* 183–4, 217; Morison, *Sources* 33, 119; Bailyn, *The Origins of American Politics* (New York, 1968) 110.

9 OED *s.v. unconstitutional* and *unconstitutionality*, from Blackstone Comm. i.245; 6 *Pennsylvania Archives*/VIII 4538; Leonard W. Labaree (ed.) *The Papers of Benjamin Franklin* xiii (for 1766; New Haven, 1969) 137; Morison, *Sources* 38, 119; Charles M. Andrews, *The Colonial Background of the American Revolution* (New Haven, 1924) 199; *Parliamentary Papers; consisting of a complete Collection of Kings Speeches, . . . a complete and correct Collection of the Lords Protests, . . .* (London, 1797) iii.441, 473, 516; Bailyn, *Revolution* 134; Bolingbroke, *Parties* 210 (Letter XVII).

10 Morison, *Sources* 119; Bailyn, *Revolution* 142 and n.44; *Lords Protests* iii.516 (7 February 1775); OED *s.v. unconstitutionality.*

11 Carl Stephenson and Frederick G. Marcham, *Sources of English Constitutional History* (New York, 1937) 646–7. In 1730 the Board of Trade used the same analogies. Cf. Stanley M. Pargellis, "The Theory of Balanced Government", in Conyers Read (ed.), *The Constitution Reconsidered* (New York, 1938) 44 n.26.

12 Bailyn, *Politics* 61 n.3, 59, 133 and n.19; Labaree, *Franklin Papers* xiii.153.

13 Bailyn, *Revolution* 276; Morison, *Sources* 7.

14 Morison, *Sources* 92, 93; Bailyn, *Revolution* 119.

15 Labaree, *Franklin Papers* xiii.136, 212.

16 C. S. Emden, *Select Speeches on the Constitution* (Oxford, 1939) 223, 225, 224.

17 Labaree, *Franklin Papers* xiii.225, 220; Bailyn, *Revolution* 217; Morison, *Sources* 127, 132, 136.

18 Morison, *Sources* 134–5; (1953) 512 Hansard (Commons)/V 195.

19 Morgan, *Political Ideas* 367; Howard Fast (ed.) *The Selected Work of Tom Paine and Citizen Tom Paine* (New York, 1945) 8, 9.

20 Morgan, *Political Ideas* 352–3, 356, 362, 369, 367–8; Bailyn, *Revolution* 94, 91.

21 Morgan, *Political Ideas* 365, 362; Bailyn, *Revolution* 94.

Plaints and Bills in the History of English Law, mainly in the period 1250-1350

Alan Harding

WRITS have always been given pride of place in the early history of English law. "Not the nature of rights, but the nature of writs", said Maitland, must be the theme of the student of English law.[1] There is no discussion in *The History of English Law before the time of Edward I* of the oral complaint as a way of beginning litigation, and the bill appears only in the guise of the Roman and Canon lawyers' libel: this is seen as a positive threat to English law, for "a libellary procedure . . . had no place either for the 'original writ' with its authoritative definition of the cause of action or for the 'issue' submitted to a jury."[2]

Now, bill procedure in the late medieval courts of Chancery and Star Chamber could perhaps be seen as stemming from this alien tradition, but parliamentary petitions or bills, going back to Edward I's reign, were undeniably part of the English way of doing things, and where (in terms of form) had they sprung from? In 1912, W. C. Bolland drew attention to bills in eyre, and in 1914 printed surviving examples of such bills, the earliest from 1286.[3] It was left for Mr Richardson and Professor Sayles in their Selden Society volume for 1941, *Select Cases of Procedure without Writ under Henry III*, to show that bills in eyre were simply the written form of oral complaints to the justices, and that such "plaints" were common from a quite early date in the thirteenth century.[4] Since 1941 Professor Sayles has provided, in the volumes of *Select Cases in the Court of King's Bench*, a mass of information on bill procedure in the common law courts in the late thirteenth and the fourteenth centuries.[5]

It seemed to me that it was time to draw some conclusions from all this work, and to identify the rôle of procedure by oral complaint and bill in the growth of English law. I shall start by trying to shift the emphasis from the invention of the first original writs in the latter part of the twelfth century to the influx of plaints in the thirteenth; and by arguing that this influx constitutes something of a second beginning for English law, or perhaps better the beginning of a second stream in English law. And I shall do this by suggesting that what was the second beginning for English law was the first beginning of French law as a centralized system.

PLAINTS, WRITS AND PRESENTMENTS

In England, a man with a grievance could go and complain to the king's chancery and get an original writ, or direct to the king's justices who might issue a judicial writ to summon the defendant. A case of the second type was what Bracton called a *querela sine brevi*, because there was no original writ; and is usually identifiable in the plea-roll from its initial words: N. *queritur quod . . .* An oral complaint of an injury for which there was an established original writ was accepted by the justices only if the injury was alleged to have occurred "within the summons of the eyre" (*infra summonicionem itineris*), thus infringing the peace of the justices and so that an original writ could not have been obtained in time.[6] The only plaints printed by Mr Richardson and Professor Sayles from the common pleas sections of eyre rolls are complaints of injury within the summons of the eyre.

For the majority of plaints on the mid-thirteenth century rolls are not instances of "procedure without writ", but of what one might call procedure without presentment (that is, the naming of criminals by local juries) or procedure without appeal (that is, the long process of criminal accusation by the injured party, beginning in the shire court and ending, in the rare cases which were carried through, in trial by battle before royal justices); and these plaints consequently appear amongst the crown pleas. Presentments must always have been based on the complaints of individuals about individual injuries, though all the hard-pressed juries could do when they came before the justices was to list common felons rather than separate felonies: "N. is a robber of fishponds" (*N. est latro in vivariis*). But occasionally the individual's complaint thrusts itself into the jury's *veredictum*, as in 1241 the complaint of H. that W. and others came by night, broke down his doors and assaulted him, thrust its way into the verdict of the jury of Canterbury.[7] Although the defendant made satisfaction to H. for the injury, the complaint came before the justices as a criminal accusation. The king was concerned with injuries only when they offended against himself, but then he was prepared to learn of them by mere complaint without formal presentment or appeal.

The plaint became established above all in special inquiries ordered by the king into the abuses of his own ministers. Amongst the few surviving returns from the Inquest of Sheriffs of 1170 is a collective complaint against the sheriff by the burgesses of Worcester that they are unjustly compelled to perform guard-service, which has cost them £24 6s. 8d.[8] The first group of plaint enrolments printed by Mr Richardson and Professor Sayles were elicited by an inquiry of 1224 into the activities of Fawkes de Bréauté and his henchmen, who had been established in control of the midland counties of England by King John a decade earlier. To take an example from the *inquisicio facta de conquerentibus* against two of Fawkes's men:

> John of Eydon complains that Vivian son of Ralph and Richard Foliot wrongfully etc. took eight marks from him because he betrothed a certain woman and took her with her chattels by night to his house; and they accused him of theft, and so on account of the oppressions and wrongs done to him he sold his land. And thereof he puts himself on the country.
>
> Moreover, John says that Richard kept him in prison in his house at Warslow for two days and he was not allowed to go out to obtain the money demanded until he had given Richard a hostage. And thereof he puts himself on the country. And he offers to prove against Richard by battle that he did this to him, as the court shall award.
>
> And Richard comes and denies the wrongful exaction and imprisonment and everything word by word. And he puts himself on the country, as also does John. And therefore let an inquest be held as before.[9]

And now put alongside this, two other pleas:

> William Haucet complains that (*conqueritur quod*) . . . Martin Clark arrested him, although he had taken the cross, and held him captive for several days in the king's prison, and would not release him even on letters from the official; and while he was captive, Martin extorted from him 5 measures of rye worth 16s. . . .
>
> The men of Verzeille complain that the men of Preixan came against them . . . in arms (*cum armis*) . . . and seized and cruelly imprisoned 4 of their number, and at length forced them to ransom themselves at 460 shillings . . .

These two examples come from the bulky registers of the complaints of the inhabitants of Normandy and Maine, Anjou and the Touraine, Poitou and Carcassonne and other parts of France, to special commissioners appointed by King Louis IX in 1247 to deal with complaints against royal officials. In Carcassonne, the *querelae* were recorded by the chaplains of villages, so that they could be shown *in scriptis* to the *inquisitoribus pro domino rege*.[10]

In thirteenth-century Castile it was the law that royal officials might not be accused by private citizens while in office, but if good men complained of them the king was bound by his office to set an inquiry on foot and find out if the complaints were true (. . . *estonce el Rey de su officio debe pesquerir, e saber la verdad, si es assi como querellassen*).[11]

The truth is that the appearance of plaints in the records of the king's justices in the thirteenth century is more than an episode in the development of English legal procedure. It represents a stage in the growth of government in western Europe. One of the main problems of thirteenth-century kings was to control the fast-growing corps of officials who acted in their name, and in sending commissions to elicit complaints, whether against their own bailiffs or against the bailiffs of the nobility, they were serving their own interests at the same time as their subjects'. In England, the king used special commissions of inquiry limited to particular counties,[12] or employed the Eyre if a countrywide hearing of complaints was needed. Plaints from individuals and communities lie behind the presentments in answer to chapters of the eyre like those introduced in 1254 concerning sheriffs and bailiffs who imprisoned men on suspicion of felony and then extorted money for their release.[13] At the Shropshire eyre of 1256 the jurors for the township of Hales presented that the Abbot of Hales imprisoned and released the men of Hales at his pleasure (*ad voluntatem suam*) and refused to replevy their goods or allow them to plead *vee de nam* in the shire court: after these presentments comes the simple statement that six of the men of Hales *queruntur de Abbate de Hales*.[14]

King and barons used the nationwide hearing of complaints at all the political crises of the thirteenth century. The eyre of the baronial justiciar in 1258 was a turning-point in the use of plaints against royal officials and others.[15] In 1261 special sections of *querele de transgressionibus* begin to appear in the eyre rolls.[16] Before the commissioners of the great administrative inquiry of 1274–5 whose harvest is in the *Hundred Rolls*, five Essex townships independently presented the same offence, which is detailed separately in a long plaint from the injured person.[17] From 1278 onwards, the writ of summons to the eyre announced that the justices were to hear trespasses and plaints concerning the king's ministers and bailiffs, the ministers and bailiffs of others, and anyone else (*et aliis quibuscumque*), and to provide remedies.[18] For three years from 1289, *auditores querelarum* sat at Westminster to receive complaints against the judges and other ministers of the king;[19] and in 1298 commissioners were sent out into the counties to deal with *querelae* of injuries inflicted upon the people in the king's name.[20]

TORT IN THE KING'S COURTS

The flow of plaints into the rolls, which becomes a flood in the second half of the thirteenth century, represents, then, a stage in the growth of government. From the point of view of legal history, I believe that it represents the bringing of torts within the scope of centralised legal systems. In the feudal monarchy of the early middle ages the cases which came into the *curia regis* were the land-disputes of the king's tenants-in-chief, or accusations of shameful crimes which involved the forfeiture of land along with blood-punishment. By 1200, the invention of original writs for land actions and of the presentment of felonies had considerably extended the scope of the king's jurisdiction in England, but I think one should beware of seeing a more or less inevitable evolution from this law of what was still essentially a feudal principality to the law of the national monarchy which to my mind existed by the end of the thirteenth century. Like Professor Van Caenegem,[21] I do not see how the king could have come in the twelfth century to provide facilities in the shape of the petty assizes for the settlement of disputes between private individuals about the possession of land if he had not first conducted a campaign against disseisins as offences against his public authority: once the king was seen to be concerned with such matters, the way was open for the private plaintiff to purchase an order for the adjudication of an alleged disseisin in his own interest. Similarly, I don't see how the law could ever have extended from the narrow field of land disputes to the substantially and socially far larger one of tort if thirteenth century kings had not taken the initiative and asked for complaints of such wrongs: not just because these wrongs infringed their authority in a general sense, but because they involved the misuse of their power by their officials.

The wrongs most commonly attributed to officials were forcible eject-ment, the seizure of stock and crops, unjust imprisonment often involving assault, defamation (in the form of the imputation of crimes or usury in order to justify imprisonment), and the extortion of money by these or other means. These torts were the by-products of more government— and of more law, which brought much arbitrary was well as much judicial distraint and arrest. Prominent amongst early complaints of trespass are also wrongs committed *against* officials going about the king's business and enjoying his special protection. Not only are abuses by the officials of liberties frequently complained of, but so also are infringements of franchisal rights, especially to keep prisons.[22]

Above all, the wrongs which were regarded as especially the concern of the king's justices, in Spain and France as in England, were those which involved the use of force. In León and Castile at the end of the twelfth century, *exquisitores* were already being appointed by the king to deal with cases of the unlawful taking of pledges and the seizure of land or goods *con armas e con fuerza* and without a judgment. In mid-thirteenth century France, people complain that others *abstulerant ei violenter cufam suam in chemino regis,* or *violenter et injuste abstulerunt,* or *ceperunt eum et verberaverunt et abstulerunt ei x solidos,* or *abstulit per vim et potenciam,* or *abstulit violenter, indebite et injuste.* In England, the allegation of *vi et armis* and the denial of *vim et injuriam* (Fr. *tort et force*) become the distinctive labels of the action of trespass.[23]

Very often, the complaint is of the arbitrary use of force by officials. In the Parliament held at Paris at the feast of the Purification in the year 1254, the bishop of Clermont complained (*conquerebatur*) of the burgesses of the town of Clermont, that they had rescued by force (*per vim*) and with the connivance of a royal officer some men he had arrested on suspicion of the murder of one of his servants. In the Parlements held at Toulouse by Alphonse of Poitiers, brother of Louis IX, villagers complained of bailiffs who seized bread from the communal ovens and extorted money for its release, committing these injuries *per vim ipsius ballivie* ("by force of the office of bailiff"): and a gentleman complained of the Count of Foix and the reeves and men of a village who had inflicted on him many violent injuries and taken his goods and animals (*plures injurias et violencias intulerunt eidem, bona sua, vaccas et alia animalia sua rapiendo*). Or the violence might have been against officials. At the Parlement at Paris at All Saints 1279 there was an inquest *super damnis, violenciis, et injuriis* inflicted by the mayor, *scabini* and men of one town upon the men of another, amongst whom there happened to be a royal servant.[24]

Not only was the substantive range of pleas greatly extended by use of the plaint, but so was the section of the population pleading in the king's courts. The men of Verzeille, the villeins of Hales, groups of merchants subjected to violence by toll-collectors; all these appear in the king's "central" courts for the first time. Often a complainant pledged his faith that he would prosecute, because he was too poor to find two persons to be pledges: *affidavit quia pauper*. It was the pressure of these new groups of complainants which required the building-up or creation of central courts in the thirteenth century. The fact that the French inquests of 1247 heard complaints of wrongs done as far back as the reign of Philip Augustus, who died in 1223, suggests that they had opened up an area of jurisdiction untouched before. In the Middle Ages, the use by a king of judicial commissioners in the provinces often ended by drawing more litigation to the centre: when the commissions lapsed, complainants took their grievances to the source of the power which the commissioners had exercised. To deal with them, Parlements sat in Paris at fixed times, perhaps from 1247 and certainly from 1250. (One thinks of the provisions made in 1258 for regular parliaments in England.) The history of Parlements at Toulouse seems to begin with the inquiry of Alphonse of Poitiers into the misdeeds of his officials in 1249.[25]

Once the king had shown his readiness to receive complaints of tort, matters which had previously been dealt with in the shire court and other local courts, where cases were always begun by oral complaint,[26] were brought before the justices in eyre. The *rotuli de querelis et transgressionibus* within the eyre rolls became inflated with complaints of trespass, *vee de nam* and nuisance, and complaints and recognisances of debt. The debt cases are presumably there because the eyre was a court of record as the shire-court was not, and it was important to have debts recorded; the other cases because poor plaintiffs who could never have afforded writs saw, with the coming of the Eyre, the opportunity of invoking the full power of royal justice against their persecutors by labelling the injuries they had suffered breaches of the king's peace. In the Statute of Gloucester of 1278, the king attempted to stem the tide of petty trespass by ordaining that the sheriffs were to hear pleas of trespass in their counties as the custom was, and that writs of trespass should not be granted for cases involving damage of less than 40*s*.[27]

But this provision had no perceptible effect: unless it is (as Mr G. D. G. Hall has suggested) the origin of the viscontiel writ of trespass. Before this time, all trespass cases in the shire court were presumably brought by plaint. After 1278, did defendants perhaps stand on its head a rule that writs returnable in the central courts would only be issued where substantial damage was alleged, and claim that writs were now required to make them answer in the shire court where more than 40*s*. was at stake? (Rather as, in the previous century, it had been established first that writs were available and then that they were essential to make tenants answer for their freeholds in the lord's court.)[28] It may also have been the rule of 1278 which made the allegation of *force and arms* invariable in returnable writs of trespass, as plaintiffs sought to label injuries involving minor damage as nevertheless cases for the central courts. By 1300 the rule is established that writs of trespass are not pleadable in the shire court where they mention wounds, imprisonment and force and arms, because these matters *tangunt specialiter coronam domini regis*.[29]

THE APPEAL, THE PRINCIPLE OF THE DOUBLE SUIT, AND TRESPASS

What ends as the civil action of trespass begins as one particular type of plaint amongst the crown pleas of the eyre, the plaint which is (to use Maitland's phrase) an "attenuated appeal". Before there were developed central courts, there seems to have been a single action in the local courts for serious private injuries, the action neither clearly civil nor criminal known as the Appeal. When the plea-rolls start in the late twelfth century we can see that every appeal which came before the king's justices began as a complaint in the shire court, where the terms of the accusation were enrolled by the coroners and the stringent processes for securing the defendant's appearance (more stringent than any available in a civil plea before the development of the action of trespass) were set in train. The appeal was a bridge carrying suits for injury from the local to the central courts, but it had two defects which needed to be remedied before it could bear much traffic. In the first place, trial was by battle between appellant and defendant, and men resorted to such a hazardous process only for the most serious injuries: as Bracton said, you didn't appeal a man for knocking the dust from your hat. In the second place, the king's clerks and judges constricted the process into the rigid appeal of felony, an accusation of crime which brought no monetary compensation even if the appellant was victorious: in fact, a majority of appellants never reached trial by battle because they were non-suited before the justices for some minor procedural mistake or a variation in their plea from what the coroners had recorded—a four-inch wound might have become a five-inch one.[30]

Yet the defendant did not go free immediately the appellant was non-suited, for the king's suit remained to be answered. A complaint of injury was neither distinctively civil, like an action by writ, nor distinctively criminal, like a presentment, so it could be both at once. In the plea rolls, appeals almost always alleged violence and breach of the peace, and in such cases the king had an interest as well as the victims. By 1250 the formula recording the non-suiting of an appellant has become stereotyped: . . . *ideo appellum nullum. Set pro pace domini Regis observanda inquiratur rei veritas per patriam. Et juratores dicunt quod . . .* The king, as the judges never tired of saying, "does not choose to fight" to prove his suit, so trial was by jury. In France, a famous ordinance of King Louis in 1259 or 1260 attempted to replace trial by battle by *tesmoinz jurez* in appeals of injury. In England this fundamental change was achieved more surely in the gradual evolution of procedure.[31]

If what the jurors said was "guilty" in one of these inquests following the annulment of an appeal, the defendant was punished, according to the plea-rolls, *pro transgressione*, for the trespass against the king's peace, though by brief imprisonment and a mere fine as opposed to the hanging which would have followed his conviction of felony. Here the victims of injuries saw a way to get redress without running the risk of battle for themselves or of a disproportionately heavy penalty for their opponents. They wanted money, not blood. The evidence that they did so is the formula which begins many eyre enrolments of the mid-thirteenth century: *N. appellavit in comitatu et nunc queritur.* A defendant in such a case will always object that he cannot be put to law *per querimoniam* or that the appellant *appellum suum non protulit modo appellacionis*, and the objection will be upheld—but he may still be found guilty of trespass. In 1255, one appellant reveals what is happening by withdrawing from his appeal and asking that the lord king might sue for him. The technique was to begin one's appeal in the shire court, and if this did not force an agreement out of court, to bring to the eyre a complaint avoiding the words of felony which would lead to battle but emphasising the forceful breach of the king's peace which would ensure that the defendant stood trial. It was this emphasis which gave civil trespass its unmistakeable labels, *vi et armis et contra pacem domini regis*.[32]

It may be that there was a collusive element in plaints of this sort: that sometimes both parties to a dispute were seeking jury-trial in a situation in which it was not normally available. *Convictum est per juratam* at the beginning of an enrolment is a sure sign of an action by plaint, so Mr Richardson and Professor Sayles tell us. This jury-trial was sought by the parties, it is *de consensu parcium*, but the king conceded it for the same reason that he accepted the plaint at all—because the substance of the complaint directly touched his authority. This is really a criminal jury, not a civil one, the jury in an action of trespass.[33]

How, and particularly when, trespass broke out of the context of the appeal to become a civil action for damages initiated by original writ—these questions will never, I think, be settled to everyone's satisfaction because they are partly questions about words and what people meant by them in the thirteenth century. The first so-called *brevia de transgressione*, in a register of the 1260s, are writs of appeal: writs which Bracton described as issuing *ad querelam appellancium* to order sheriffs to make up for their failure hitherto to attach the *appellati*. These writs give rise to many enrolments amongst the crown pleas which begin *appellat per breve domini regis*, and at least two, which Mr Fifoot took to be the first references to writs of trespass, begin—paradoxically—*queritur per breve domini regis*. Appeals by writ, like appeals *per querimoniam*, did very often fail to comply with the rules of the appeal and lead to fines *pro transgressione*. The writ of appeal was perhaps invoked more often because the complainants had failed to pursue the appeal process sufficiently closely even to gain attachment than because the sheriff had failed to do his part.[34]

Many appeals by writ concerned unjust imprisonment by royal officials or the officials of liberties. For instance, in the Kent eyre of 1255, R. appealed four men by the king's writ *de inprisonamento et pace domini Regis infracta*, alleging that they kept him confined for eight days and tortured him *igne et aliis tormentis*. The accused objected that R. had specified no day or hour, and the appeal was annulled. On inquiry for the sake of the king's peace, the jurors of the hundred of Maidstone related that R. had been taken by the hue and cry on suspicion of burglary, and that the accused had come to the prison by night and tortured him and almost killed him by piling planks and tables upon him. In the same eyre, I. appealed Adam the headborough of imprisonment, doing so by the king's writ. The appeal was annulled this time because the appellant did not offer battle and *hoc petit sibi emendari*. The jurors said that the hue had been raised against I. and that it was then that the headborough arrested him. In the Hampshire eyre of 1256, a brother and sister appealed a man by writ, alleging that he had arrested them *in regali via*, taken

F

them to his manor-house, hung them up by the feet *et quodam cultello punxit eos per totum corpus*. They asked for damages. The accused did not object to the form of this "appeal" but denied the allegation, and the jurors of two hundreds found him not guilty: the appellant had been arrested by the accused's serjeant on suspicion of theft and handed over to the tithing to guard until the next meeting of the seignorial court. When, in 1257, R. appealed N. and others by the king's writ *de inprisonamento et pace domini regis infracta* and then before the justices in eyre complained (*conqueritur*) that they kept him shut up for two days over a midden, the appeal was annulled because of the change of procedure. But the accused was found guilty on trial *pro pace* . . . and on this occasion he was ordered to make satisfaction to the plaintiff.[35]

Fleta could still remark that: "In appeals of mayhem, wounding and imprisonment, one may proceed criminally or by complaint, complaining of the injury civilly by writ of trespass (*conquerenti civiliter, conquerendo de injuria per breve de transgressione*)." It seems to me likely, then, that the writ of trespass emerged from the writ of appeal in the context of imprisonment and the violence which often went with it. The eighth chapter of the Statute of Gloucester, which is entirely concerned with trespass, makes special mention of cases of beating, which it assumes will be the subject of plaints, and of "wounds and maims", for which writs shall be available as before.[36]

Professor Milsom demonstrated some years ago that there was no more unity to civil trespasses than the label, "breach of the peace". Trespass, tort, consists in the offence to public authority which is alleged in order to gain redress for private injury. The principle of the double suit of king and private plaintiff came from the appeal, but the idea that in an action for trespass the plaintiff prosecuted both suits at once, *tam pro domino rege quam pro seipso*, could only have come from the plaint, in which the criminal and the civil were not distinguished. That is why the appeals which were turned into plaints seem particularly significant. For the general history of the period, it is also significant that most of these cases concerned the arbitrary use of imprisonment or distraint by officials and the attendant violence, or sometimes attacks upon officials or the infringement of rights to imprison or distrain; that they arise directly from the growth of government and law.[37]

BILLS

The writing down of complaints and the presenting of petitions seems to have become widespread only in the second half of the thirteenth century, surely as a result of the royal inquiries into administrative abuses. In 1247, the chaplains of French villages were writing down the *querelae* of the people for the king's inquisitors, and these survive in a Latin record.[38] Some twenty years later, the "Plaintes contra Geoffroi de Roncherolles, Bailli de Vermandois" are registered as they were presented, and are almost all in French:

> Sengneurs enquesteurs de par le roi, sires Hues li Fruitiers, bourgois de la commune de Compiègne, se plaint et dit encontre le roi. . .
>
> C'est la peticion Henri le Lorgne, de Compiengne.—Sire, il avint que Henris li Lorgnes aloit à Soissons . . . (There follows the story of a quarrel, which resulted in the bailli fining Henri more heavily than was customary.)[39]

From about the same time as these early bills from France, we have this bill from some Northumbrian sokemen against the king's warden.—

> A nostre seignur le Rey les sokemen de Sunderlaunde et de Schoston' se pleynient de sire Robert de Nevile . . . ke il lur ad fet si grant tort ke eus ne poient sustener . . . por quey il prient a nostre seignur le Rey ke il lur face tenir en lur usages et en lur Custumes . . . [et] il prient por lamur de deu siluy plest ke il lur face aver dreyt de lur tortenuses fez. . .[40]

In 1286 we come upon the first surviving bills to the justices in eyre, and these are found to correspond to cases in the *rotuli de querelis* of the eyre rolls. Some bills in eyre are rambling and ungrammatical, but mostly they are terse and business-like.—

> J. sey pleynt . . . de ceo ke R. . . . vint en le haut Chemin en E. a tort e a force e as armes en countre la pes e ly baty e malement naufra a ces damages xl s. ke a graunt peyne eschapa la mort e ceo vous prie pur deu e vostre alme ke seyt enquiz par bon pays.[41]

It seems to me that the most significant thing about these bills is the most obvious: they are in French, the litigant's vernacular, not in the professional Latin of chancery clerks or Westminster lawyers. The plaintiff by writ must have defined the legal substance of his case in order to get the appropriate writ from chancery; the plaintiff who took his bill to the justices was relying less on definite rights in private law than on the king's known concern for justice and public order.

The formulation of writs had marked off clearly civil categories of trespass, but bills of trespass continued to combine civil and criminal elements, to obtain damages for the injured parties and form the basis of indictments at the same time. During the trial of the judges before the *auditores querelarum* of 1289, the charge was made against Solomon of Rochester that as a justice in the Suffolk eyre of 1286 he maliciously arranged for bills to be presented against one Henry of St Edmunds. Answering the charge, Solomon said that it was the custom in the eyre that for the preservation of the peace (*pro pace observanda*) any person (*quicumque de populo*) might take a bill to one of the justices, who was bound to receive it and pass it to the presenting jurors, so that if it was true they might include it in their *veredictum* and if it was not, reject it. One of the bills of 1286 printed by Bolland is endorsed *Ista billa est vera . . .* , and it looks as though the standard method of indictment, the finding of a true bill by a grand jury, originated in the eyre.[42]

Bills and juries were linked from the beginning because complaints were so often in answer to special inquests set on foot by the king. It may have been the measures for restoring order after the barons' war which were decisive in encouraging the writing down of complaints and suit by bill. On the eyre rolls of the late 1260s there often appears an order to the justices that *per sacramentum proborum et legalium hominum per quos rei veritas melius sciri potuerit diligenter facerent inquisicionem de transgressionibus factis . . . tempore turbacionis* to a named complainant. The findings of the juries appear in the roll, or occasionally on a schedule sewn to it, as series of articles, and Mr Richardson and Professor Sayles have shown the importance of these in the history of the bill. Early in the next century, the abbey of St Augustine, Canterbury, is found employing one of its four attorneys in the Kent eyre to act for it in bill-cases; and at the same time seeking out confidants within the presenting juries to discover if any *veredicta* against the abbey were under consideration.[43]

The General Eyre ground to a halt in the 1290s under the burden of its own popularity as a dispenser of all-round justice. There were to be further eyres in London and Kent, with their rolls of *placita de querelis et bilettis* or *de querelis et transgressionibus* (35 membranes in the London Eyre roll of 1321, to the same number of *placita per brevia*).[44] Over most of the country, however, bill jurisdiction passed to the justices of trailbaston, the court of King's Bench and the justices of the peace. The commission of Trailbaston, first issued in 1305, looks as if it was devised to take over the bill-jurisdiction of the Eyre, extended somewhat by concern for the particular evils of that time of crisis, such as maintenance and attacks on jurors for telling the truth: in these cases of "enormous trespass" the justices were told that the defendants were always to answer at the king's suit if the *pars querens* failed to prosecute.[45] All cases of trespass in the trailbaston rolls were brought by bills, but the bills were dealt with in three different ways. Some cases (where the presenting jury approved the bills and the complainant did not prosecute) were tried at the king's suit, some at the suit of the party, and some at both. A private person might act as king's attorney and sue for the king alone, but more usually he sued (according to a formula with a great future) *tam pro domino Rege quam pro seipso*.[46]

Bills came into King's Bench because the court was used as a makeshift eyre in the early fourteenth-century crisis of order. In 1305, the justices *coram Rege* were used as justices of trailbaston and assize in the home counties; in Kent they dealt with 21 membranes-worth of assizes and essoins and 15 membranes-worth of trespasses by *peticionibus et querelis* or *querelis et bilettis*. In 1323, the court was given a permanent trailbaston commission throughout England, and in 1336 it had a separate division to cope with bills.[47] In King's Bench the bill made possible public prosecution conducted by the king's law officers. The writing down of criminal accusations as bills opened up new procedural possibilities, just as the writing down of civil claims as writs had done. An indictment consisting of a bill submitted *ad patriam* and endorsed *billa vera* by the "grand inquest" or "triers" set out a charge in more detail than the *veredictum* of the presenting jury could ever have done.[48] Moreover, a separate bill could be carried and prosecuted by an attorney—and the king now had his own serjeants and attorneys. In the London eyre of 1321, the King is found suing a bill of trespass by Geoffrey le Scrope, his serjeant.[49] The rôle of the king's attorney was to take over a prosecution in King's Bench when a private complainant withdrew, or to put in a bill of information himself. When William Cary was committed to the Marshalsea by the king's council in 1373, and then brought into King's Bench, "Thomas de Shardelowe, qui sequitur pro domino rege, protulit quandam billam pro ipso rege versus prefatum Willelmum in hec verba:

> A justicz du baunk nostre seignur le roi moustre Thomas de Shardelowe, qi suist pur nostre seignur le roi, qe . . .",

and he relates how William took his case to Rome against the king's prohibition.[50] The private individual's complaint "for the king and for himself" grew into the bill of information (what the Tudors called the "penal and popular action") which secured a statutory reward for the informer who gained a conviction.[51]

The bills of ordinary people naturally went to the local justices of the peace. In the course of the fourteenth century, the J.P.s were barred from hearing suits of the party. Defendants were therefore always tried at the king's suit, and their trespasses were recognised as a second category of crimes, below felonies, to which a later generation of lawyers gave the name of misdemeanour.[52] In the complaint of trespass the citizen first used the concept of public wrongfulness to get redress for private injuries, so creating the category of tort; and then the king used the complaint of private injury by bill of trespass as a way of bringing new types of offender to prosecution, so creating the category of indictable trespass or misdemeanour. Both processes rested on the basic principle of the double suit which had first come to the surface in the appeal of felony, the principle that a violent injury which was the subject of a private complaint was also a trespass against the king's peace which the king must prosecute *ex officio suo*.

COMMISSIONS OF OYER AND TERMINER AND IMPEACHMENT

Trailbaston was a member of a huge class of commissions known as commissions of *oyer and terminer:* the justices were to *"hear and determine . . .* felonies at our suit, and . . . trespasses, oppressions, extortions, conspiracies, outrages, injuries and grievances as well at our suit as at the suit of others wishing to complain of them . . ." Commissions of oyer and terminer were designed to deal with plaints and bills of trespass: a writ had only to be read to know how the case was to be determined, but a complaint had to be heard before it was even certain what the action was. There was a whole range of such commissions, which might be instructed to deal (like Trailbaston) with felonies and trespasses throughout the country, or with trespasses of a particular type committed in a single county, or with trespasses committed by particular royal ministers, or with trespasses committed against particular complainants. For instance, in 1254 three justices were ordered to hear the complaints of all who wished to complain of trespasses and injuries committed by a past sheriff of Yorkshire; and in 1258, Giles of Erdington was commissioned to hear and determine the complaints of one Walter, a man of the king's manor of Bromsgrove, of trespasses done to him in lands and chattels, the commission being granted out of compassion for the simplicity and poverty of the said Walter. Later examples are the *auditores querelarum* of 1289; the commissions of 1298 to hear and determine grievances inflicted on the people in the king's name; the trailbaston commissions; and the commision of 1309, issued *ex querela quorumdam Insulanorum,* to deal with the complaints of all Channel Islanders wishing to complain of trespasses and injuries committed by the bailiffs of the Isles.[53]

Complaints of official abuses were frequently matter for commissions of oyer and terminer. I find especially interesting the powerful commission, including the chief justices of both benches, appointed in 1307 to hear and determine the complaints of all those wishing to complain of the abuses of Walter Langton, bishop of Coventry and Lichfield, committed when he was Edward I's treasurer. This commission was issued because of the *clamor* of "innumerable complaints" and Edward II's wish to answer "the petitions of the people".[54] Surely Walter Langton was as much "impetitioned" or "impeached" by "the clamour of the commons" in 1307, as William Latimer was in 1376? It was standard form for commissions of oyer and terminer of trespass (which are prominent amongst writs of trespass in the Register) to say that they issued *ex gravi querela* of an individual or *ex clamosis querimoniis diversorum bonorum.*[55]

In an important article, Miss Lambrick has shown how the parliamentary impeachments of 1376 fit into the categories of a group complaint of the men of Abingdon against the Abbot of Abingdon in the 1360s. The Abbot was expressly said to have been impeached before justices of oyer and terminer: *idem Abbas occasione cujusdam presentacionis . . . super ipsum facte . . . impetitus extitit.*[56] But there is no reason to think that this process was at all new. A form for it exists in the *Register* in a writ, apparently issued in 1336, ordering the sheriff of Hampshire to summon juries to present the trespasses committed by the bishop of Winchester, since the king, moved by the *clamosis querimoniis* of the men of the county, has assigned justices *ad querelas omnium et singulorum pro nobis vel pro se ipsis inde conqueri et prosequi volencium . . . audiendas et terminandas . . .*[57] Impeachment could be by one bill, as William of Rouceby was *impetitus* in Chancery in 1354 by the bill of a Genoese merchant whose ship he had arrested off the Scillies, or by many. Many bills added up to "the clamour of the commons" and made you *impetitos et notorie rettatos*, like the forgers whose arrest was ordered in 1367. At the trial of chief justice Willoughby in 1341 before a commission of oyer and terminer "several bills were read which were not supported by pledges and to which nobody made suit", and it was ruled that indictments or suits of the party were not essential: the commission was sufficiently "informed by the clamour of the people".[58]

It must have looked at the beginning of the fourteenth century as though the English judicial system was being reorganised around the bill and the commission of oyer and terminer, both ambiguous in being civil and criminal at once. But the gentry used judicial commissions too much as weapons rather than remedies. The notorious local struggles of later medieval England were conducted to a considerable extent by firing-off bills to accuse one's rivals of conspiracy, riot and the corruption of justice, procuring indictments against them often found to be malicious, and obtaining commissions of oyer and terminer as the heavy artillery, equal to whole armies of retainers. The community of the realm protested to Edward II that commissions of oyer and terminer of trespass were being granted more lightly and commonly than before and causing great evils and oppressions, for when a *grant Seigneur, ou homme de poer*, wished to ruin someone he alleged a trespass against him and purchased commissions of oyer and terminer to people favourable to himself. The king's reply was to say that commissions should only be issued for enormous trespasses.[59] Despite such abuses, special commissions to deal with bills did add a valuable new dimension to the judicial system. By a statute of 1340, a prelate, two earls and two barons were to be appointed in every parliament to receive the petitions of "all those who wished to complain" (a time-honoured phrase) of delays in Chancery, King's Bench, the Common Bench, Exchequer and other courts. The commission, which was still at least remembered in 1377, was to scrutinise the record of a case in which "the diverse opinions of the judges" or other difficulties prevented a decision, take advice from the chancellor and other members of the king's council and then instruct the original court as to the judgment it should give. There is a case, that of Geoffrey of Stanton, printed by Professor Sayles from the King's Bench rolls, which seems to show the procedure in action.[60]

BILLS IN EYRE, PARLIAMENT, AND CHANCERY

In many respects the activities of Parliament were a continuation of common law processes by bill. Like bills in eyre, bills in parliament are couched in French and use the verbs *se pleynt* and *moustre*. More importantly, bills in parliament were like bills of trespass in identifying royal interests with individual private wrongs. The insistence of the Commons at the impeachments of 1376 that they were in fact suing for the king stands in a very old tradition. The common petition was a realisation of the political possibilities of the bill from a village or shire community to the justices in eyre. Instructions might be given in Parliament itself for hearing and determining *querelas* against named persons; and the "complaints of those who wished to complain" of royal servants who contravened the Ordinances of 1311 were ordered to be heard and determined by a bishop, two earls and two barons in each subsequent parliament (this is an obvious precedent for the parliamentary commission of 1340).[61]

The majority of individual petitions on the parliament rolls are concerned with justice. Some are straight complaints of trespass, but in these cases the complainant was usually instructed to sue at common law: "Ad Petitionem H. conquerentis, quod R. et quidam alii Malefactores, ipsum H. apud R. verberaverunt, et imprisonaverunt quousque Finem fecerat cum eo pro xx libris. Et ad aliam querelam . . . quod ipsi uxorem suam apud E. et alia bona et catalla sua ad valenciam cc librarum ceperunt et abduxerunt; Ad utramque Petitionem responsum est: Quod sequatur ad communem Legem." The business of Parliament was not to hear cases itself but to see that the common law dealt with enormous trespasses properly, and it often did this by telling the petitioner to go to Chancery and get a commission of oyer and terminer: *Adeat Cancellarie, et habeat ibi Justiciarios ad audiendum et terminandum per Finem;* and "Eit Brief de trespas a la commune Ley, ou de oier et terminer par fyn faire s'il voet." Conspicuous amongst cases treated in this way are trespasses against groups and communities such as foreign merchants and the Channel Islanders.[62]

In this way the duty of seeing that the law coped adequately with the enormous trespasses characteristic of the fourteenth century passed from

Parliament to Chancery. So-called "parliamentary petitions" were addressed to the king and his council. Now, Professor Wilkinson tells us that in the early fourteenth century the council was barely distinguishable from chancery, and chancery was the institution with the longer tradition and greater resources. What a "parliamentary petition" was usually asking for was something it was the chancellor's to give, either formally, on a warrant from the king, or substantially, on his own decision though in consultation with members of the council if need be.[63] People applied to the chancellor direct for relief against violence, maintenance and the corruption of justice, and the results of commissions issued by Chancery were often returned into Chancery.[64] So, the commissioners of oyer and terminer for the complaints of the men of Cirencester against the Abbot of Cirencester returned their proceedings in 1342, the Abbot being ordered to answer in Chancery.[65] The jurisdiction of Chancery as a court can be watched growing from the ancient function of Chancery as an office to issue writs in answer to the complaints of aggrieved parties. The crucial writ was the commission of oyer and terminer, which issued *ex gravi querela* to deal with *querelae* of trespass. In 1450, John Paston petitioned the Chancellor.—

> Please it your reverent Fatherhood to grant unto your said beseecher . . . a special assize against the said Lord Moleyns . . . and others to be named by your said beseecher, and also an oyer and determiner against the said Lord Moleyns . . . and others of the said riotous people in like form to be named, to enquire, hear and determine all trespasses, extortions, riots, forcible entries, maintenances, champerties, embraceries, offences, and misprisions by them or any of them done, as well at suit of our sovereign Lord the King, as of your said beseecher . . . or of any other the King's lieges: at reverence of God, and in way of charity.[66]

In the fifteenth century, however, Chancery became increasingly absorbed in the substantially new area of uses, and the king's council had to resume direct responsibility for hearing bills alleging enormous trespasses. The Council in Star Chamber heard cases "at the suit of the party", but the party had to label the injury as a riot to get his bill accepted, just as a thirteenth century complainant of trespass had to label the injury a breach of the peace. In both instances the real issues were usually ones of land-tenure, and in proportion as the alleged riot was fictional it needed to be given colour in phrases which seem to grow directly from the *vi et armis* of trespass. The trespassers "in Riotous manner arrayed in form of war, that is to say swords, sharp daggers and gloves of mail", who attacked "your said orator in God's peace and yours" at Bexhill in a Star Chamber case of 1500, were already on the march "with hauberks, iron gloves, swords, bucklers, and other arms, arrayed against the peace of our lord the king" in a bill in Chancery in 1388, and "with force and arms, to wit bows, arrows, hauberks and habergeons" in Bolland's bills in eyre. Whether in Eyre, Parliament, Chancery or Star Chamber, all bills had this in common, the label of public wrongfulness which directed them to the most effective royal court available.[67]

BILLS AND WRITS

Perhaps I may conclude with the remark that if Maitland's student of English law wants to put the growth of that law in a wider historical perspective, not writs but bills must be his theme. For plaints and bills were what English law had in common with French, Spanish or Scottish law. In thirteenth-century León and Castile, the legal historian will find the principle that royal officials might not be directly accused by private persons, but that if good men complained of them to the king, he was bound by his office (*de su oficio*) to prosecute and discover if the truth was as they complained (*e saber la verdat, si es assi como querellassen*). The legal historian will also find in Spain a system of *pesquisas* which, as Miss Proctor describes them, sound very like English commissions of oyer and terminer concerning trespasses, for the parties of *pesquisidores* were instructed to deal with cases such as the unlawful taking of pledges and the seizure of land and goods *con armas e con fuerza* in particular areas.[68] In France, he will find nation-wide inquests into complaints of official violence, which merge around 1250 into regular *parlements*.

The comparison between England and Scotland will be found particularly interesting, because in Scotland the same basic writs (or "brieves") were used as in England but royal justice was relatively weak when complaints of trespass began to pour in. The Scottish council was probably hearing plaints before 1290, when Edward I appointed four Englishmen *ad querelas diversorum hominum . . . audiendum et terminandum*. There survives a roll of pleas in the parliaments of King John at Scone in 1292 and Stirling in 1293, which includes amongst its twenty or so items a bill from the abbey of Reading (*A nostre seingnur le Rey de Escoce e a soun Counsail mustrent . . .*), and three pleas of trespass. In 1318, twenty years after Edward I's appointment of commissioners in England to hear on indictment and at the suit of the party injuries done to his people in his name on account of the war, King Robert I of Scotland gave orders *De transgressionibus venientibus ad exercitum*, that each trespasser should be attached to answer before the justiciar, *ita bene ad dampnum partis sicut ad indictamentum domini Regis*. In 1341, there were two "auditores deputati ex parte . . . regis et parliamenti ad audiendum et terminandum supplicaciones et querelas que in parliamento non fuerant terminate"; and in 1425 there was an attempt to divert *querellis* from the overburdened council to regular *sessions* of the chancellor and certain discreet persons of the three estates. From these expedients there grew eventually the Court of Session, in much the same way as Parlement in France and Parliament, Chancery and Star Chamber in England had grown, on a diet of bills.[69]

If the preoccupation with the writ is put aside, England can be seen to take its place in the general thirteenth-century move from accusation to inquisition, and growth of centralised systems of justice fed by plaints and bills of trespass and capped by judicial parliaments.

NOTES

[1] Maitland CP ii.110.

[2] PM ii.560.

[3] Bolland, *Eyre of Kent* ii (1912) 27 SS xxi–xxx; *Bills in Eyre* (1914), 30 SS.

[4] *Procedure without Writ* (1941) 60 SS. "Plainte ou clameur est quant aucun monstre a la Justice, en plaignant soy, le tort qui luy a esté faict afin qu'il en puisse avoir droit en Cour." This definition in the *Summa de legibus Normannie* is quoted by Roger Grand in "Justice Criminelle, Procédure et Peines dans les Villes aux XIIIe et XIVe Siècles" (1941), 102 *Bibliothèque de l'Ecole des Chartes* 70 n.2.

[5] Sayles, *King's Bench Cases*, especially vol. iv 74 SS lxvii f. See also G. J. Hand in [1961–3] *Proceedings of the Royal Irish Academy* on plaints and bills in Ireland.

[6] One of the charges against Justice Richard de Boyland in 1290 was that in the Eyre at Gloucester he had entertained a bill alleging false imprisonment which had not taken place *infra summonicionem itineris*: see Tout and Johnstone, *State Trials* 5–6.

[7] *Procedure without Writ* 67: PLACITA CORONE CIVITATIS CANTUARIE. VEREDICTUM VENIT PER XIJ[CIM]. Hamo le Queller queritur quod Walkelinus le Gayoler, Iohannes Fareman, Adam le Waller et Simon Myngnot venerunt de nocte ad domum ipsius Hamonis et hostia sua fregerunt et ipsum Hamonem wulneraverunt, verberaverunt et male tractaverunt . . . On the relationship of plaints to presentments, cf. p. 68 and note 17 below.

[8] *Procedure without Writ* lv.

[9] *Ibid.*, 49, 52.

[10] Delisle, *Enquêtes* 74: "Guillelmus Haucet conqueritur quod, cum esset plegius pro quodam homine, Martinus Clericus cepit eum, licet esset crucesignatus, et tenuit eum captum in domo regis per plures dies, et noluit eum liberare per litteras officialis, et dum captus esset, Martinus abstulit ei v minas siliginis, valoris xvi solidorum, et in allis dampnificatus est ad valorem xv solidorum. Duo anni sunt."
Ibid. 303: "Conqueruntur homines de Verzelano, dicentes quod, post guerram vicecomitis et comitis Tholosani, scilicet post duos dies, et factas et datas treugas in die mercurii, homines de Prixano venerunt super homines de Verzelano et invaserunt eos cum armis, scilicet in die veneris, et ceperunt IIII[or] homines . . . et crudelissime detinuerunt eos, et tandem redimere [coegerunt], et extorserunt ab eis pro redemptione CCCCLX solidos melgoriensium, et pro missionibus in carcere factis XII [CIM] solidos melgoriensium, et tenuerunt eos captos per VII ebdomadas . . ."
Ibid. 301: ". . . Nos F. et J. rectores ecclesiarum de Cofolanto et de Monte Claro, de mandato venerabili patris Clarini, Dei gratia Carcassonensis episcopi, citavimus per litteras nostras in locis a nobis assignatis conquerentes de domino rege vel senescallis, vicariis vel baiulis vel aliis servientibus pro domino rege, ut, si aliqui vellent facere querimonias de praedictis, venirent coram nobis diebus assignatis et ostenderent nobis injurias eisdem illatas vel dampna, et nos redigeremus in scriptis et ostenderemus venerabili patri nostro praedicto vel inquisitoribus pro domino rege, et nos omnes infrascriptos conquerentes fecimus jurare de dicenda veritate."
Cf. for some more examples pp. 73–4: "QUERIMONIAE CENOMANNORUM ET ANDEGA-VORUM . . . Hamelotus le Pevrier conqueritur quod Petrus le Ber arrestavit eum, imponens ei quod non iverat in exercitu, quod non debebat, quia erat homo Templi. Novem anni sunt.
"Oliverius le Pevrier conqueritur quod Tranchant et Mocart ceperunt eum et verberaverunt, et abstulerunt ei X solidos, et fecerunt eum, cum esset in vinculis, jurare quod de cetero non ferret super hoc clamorem. Circa Pasca, duo anni sunt."

[11] *Los Codigos Españoles: Codigo de las Siete Partidas*, iii (Madrid, 1848), 265 (La Setena Partida, tit.I, ley xi). Cf. E. S. Procter, *The Judicial Use of the Pesquisa in León and Castile* (EHR Supplement no. 2), 32.

[12] CPR (1247–58), 372 (4 August).

[13] Cam, *Studies* 24, 94 (no.53). Miss Cam somewhat oddly describes the chapter as concerning sheriffs who connive at the escape of indicted criminals.

[14] JI 1/734, m.25.

[15] See E. F. Jacob, *Studies in the Period of Baronial Reform and Rebellion, 1258–67* (Oxford, 1925).

[16] *Procedure without Writ* 114.

[17] Helen M. Cam, *The Hundred and the Hundred Rolls* (London, 1930), 43. Cf. H. M. Chew and M. Weinbaum (ed.), *The London Eyre of 1244*, (1970) 6 Lond. RS 133–4 (nos. 341 and 345): in 1244 the City of London had answered the chapter "De imprisonatis ad voluntatem ballivi sine causa racionabili et liberatis sine warranto" by referring to the complaint of one Alfred of Pinchbeck enrolled immediately after the presentment in the form *ostendit justiciariis*.

[18] Cam, *Studies* 136; cf. SR i.44. See also Cam, *The Eyre of London 1321*, i (1968) 85 SS 3.

[19] Tout and Johnstone, *State Trials*.

[20] CPR (1292–1301), 338; W. S. Thomson (ed.), *A Lincolnshire Assize Roll for 1298*, (1944) 36 Linc. RS.

[21] R. C. van Caenegem, *Royal Writs in England from the Conquest to Glanvill* (1958–9/1959) 77 SS 283ff.

[22] Cf. Procter, *Pesquisa* 26–7.

[23] Procter, *Pesquisa* 21; *Siete Partidas* iii.347 (La Setena Partida, tit.x, ley viii); Delisle, *Enquêtes* 74, 75, 257 etc. There seems to have been an international legal vocabulary of trespass made up of terms like force and arms, *tort et force, vulneravit et verberavit, domos fregerunt* . . .

[24] Comte Beugnot (ed.), *Les Olim ou Registres des Arrêts rendus par la Cour du Roi*, i (Paris, 1839), 417–18; P.–F. Fournier and P. Guébin (ed.), *Enquêtes administratives d'Alfonse de Poitiers: Arrêts de son Parlement tenu à Toulouse et Textes annexes, 1249–71* (Collection de Documents inédits sur l'Histoire de France), 14, 20–21, 302; C.–V. Langlois, "Nouveaux Fragments du *Liber Inquestarum*", (1885) 46 *Bibliothèque de l'Ecole des Chartes* 446. A basic meaning of *vis* seems to have been an actual force of armed men.

[25] Delisle, *Enquêtes* 15; F. Lot and R. Fawtier, *Histoire des institutions françaises au Moyen Age*, ii (Institutions royales, Paris, 1958), 472ff.

[26] G. J. Turner (ed.), *Brevia Placitata* (1947/1951) 66 SS xliv; BNB no. 1730. The one criticism which might be made of Mr Richardson and Professor Sayles is that they give an impression of the *querela* as a technical alternative to the writ, whereas it was originally the simple and basic way of beginning a case over the whole of western Europe. The word is found at least from Carolingian times as the usual term for a *quarrel* between two parties pursued in a judicial way. At the same period it could already mean complaint: in 847 the Frankish *missi dominici*, in an interesting anticipation of the instructions to justices in eyre, were ordered to hear *querele pauperum*. See C. Manaresi, *I Placiti del "Regnum Italiae"* (Rome, 1955), 774; A. Boretius (ed.), *Capitularia Regnum Francorum*.

[27] See *Early Registers* cxxx–cxxxi for a comment on the contribution of the local courts to ideas of tort and contract; Cam, *Eyre of London* i. lxxxviii for an analysis of the cases brought by bill. For the Statute of Gloucester, cap. VIII, see SR i.48: "Purveu est ensement, qe Viscuntes pleident en Cuntez les plesz de trespas ausi com il soloient estre pleidez. Et qe nul eit desoremes bref de trespas devaunt Justices (se il na fie) par fei, qe les biens enportez vaillent qaraunte soul ai meins. E si il se pleint de Baterie afie par fei qe sa pleinte est veritable. De plaies e de mahems eit em bref si com em soleit aver . . ."

[28] *Early Registers* cxxxii; cf. the paper by John S. Beckerman in this volume. It is difficult to see what use there would have been for writs in order to bring trespass cases in the shire court before the Statute of Gloucester, the received version of which specifically says "*plesz* de trespas" before the sheriffs (see previous note), where the version in a fourteenth-century MS. says "*brefs* de trespas" (National Library of Wales, Peniarth MS. 330A).

[29] *Brevia Placitata* lxiv; *Early Registers* cxxxii.

[30] *Procedure without Writ* cxxxiii; R. F. Hunnisett, "The Origins of the Office of Coroner" (1958) 8 TRHS/V 96; Bracton ff.101v–102, 138 (Woodbine–Thorne ii. 291, 388).

[31] For the king not choosing to fight, see J. M. Kaye (ed.), *Placita Corone*, (1966) 4 SSSS 18, 23; for Louis XI's ordinance, P. Viollet (ed.) *Les Etablissements de Saint Louis* (Paris, 1881), ii.8–10: "Nous deffandons batailles par tout notre domoine en toutes quereles . . . et en leu de batailles, nous metons prueves de tesmoinz . . ."; cf. Lot and Fawtier ii.317.

[32] JI 1/361, m.36 for the case of 1255 (from the eyre in Kent). In the same eyre (m. 56d.) Nicholas Ferthing who *appellavit in comitatu . . . de roberia, verberatura, plagis et pace domini regis infracta*, comes before the justices and says that the accused *ipsum verberaverunt, vulneraverunt et maletractaverunt contra pacem etc.* The appeal is disallowed because Nicholas has not pronounced the words of felony. The jury finds that the parties have come to an agreement, so they are both imprisoned. Cf. JI 1/568, m.3 (Norfolk, 1257), where the complainant asks for damages (*Et hoc petit sibi emendari etc.*), but sees his suit disallowed for variance *eo quod alias appellavit per verba appellacionis et modo queritur* and the accused found not guilty *de aliqua verberatura*. In the Oxfordshire eyre of 1261 (JI 1/701, m.24d.) a woman appeals four brothers. *Et quod hoc fecerunt in roberia et contra pacem petit quod inquiratur per patriam.* The brothers successfully object that she *non offert disracionare versus eum sicut mulier versus hominem*, but *pro pace domini regis observanda inquiratur rei veritas per patriam*. The jury finds that the accused entered the woman's house by force and took her goods, but on account of arrears of rent and not in robbery. So they are quit *quo ad vitam et membra* but have to make fine *pro transgressione* and satisfaction to the appellant for what they took. For another case in which the accused successfully objects that the appellant *alias ipsum appellavit in Comitatu et modo queritur* but is punished *pro transgressione*, see JI 1/235, m.15d. (Essex, 1255). In another case on the same roll, the appellant *appellavit in Hundreto et modo queritur* (m.20d.)

[33] *Procedure without Writ* xv, xlv; see the case of John of Eydon (above, p. 67), an early complaint against officials in which the complainant seems uncertain as to whether it is appropriate to offer battle or seek jury trial; cf. also the formula found in the trailbaston rolls of the next century: *Compertum est per inquisicionem* upon which the *querens* and the *defendens* put themselves (e.g. JI 1/509, m.4d.) In some respects the situation was the reverse of what Maitland thought (p. 65 above): the purpose of the common-law bill was precisely to get an issue tried by jury

[34] G. D. G. Hall, "Some Early Writs of Trespass", (1957) 73 LQR 72, writ B.8: *de transgressione de raptu et de pace regis infracta*. In a register of some ten years earlier a writ of appeal *de mahemio et pace domini regis fracta* is given as a variant of a writ of trespass (*ibid.* 67, writ S.1). For Bracton's description of the writ of appeal, see f.149 (Woodbine–Thorne ii.420). At the Northamptonshire eyre of 1253 (JI 1/615, m.13d.), a man *appellat per breve domini regis*, offering *disracionare versus* the accused *ut homo qui etatem transiit*. The appeal was annulled because the hue and cry had not been raised, but also because the writ made no mention of felony: this appellant was taking extra care to avoid battle. On inquiry *pro pace domini regis*, the accused was found guilty of wounding the appellant and fined half a mark. Mr Fifoot's two cases beginning *queritur per breve domini regis* are on this roll: Fifoot, *Sources* 54; the cases were printed by Richardson and Sayles, *Procedure without Writ* 61, 75. In one of them, Henry Organ *conqueritur per breve domini regis* that the defendants assaulted him *vi et armis et contra pacem*. In each case the defendants object to the process as a defective appeal: these seem to me to be not early writs of trespass but examples of the sort of "attenuated appeal" which gave rise to the writ of trespass. At the Herefordshire eyre of 1292 (JI 1/303, m.74), William de Norton, who had got his opponent into gaol by writ of appeal, came and said that he did not wish to proceed *per formam appelli, immo per formam transgressionis*. The defendant successfully objected that they had made a concord concerning all the trespasses and contentions between them.

35 JI 1/361, m.52 (two cases); JI 1/778, m.57d.; JI 1/568, m.18d.

36 Fleta i.40 (72 SS 9); for the Statute of Gloucester, see note 27 above. The line between beating and wounding was naturally a fine one. At the eyre of Norfolk in 1257 (JI 1/568, m.3), an appeal *de verberatura, mahemio et pace etc.* was changed to a plaint that the defendants *verberaverunt et malectract-averunt* the plaintiff *contra pacem* and a claim for damages.

37 S. F. C. Milsom, "Not Doing is no Trespass", [1954] CLJ. For an action by writ of trespass alleging assault on a man *qui deputatus fuit ad colligendum teolonum domini regis*, see JI 1/361, m.27 (1265); alleging the seizure of a hand-having thief from the prison of a liberty, see JI 1/820, m.18 (1258); alleging breach of close committed against a man *in servicio domini regis* and enjoying the king's special protection, see the same roll, m.19; alleging distraint to suit of court, against the provisions of Westminster, JI 1/701, m.6 (1261); alleging distraint on goods in the plaintiff's shop so that he was forced to close, see the same roll, m.12d. Writs of trespass alleging false imprisonment are numerous.

38 Above, p. 67.

39 Delisle, *Enquêtes* 698-9.

40 C. M. Fraser, *Northumberland Petitions*, (1966) 176 Surtees Society 109-10.

41 Bolland, *Bills in Eyre* 71.

42 Tout and Johnstone, *State Trials* 68; Bolland, *Bills in Eyre* 79.

43 JI 1/237, m.2; *Procedure without Writ* lxii–lxiv; F. Pegues, "A monastic society at law in the Kent eyre of 1313-14", (1972) 87 EHR 554, 558.

44 Cam, *Eyre of London* i. lxxxviii.

45 *Rot. Parl.* i.178.

46 See JI 1/509 (Lincolnshire, 1305): PLACITA CORAM . . . JUSTICIARIIS DOMINI REGIS AD DIVERSAS FELONIAS ET TRANSGRESSIONES IN COMITATU LINCOLN' FACTAS AUDIENDAS ET TERMINANDAS ASSIGNATIS. For examples of the various formulae, see m.4d.: *Compertum est per inquisicionem in quam W. querens et J. defendens se posuerunt; m.7: ad presentacionem xii etc. et ad sectam W. querentis compertum est per inquisicionem in quam P.* (the defendant) *se posuit; m.15: presentatum fuit alias* that R. extorted money from G. by menaces, now *G. non sequitur, ideo pro pace domini regis observanda inquiratur rei veritas; m.18:* H. and R. *attachiati fuerunt ad respondendum domino regi de placito conspiracionis . . . unde S. miles qui sequitur pro rege; m.21:* B. and others were attached to answer *tam domino regi quam W. filio J. de placito quare . . . Et unde W. qui sequitur tam pro domino rege quam pro seipso . . .*
   The following is a bill to the justices of trailbaston in Gloucestershire in 1321 (E 36/88, no.29):
   A les Justices nostre seignur le Rey moustre et se pleynt R. that P. and others assaulted him and extorted from him *a force et as armes* and *par leur manasses*, including a threat of false indictments, the damages he had recovered in a previous trailbaston plea of wounding. *Cest tort et cest trepas ly firent . . . a tort et encontre la pees nostre seignur le Rey as greves dampniages de mesmes celuy R. de lx livres . . .* (The bill is endorsed:) *Affidavit quia pauper;* names of two pledges each for the four defendants; *nulla transgressio ad patriam; postea non prosecutus; misericordia xl d.; Finits.*

47 Sayles, *King's Bench Cases,* iv, introduction (74 SS lxvii–lxviii); JI 1/379.

48 See the endorsements of the bill of 1321 cited in n.46 above. For a good example of a King's Bench indictment file of 1338, see KB 9/155.

49 Cam, *Eyre of London* ii.143.

50 Sayles, *King's Bench Cases,* vi (82 SS 168).

51 Holdsworth, HEL ix.236ff.; Sayles, *King's Bench Cases* ii (57 SS lxxxv); C. G. Bayne and W. H. Dunham *Select Cases in the Council of Henry VII* (1956/1958) 75 SS lii; T. F. T. Plucknett, "Some Proposed Legislation of Henry VIII" (1936) 19 TRHS/IV.

52 Bertha H. Putnam, *Proceedings before the Justices of the Peace in the Fourteenth and Fifteenth Centuries* (London, 1938), xxvi, clviii.

53 Sayles, *King's Bench Cases* v (76 SS 49); CPR (1247–58) 372; CPR (1258–66) 53; notes 19 and 20 above, for 1289 and 1298; for 1309, *Rot. Parl.* i.464; Bolland, *Bills in Eyre* 137ff. Cf. the writ of summons to the eyre from 1278 (p. 68 and n.18 above) and the related Statute of Rageman SR i.44): Justices are to go *parmi la terre, a enquere e oier, e terminer les pleintes, e les quereles de trespas feez dedenz ses xxv aunz passez . . .*

54 Alice Beardwood (ed.), *Records of the Trial of Walter Langeton, Bishop of Coventry and Licnfield, 1307-1312* (1969) 6 RHS Camden/IV. In Latin *querela* and *clamor* are synonymous, as are *plainte* and *clameur* in French: see above, note 4. Written bills were presented against Langton, for example:
   J. porrexit super Walterum de Langeton . . . quamdam querelam in hec verba. A nostre seignur le Roy se pleint Johan Sampson Deuerwyk de Wauter de Langeton [and others] qe par leur fausse conspiracie e compassement fesoient une Margerie de Silkeston appeler le dit Johan de la mort son baroun pur le quel faux appel le dit Johan feust enprisoun troys auntz e demy en le chastel Deuerwyk en le garde le visconte qui fu en daunger levesque adonqe Tresorer le Roy . . .

55 The commissions of oyer and terminer of trespass in the Register as printed by William Rastell (London, 1531) begin at f.123. For an oyer and terminer of trespass beginning *Ex gravi querela H. accepimus quod . . .* see *Early Registers* 185. Another common trespass writ began *Audita querela,* and ordered justices to give a remedy "having heard the complaint": *Early Registers* 173.

56 Gabrielle Lambrick, "The Impeachment of the Abbot of Abingdon in 1368", (1967) 82 EHR 258 n.4.

57 f.125v.; CPR (1334–8) 291 (2 June).

58 Lambrick, "Impeachment" 266ff.; T.F.T. Plucknett, "Origins of Impeachment" (1942) 24 TRHS/IV. M. V. Clarke noted that the word *empeschement* came into vogue in Edward II's reign ("The Origins of Impeachment", *Oxford Essays in Mediaeval History presented to H. E. Salter* (1930) 164). A pardon of 1321 said that the Welsh marchers were not to be "impeached, aggrieved or molested" for felonies or trespasses committed against the Despensers (CCR(1318–23) 495); and in 1325 the men of Chester were not to be *empeschez* for acts done in the king's service in 1322 (*Rot. Parl.* i.438). These were years when the justices of trailbaston were very active, hearing bills of felonies and trespasses.

59 *Rot. Parl.* i.290.

[60] SR i.282; Sayles, *King's Bench Cases* vi (82 SS 1–11); *Rot.Parl.* ii.122–5.

[61] H. G. Richardson and G. O. Sayles, *Rotuli Parliamentorum Anglie hactenus inediti, 1279–1373* (1935) 51 RHS Camden/III 3: *Radulfus de Hengham et socii sui audiant querelas contra Eliam de Hauville et terminent; Rot. Parl.* i.286.

[62] *Rot. Parl.* i.376 (nos. 43–5), 464, ii.396; CChW 339, 346 (a mandate to appoint two named persons as justices to hear and determine a trespass against Alyne Lovel, to which is attached Alyne's bill in *moustre et se pleynt* form); Richardson and Sayles, *Rotuli* 2, 6, 20 etc.

[63] B. Wilkinson, *The Chancery under Edward III* (Manchester, 1929), 26–40.

[64] B. Wilkinson in J. Willard and W. A. Morris, *The English Government at Work, 1327–1336* (Cambridge, Mass., 1940), 190ff.

[65] Lambrick, "Impeachment" 265.

[66] James Gairdner, *The Paston Letters* i (London, 1908) 144–5.

[67] S. E. Lehmberg in (1961) 24 *Huntington Library Quarterly* 189; Bayne and Dunham, *Council Cases* 123–7; W. P. Baildon, *Select Cases in the Court of Chancery* (1896) 10 SS 7; Bolland, *Bills in Eyre* 88. See S. F. C. Milsom, "Trespass from Henry III to Edward III" (1958) 74 LQR 222, for the formula *vi et armis scilicet gladiis arcubus et sagittis.*

[68] Above, note 11; Procter, *Pesquisa* 21. Another example of the growth of courts from the hearing of complaints against officials is provided by Sicily. At Messina in 1234, the Emperor Frederick II set up *curias solemnes* whih were to meet twice yearly in five named towns. There anyone might complain of injuries (*conqueri de damnis et injuriis*) inflicted on him by officials of the province (J. L. A. Huillard Bréholles, *Historia diplomatica Frederici secundi* (Paris, 1852–61), iv.460–63).

[69] See A. A. M. Duncan, "The Central Courts before 1532" in *An Introduction to Scottish Legal History* (1958) 20 Stair Society 321–49; *Acts of the Parliament of Scotland* i.107, 445–9; A. Harding, "The Medieval Brieves of Protection and the Development of the Common Law" (1966) 11 *Juridical Review* 146.

A View of the Admiral Jurisdiction: Sir Matthew Hale and the Civilians

D. E. C. Yale

In 1661 Dr John Godolphin, who had been an Admiralty Judge during the Commonwealth, published a little book entitled "A View of the Admiral Jurisdiction."[1] I have borrowed both his title and his topic, and propose to-day to take a view of the Admiralty jurisdiction during the latter part of the seventeenth century.

There are, it seems to me, many different standpoints not only of time, but of place from which one can view a jurisdiction and the working of a court. I choose the seventeenth century and approximately the period 1650–1700 because it was especially critical for the Admiralty jurisdiction. I choose mainly the standpoint of lawyers, common law and civilian, because they had the most to say and much to do with the story. But of course theirs was not the sole standpoint. One may view the court from a non-professional standpoint, that of the litigants, actual or potential, or that of persons in political and public life, or even from the standpoint of the ordinary casual spectator.

One onlooker was Samuel Pepys who one day in March 1663 witnessed a session of the criminal jurisdiction of the Admiralty. He was not complimentary. "To St Margaret's Hill in Southwark", he wrote in his Diary,[2]

> where the Judge of the Admiralty came, and the rest of the Doctors of the Civil Law, and some other Commissioners, whose commission of oyer and terminer was read, and then the charge given by Dr Exton, which methought was somewhat dull, though he would seem to intend it to be very rhetorical, saying that justice had two wings, one of which spread itself over the land, the other over the water, which was this Admiralty Court. That being done, and the jury called, they broke up, and to dinner in a tavern hard by, where a great dinner and I with them; but I perceive this court is yet but in its infancy, as to its rising again, and their design and consultation was —I could overhear them—how to proceed with the most solemnity, and spend time, there being only two businesses to do, which of themselves could not spend much time. In the afternoon back to the court again where, first, Abraham the boatswain of the King's pleasure-boat, was tried for drowning a man, and next Turpin, accused by our wicked rogue, Field, for selling the King's timber. But after full examination they were both acquitted, and so I was glad of the first, for the saving the man's life, so I did take the other as a very good fortune for us; for if this Turpin had been found guilty it would have sounded very ill in the ears of all the world, in the business between Field and us.

We need not pursue the interest of the Navy Office and their Clerk of the Acts in this latter prosecution, and acquittal.[3] We should rather listen to Exton's figure of speech, the two wings, one over the sea, the other over the land, which hinted at the main issue of contention between the common law and Admiralty jurisdictions, and to note that Pepys heard the civilians in a mood of resurgence, the "rising again", as he put it, of the Admiralty jurisdiction. It was not just that they were overjoyed with the restoration of the King and the Latin language; they expected more substantial benefits. This hope did not, in the long run, come to fruition, but clearly the civilians were in an optimistic mood. Godolphin introducing his book described himself in his literary venture as now being

> free to sail from the law to the jurisdiction of the Admiralty, being the port of discharge in the design of this adventure; the wind seems fair, the sea well purged of rovers, and Nereus re-invested with his trident . . .

Godolphin's, too, was not the only literary venture in this "fair wind". Richard Zouch, a former Admiralty Judge, published a lengthy vindication of the Admiralty in 1663,[4] designed to combat the influence of Sir Edward Coke's Fourth Institute and its damaging interpretation of Admiralty jurisdiction, and Exton, the current judge, followed in 1664 with his *Maritime Dicæologie*.[5] These works, Zouch's and Exton's, are replete with erudition and not wanting in aggressive spirit, nor were they alone. They found themselves, perhaps somewhat surprisingly, in alliance with William Prynne who later in the decade published his *Animadversions* on Coke's Fourth Institute,[6] and outdistanced them both in erudition and aggressive spirit. At sight this "battle of the books" appears one-sided, and the other side of the case seems almost a default of appearance and answer, but Godolphin's "rovers" were not beaten. Coke and Hobart might be dead and gone, but they had their successors, and the civilians were by no means without opposition.

Broadly speaking, in later Tudor and earlier Stuart times, the jurisdictional conflicts between the Admiralty and the courts of common law had been, temporarily and from time to time, resolved by conciliar fiat, and when the trouble grew really acute, by conciliar arbitration. In 1575, 1611 and 1633 the common law judges and the civilians had been summoned into conference and some compromise obtained and ratified by the authority of the privy council. These compromises had generally favoured the civilians' case, but had never cured the irritation and abrasions between the two jurisdictions. Practically, and superficially, the trouble was about the use and abuse of writs of prohibition, but more deeply, the civilians (despite the erudition of Exton and the rest) do not seem to have fully appreciated the strength of Coke's position and that of like-minded common law judges. The medieval statutes, of 1389 and 1391,[7] which delimited the Admiral's jurisdiction were no doubt open to some argument by way of interpretation, but the basic criterion they laid down was not one concerning the nature of the cause of action but one of location. Thus a contract to furnish or repair a ship in the port of London was manifestly a maritime matter, but such a contract did not arise nor was it to be performed on the high sea and outside the body of an English county, as the statutes required. Therefore, according to Coke, a prohibition could be had to stop the Admiralty adjudicating on such a contract, as either made or performable upon land or within the body of a county. Coke certainly allowed that the Admiralty might execute its process within the body of an English county (there was plain yearbook authority for that), but with regard to cognisance of causes of action he was adamant. Moreover, he had affirmed that the common law judges were the ultimate arbiters upon the interpretation of statutes. This was the vital question, who was to have the last word in interpretation and so fix the bounds of jurisdiction? The common law position was that the last word belonged to the common law judges, and they were equipped with prohibition and other such writs to enforce that last word.

Against the common law position, based as it was on the authority of statute and on the assertion that the common law judges were in the last resort the interpreters of statutes, the Admiralty lawyers had their sheet-anchor in the Lord Admiral's patent. The medieval patents had been simple enough texts and generally confined themselves to, and contented themselves with, reciting the statutes of Richard II, but the Tudor patents, and the later patents down to Buckingham's in 1618, were much more elaborate grants, and what is more they were fortified with sweeping non-obstante clauses.[8] The Admiralty lawyers placed their faith largely therefore on the strength of the King's patent, the grant of a great franchise jurisdiction, and copies of these patents surviving in archives show that they annotated and studied its clauses with loving care. The terms of the patents enabled for instance, the Admiralty lawyers to claim jurisdiction over transmarine or ultra-marine contracts. True, their case seemed to involve them in two inconsistent propositions: (i) they asserted that the Admiralty jurisdiction thus conferred did not infringe the statutes of Richard II, (ii) they asserted also that the non-obstante clause was valid and authorised the Lord High Admiral to exercise all jurisdiction conferred by his patent even if that jurisdiction was in part not reconcilable with the statutes. With regard to transmarine contracts Coke's argument in the debate of 1611 may be taken as illustrative of the common law position. Where the Admiralty lawyers complained of prohibitions upon "bargains and contracts made beyond the seas wherein the common law cannot

G

administer justice", he replied that the jurisdiction of the Admiral "is wholly confined to the sea which is out of any county", and with regard to transmarine contracts where the common law could not provide, the civil law jurisdiction of the Constable and Marshal was appropriate, and further he asserted "if any indenture, bond or other specialty, or any contract, be made beyond sea for the doing of any act or payment of any money within this realm, or otherwise, wherein the common law can administer justice, and give ordinary remedy", then, he claimed, the common law had exclusive jurisdiction. Needless to say, he denied roundly the validity of non-obstante, and in so doing he had, exceptionally, the whole hearted support of Prynne a generation later, who devoted much ink and effort to demonstrating that all such clauses "are void in law to all intents and detestable public nuisances."[9]

I do not intend to discuss the various conciliar arbitrations, the first in the reign of Elizabeth, the second under James, the third under Charles in 1633. Each broke temporarily the deadlock but each failed to endure. The last settlement, that of 1633, may be briefly summarised.[10] Of its five points, the first prohibited prohibitions "upon contracts made or other things personally done beyond or on the seas." The second article provided that no prohibition should issue on suits for freight, or for mariners' wages or for breach of charterparty in respect of overseas voyages. The third article preserved from prohibition all Admiralty actions in rem for building, supplying or repairing ships in or out of the kingdom. The fourth and fifth articles dealt with disputed questions of jurisdiction over navigable rivers and the use of habeas corpus for persons committed to the custody of the Admiralty Marshal.

These articles did not comprehend the range of Admiralty actions but they covered the areas where abrasion had been most severe, and they were by and large kept for about ten years. Naturally the settlement depended for its efficacy upon the authority of King and Council, certainly not on a genuine resignation of either side to the arguments and claims of the other. When Crown and Council disappeared, the office of Lord High Admiral itself was transferred to a Council of State. It was no novelty that the office of Lord High Admiral should be vested in a plurality of persons, put into Commission, but the inception of the republican Commonwealth initiated a new situation potentially perilous for the Admiralty jurisdiction. In fact the Court was suffered to survive but was placed under certain restrictive regulations. Without relating the various regulations of the Interregnum, it is enough to say that the Long Parliament passed a regulatory ordinance in 1648 and this was kept on foot by periodic measures of the Commonwealth.[11] This legislation was in certain respects surprisingly liberal. It assured to the Court its jurisdiction in rem in respect of maintenance and supply of ships, bottomry hypothecations, and even foreign contracts concerning shipping and navigation. It secured to the Court cases of charterparties, or contracts for freight, bills of lading, mariners' wages, damage to cargo, collisions and damage caused by anchors and buoys dangerously placed. Litigation on bills of exchange and mercantile accounts was expressly excepted. Moreover, the legislation expressly affirmed the civilian procedure and the Court's authority to execute its decrees and sentences. There were, however, many cautious features. The legislation was never more than temporary and renewable, the Court was staffed by three judges, instead of the traditional single judge, and they were enjoined to give reasons for their decisions.

This ordinance did not reflect much fresh thinking on jurisdictional problems, but it set the pattern for many of the post-Restoration legislative proposals. Also the very survival of the Court testifies to the strength of demand; this had been exerted at ambassadorial level, and the legislation of the Interregnum had reflected other pressures too. Shipmasters had complained that discipline at sea could not be maintained without the effective backing of an Admiralty Court. Shipowners had complained that they could not control maritime ventures where (as was commonly the case) the shipmaster was a part owner, unless the advantages of an Admiralty jurisdiction were available to them. More significantly, numerous merchants had preferred petitions. The mercantile interest indeed took different directions. Some merchants certainly were not well disposed to the Admiralty jurisdiction, which they thought tended to prefer the interest of mariners to merchants, and during the Commonwealth there was a certain and not negligible pressure from the mercantile interest to supersede the Admiralty in matters of foreign trade and commerce.[12] But the civilians were not dislodged. Neither the government nor the strictly maritime interests of owners and seamen favoured that. Probably the Commonwealth establishment was a matter of hard necessity. At the end of his life, in 1685, Jenkins wrote to Pepys a letter[13] in which he discussed the legislation of the Interregnum. Mere necessity, he thought (looking back 30 years) extorted the concessions, in the interests of trade and navigation, and because it was realised that without the proper protection of mariners and materialmen there would have been "decay and ruine in Shipping and Foreign Trade".

But the Restoration brought times which, as we have seen, seemed more propitious. The office of Lord High Admiral was now vested *de facto* as well as *de jure* in the King's brother. Moreover, James had married Clarendon's daughter and Clarendon was now Lord Chancellor. Accordingly the civilians were hopeful of a legislative settlement, and looked first towards the House of Lords. No doubt there were other considerations. The House was itself a body with judicial experience, and as Jenkins later wrote, therefore "the most competent judges of the proper bounds and limits of jurisdictions that clash".[14] Another practical consideration may well have been that the interest of the common lawyers was more strongly entrenched in the lower than the upper House. The first attempt in the Lords, in 1662, nevertheless failed.[15] Next year, the point of attack was shifted to the Commons. But there the civilians' bill was killed stonedead by the arguments and eloquence of the Solicitor-General, Sir Heneage Finch.[16] Backed though it was by the usual shoals of petitions, the civilian initiative failed in both Houses. Both measures had been largely modelled on the conciliar settlement of 1633, and the Parliamentary ordinance and Commonwealth Acts. On the face of it, it seems an unexpected reverse. If the Admiralty cause had gained at least a limited measure of success under the Commonwealth regime, how was it that in the early 1660s no success whatsoever was achieved?

The probability of the matter may be that the civilians failed because they had placed too much trust in princes and Lord Chancellors. With regard to James there is good and positive evidence that he assumed a position of neutrality.[17] Certainly his interest in his office of Admiralty was first and foremost a naval one, and it seems that at this critical juncture of forces he deliberately stood aloof and apart. Former Lord Admirals had been keenly alive to their financial interest in their jurisdiction. One cannot study the tenures of, for example, Nottingham and Buckingham without being aware of such a concern. But James does not appear to have displayed any anxiety on this occasion on this aspect of the matter. But of course the financial interest of the Lord High Admiral lay mainly in his droits of Admiralty and in his shares in prize, not on the instance side of his court. With regard to Clarendon, the evidence is more problematic, but it seems probable that he was influenced by a conviction that nothing should be done to antagonise the interest of Church and State. True, as a court the Admiralty had nothing to do with the Anglican establishment, but as a profession the civilians had a great deal to do with it. There is a long passage in Clarendon's *History of the Rebellion*[18] reflecting on the position of the civilians in the days of the Long Parliament and upon the dire consequences which resulted from the animosities which existed between the two legal professions at that time. But whatever the reasons, both Lord Chancellor and Lord Admiral stood aside. And without their active support the measures of 1662 and 1663 came to nothing.

Defeat in both Houses made further effort for the time futile. Nor was the resort to the Privy Council after the Restoration a solution, understandably enough in the eyes of the civilians, for they saw that the authority of the Council was not what it had been. True, the Council concerned itself with demarcations on droits and continued active in the area of prize, but no move in that area of authority was attempted on the broader issues of jurisdictional dispute. The campaign was not reopened till 1670. Then two draft bills were prepared, one by Jenkins as Judge,[19] the other by the King's Proctor and the King's Advocate, the latter accompanied with a schedule of all prohibitions issued to the Court over the past ten years.[20] Jenkins' draft was adopted; it was indeed very much the bill of 1662 as amended then in Committee. Introduced into the Lords it was committed and certain common law judges and civilians were summoned to attend to discussions of the Committee. Jenkins' speech[21] to the Committee on that occasion is perhaps the most powerful argument on the Admiralty side ever delivered, and in many respects is the *locus classicus* for the civilians' case.

This speech contains much that was common material in the controversy, the minutiae of statutory interpretation, but it was not essentially an argument before lawyers but a speech addressed to legislators. The emphasis was on what was seen by Jenkins to be the rational solution, what was the reasonable reconciliation between the two jurisdictions.

Mere locality, Jenkins argued, did not make a cause maritime. The geographical position of the parties or their property should not be the controlling criterion. And he then proceeded to speak to the maritime causes set out in the bill, seeking to establish with much citation and argument that each was properly within the cognisance of the Admiral's jurisdiction. A great part of Jenkins' argument is concerned with these various causes of action, e.g. foreign contracts, secondly, mariners' wages, freight and breaches of charterparty, and thirdly, ship building and supply of tackle and victuals. In historical retrospect Jenkins naturally placed emphasis on the 1633 settlement which he said "was punctually observed as to the granting and denying of prohibitions till the late disorderly times bore it down as an act of prerogative prejudicial (as was pretended) to the common law and the liberty of the subject." Having then surveyed the intervening period of Interregnum and Restoration, he turned to the positive reasons in favour of a legislative settlement. First, such a settlement would cure existing uncertainties, and secondly it would protect the interests of litigants from the incompetency of the common law courts to give effective remedy and relief in maritime causes. Jenkins no doubt was accurate enough in referring to the greater convenience for litigants of Admiralty process. "Nothing" he declared "can be more pernicious to seafaring and trading men than delays in their law-suits." And the difficulties were greatly exacerbated by intercurial conflict. He referred to a case a year earlier "where one Rand brought his action in the Admiralty against Gosling's ship for his wages, having been hired as master of the ship from London to Lisbon and back again, and also for disbursements made at Lisbon to the ship's use, and sentence given for Rand. Gosling appeals to the Delegates, and they affirm the first sentence, and Gosling being taken in execution pays the money with costs of suit. But the matter ended not here, for Gosling brings his action against Rand for double damages, as having sued in the Admiralty against the statute, 2 Hen. 4 [c.11]. The trial being at the Guildhall, the jury found for the plaintiff Gosling, and he recovered £80 not from Rand (for he happened to die pending the action) but from his poor relict and administratrix." And for good measure, Jenkins added, such a penal action might be against the Judge, Registrar or Proctor as against the libellant, for, he said, "there is not that sort of action to be named wherein the Admiralty has not been some time or other prohibited, either for want of being heard, or else the matter was not fully before the court." So apart from the risk of being deprived by prohibition, the libellant ran the risk of being penalised by action, and having to pay damages in a sum likely to be in excess of the costs incurred in prosecuting his claim in Admiralty.

Merchants as well as mariners might also suffer. Suppose, he argued, the case of a foreign merchant who is my debtor. His ship or goods being within reach of arrest, I arrest them and then they are in the ordinary course released on bail. When I come to proceed in Admiralty for the claim, freight money, breach of charterparty or the like, prohibition is obtained on the suggestion that the contract was not made *super altum mare* but in some Spanish port. My debtor is in Spain, the ship is gone and the bail cannot be sued on in another court. I am practically without remedy. An even more frequent case was where an English merchant owed money to a foreigner, say, a merchant in Spain. The Spaniard sues in Admiralty and the Englishman obtains a prohibition and the Spaniard is forced to sue at common law on his bond or other security. If the defendant pleads *non est factum*, the difficulties are almost insuperable, because the Spanish notary will not part with the original and the notarial copy is not receivable in evidence. Nor are witnesses available for *viva voce* examination, whereas in Admiralty there is no difficulty as to the evidence either in receiving the notarial copy or in getting the Spanish evidence by commission abroad. "A sad discouragement to trade" Jenkins thought, as well as amounting to a failure of justice.

Perhaps the principal sufferers were the materialmen, the repairers and suppliers of ships. Moreover their difficulties involved a wider interest, the employment and mobility of English shipping. The hand of prohibition had fallen with particular severity on them. No doubt they were English residents, but shipwrights and others were especially hurt by prohibition because Admiralty arrest and bail effectively enabled them to work on credit, and this was especially the case in respect to the goods and services supplied to foreign ships. With regard to the building of ships in England, the security in rem was of particular importance on account of the fact that ships were ordinarily built for several part-owners, some of whom might live in distant parts and whose shares might vary enormously in fractions of the whole hull.

Jenkins' speech was forceful but temperate. He was not asking that Admiralty should be immune from prohibitions, only that they should be used against a background of settled jurisdictional limits and not abused by being employed to secure a sort of irregular or illegitimate appeal. This argument was a valid one, and not unlike that argument Coke himself had used fifty years earlier against common injunctions out of Chancery. The real question, of course, was who was to decide the proper limits of jurisdiction, Parliament or the judges in Westminster Hall? But the bill failed to make progress and this second initiative came to nothing.

In 1673 as a result of the Test Act James was evicted from his office of Admiralty which thereafter went into commission, and the question was left undisturbed till 1685, when James acceded as King and also reassumed the Admiralty. Yet another attempt was put on foot. A printed list was prepared of the causes which the civilians considered legitimately the business of the Admiralty.[22] Seven categories were set out. First, mariners' wages. The principal reasons were the facility of joinder of claimants, the expeditious procedure in Admiralty, and the security of the process in rem. Moreover in Admiralty the employer's oath authenticated the contract, whereas at common law the contract had to be proved by witnesses.

Secondly, freight and charterparty cases. The thrust of the argument here was the interdependence of freight and wages. That freight was the mother of wages was an age-old Admiralty principle.

Thirdly, all claims against the ship on grounds of repair and supply, as well as construction. The primary and sufficient reason here was that such goods and services were delivered and rendered on the credit of the ship.

Fourthly, bottomry. The common law did not provide for non-possessory liens. Such hypothecation by maritime lien was necessary in the interests of navigation, especially where the ship was supplied in a foreign port.

Fifthly, collision and damage cases. The snag here was that the common law could only provide remedy against master and mariners, and such persons might be hard to find or worthless to sue. The Admiralty remedy in rem on the other hand, was an effective remedy.

Sixthly, transmarine contracts, and seventhly, nuisances in navigable rivers.

This bill was drawn by Bedford, the Admiralty Registrar.[23] Jenkins now in retirement and failing health could not speak in support but wrote letters and made interest where he could. He was particularly keen on that clause of the bill which secured to the Admiralty sole right to arrest in ports and navigable rivers. Not that the Marshal had been much interfered with. In 1684 Saunders remarked judicially as C.J.K.B. that "nothing is more frequent than for the Admiralty to arrest ships riding in the river, [and] that it was done every day for mariners' wages and other maritime causes."[24] But, wrote Jenkins in a letter to Pepys,[25] Doctors' Commons considered this clause absolutely vital. The Sheriffs of Kent and Essex and the officers of the City had taken to arresting cargoes in the river, and wrote Jenkins, "he that arrests or executes men or goods in a ship hath the better end of the staff; he needs not in that case to sue for a prohibition, for the courts at Westminster do not use to prohibit one another, much less will anyone of them prohibit itself when the arrest is made by process out of it."

Jenkins recommended that the King's interest be engaged and that he be encouraged to "dispose my Lord Keeper and my lords the Judges to favour the passing of it, there being no cause, action or judgment pretended to in this bill but may and will come before them whenever either of the parties do appeal, and my Lord Keeper do (as always he does) put the judges into the Commission of Delegates." He recommended also that the bill be entrusted to "some noble hand that will have a care of it and affection for it". But there is no evidence that the bill came to any "noble hand"; it is certain that it was not even formally introduced. The parliamentary sessions of 1685 were too short and no further opportunity occurred during James' reign.

1685 was the last opportunity, and after the Revolution legislative moves were abandoned.[26] The office of Lord High Admiral was placed in commission, and the civilians seem to have tacitly conceded failure. Probably by the end of the century they realised hope of such a settlement must be abandoned. Sir Nathaniel Lloyd, King's Advocate and Judge in the early eighteenth century, extracted into his common-place books certain items culled from the calendars of the Admiralty office, and added the melancholy note "By perusing this calendar it will appear that the Admiralty had a large Jurisdiction. Quomodo evanuit?"[27] How it disappeared, and where it went, are certainly questions to be asked, and involve us in retracing our steps.

*   *   *

During the seventeenth century these attempts, conciliar and parliamentary, to reach an enduring settlement failed, as we have seen, despite numerous opportunities. The reasons for failure are, no doubt, likewise numerous, and some of them speculative. But largely among them must be rated the professional divide separating Doctors' Commons from the Inns of Court. The civilians never tired of insisting that the Admiralty was the King's Court as much as his courts in Westminster Hall,[28] they even countered the argument that the civil law was an un-English body of rules and principles, by asserting that their law was the common law, not the common law of the land, but the common law of the sea, and maintaining that the civil law was for them no more than an auxiliary source to assist the administration of maritime law and custom. But all the verbal fencing appears a superficial skirmishing, a surface upon the deep professional division which kept both sides apart. This is no place to argue the advantages and disadvantages of it. In the last hundred years the disappearance of Doctors' Commons has had its effect on the theory and practice of maritime law. In the sixteenth and seventeenth centuries the institution of Doctors' Commons was certainly one factor in the jurisdictional jarring. The fact that Admiralty applied rules and principles, and used a procedure, different from those of the common law was probably not in itself a cause of hostility. The Court of Chancery had developed a body of principles, and used a procedure, which was not that of the common law, yet despite some crises the common lawyers lived with it amicably enough. The fact is they worked in it, practised in Chancery, acted judicially in the Court, and one sees a similar situation in the conciliar courts. But with the church courts and in Admiralty there was no such assimilation and reciprocity, at least to such a degree as appears in Chancery, in the conciliar courts. And the differences must be largely attributed to the professional separation. There was no Chancery Bar, no Star Chamber Bar, no separate career, for the lawyers who appeared before those Courts. But it was otherwise with the doctors and it was otherwise also with the proctors. Contact was not indeed entirely lacking. Civilians might have audience in Westminster Hall and argue at the bar of a common law court on points raising questions of civil law, and there was a certain (though limited) mutuality among the judiciary. In the latter part of the seventeenth century common law judges joined in commission with the civilians e.g. on appeals before Delegates,[29] and in criminal cases tried at Admiralty sessions both common lawyers and civilians sat together. It is true that in prize the common law judges were not concerned, appeals there lay to a committee of the privy council, but then there never was any serious jurisdictional controversy over prize. Though highly lucrative, the prize jurisdiction was not in contest. It was on the fate of the instance side that the future of the commercial law of the country turned.

The all important factor was the attitude of the common law judiciary. More important, so it seems to me, than the attitude of litigants. Normally, no doubt one must bear in mind that a court can only decide a case if the layman or his legal adviser decides to go to that court; such a factor is crucial, for example, if one is considering the intercurial contest between the King's Bench and Common Pleas at this time over bills of Middlesex and *ac etiam*. But with an issue of prohibition it was not a question of attracting litigants, but a question of barring their suits in another court. One side or the other has lost or looks to lose a case in Admiralty; there is every encouragement to him in the possibilities of prohibition. The common law judges cannot lack opportunity to decide what may be litigated in Admiralty and what not.

It is worth bearing in mind that the party seeking prohibition was not necessarily a person who fled into Westminster Hall at the first sight of the Admiralty Marshal. The writ of prohibition[30] was, if one can be allowed the figure of speech, very much the trump card in the pack, and a card which could be played at any stage of the game. Indeed prohibition could be had after definitive sentence in the Admiralty, and even after an appeal to Delegates. And what seems even more remarkable, and certainly to the civilians appeared specially reprehensible, the writ could be had by that party who had initiated proceedings in the Admiralty in the first place. The availability of prohibition after sentence and appeal was naturally a very sore point with the civilians. They complained of it in the sixteenth century. The admiralty complaint of 1575 asked "that after judgment or sentence definitive given in the Court of Admiralty, in any cause, and appeal made from the same to the High Court of Chancery, that it may please them [the common law judges] to forbear granting of any writ of prohibition, either to the judge of the said Court, or to her Majesty's Delegates, at the suit of him by whom such appeal shall be made, seeing that by choice of remedy that way, in reason he ought to be contented therewith and not to be relieved any other way." On that occasion the judges did indeed promise that no prohibition should issue after an appeal to Delegates, nor indeed after two terms elapsed since sentence in Admiralty. But as with other undertakings this concession did not endure. A century later Jenkins was complaining of the practice of prohibiting after sentence.[31]

One cannot explore the attitudes of the many common law judges who in the seventeenth century had a part in such decisions. There was inevitably a diversity, there were (in modern parlance) some who were "hawks", and some who were "doves". By no means all the judges took the stern attitude of such chief justices as Coke and Hobart. A sample may be taken by considering common law attitudes to the vexed question of transmarine contracts. The Lord Admiral's patent certainly extended to contracts of a maritime, or mercantile and maritime, nature made abroad. Coke equally certainly denied the validity of the grant of such jurisdiction, but the cases he cited do not establish his case, and the Admiralty both in the sixteenth and seventeenth century habitually exercised jurisdiction over such cases. The 1575 settlement had affirmed the jurisdiction over "all contracts and other things arising as well beyond as upon the sea". So in 1589[32] the King's Bench refused to prohibit a suit started in the Admiralty upon a bond "supposed to be made and delivered in France." The judges indeed affirmed a concurrent jurisdiction, but they refused to interfere on the sensible ground that "the witnesses of the plaintiff are beyond sea, which may be examined there, but not here." Coke's accession to the Chief Justiceship of the Common Pleas meant that that court, which had only very recently started issuing prohibitions at all,[33] took a strict line upon the medieval statutes, but the contemporary judiciary were much divided. In 1610[34] Fleming C.J.K.B. thought that an Admiralty suit on a maritime contract made in France should not be prohibited, because the matter could not be tried at common law. But his puisnes, Yelverton and Williams JJ., overruled him on the ground that the venue could be laid in an English county. Next year in 1611[35] the Common Pleas were divided in the case of a suit where a charterparty had been made in a North African port and the cargo of sugar had been spoiled at sea. A prohibition was awarded, but Walmesley and Warburton JJ. were of the opinion that a prohibition should not issue where the case was not triable at common law. They certainly stated that the common law remedy when available was to be preferred, but they did not adopt Coke's view that the Admiralty was not entitled to such a jurisdiction. Hobart, who succeeded Coke as C.J.C.B., spelled out his predecessor's doctrine with full rigour. In 1614[36] he announced "that the Admiralty court hath no power over any cause at land, for both by the nature of the court and by the statute it is only to meddle with things arising on the high seas. And further that these things done must be of the same nature and respect." In short, he laid both conditions upon the Admiralty, the locality test of the high seas and also the requirement that the cause of action be of a maritime nature. Failure on either count disentitled the Admiralty.

But the authority of Coke and Hobart did not settle the question. In 1625[37] the King's Bench denied a prohibition in a case where a bond had been given in Virginia for the delivery of a cargo in a Virginian port, and where the Admiralty had awarded damages for non-delivery. Doderidge J. held that the Admiralty had jurisdiction over such a cause of action arising in Virginia. Whitlock J. agreed that it was not reasonable that the common law should adjudicate on contracts and things done abroad where another law, usually the civil law, prevailed. Jones J. however pointed out, as indeed Coke had done before, that the common law court in England could apply foreign law. As we should say to-day in a matter of Conflicts, he distinguished between a question of jurisdiction and a question of applicable law. The 1633 agreement restated the rule of 1575, and for a while held. In 1635[38] the King's Bench declined to prohibit an Admiralty suit for breach of a foreign contract to transport goods from the West Indies to England, but in the early 1640s prohibitions were resumed.[39] After 1660 the civilians, as we have seen, failed to establish by legislation their case for cognisance over transmarine contracts, and the only post-Restoration case which may be considered of importance is important only because it represents the driving home of the last nail by way of prohibition. Indeed it marks the end effectively of Admiralty jurisdiction in affreightment cases. In *Jurado* v. *Gregory* (1669)[40] the contract of lading had been made in Malaga. The cargo had been refused there and a Spanish Admiralty Court had ordered that the contract be performed. A suit was brought in the English Admiralty charging the defendant with breach of that order. A prohibition was prayed, "because it appears that the contract was made upon the land." Sir Heneage Finch, then Solicitor-General, argued for the defendant in prohibition and urged that "where sentence is obtained in a foreign Admiralty, one may libel for execution thereof here, because all the Courts of Admiralty in Europe are governed by the civil law, and are to be assistant one to another, though the matter were not originally determinable in our Court of Admiralty." The King's Bench agreed with this reasoning (as well they might on previous precedents[41]), but avoided its conclusion by holding that the Spanish decree was not final but only interlocutory. The English libel was therefore in nature of an original suit and they issued a prohibition. A consultation was later refused. This was the end; it was indeed the last prohibition ever required on an affreightment contract. In the year following, 1670, occurs the last reported prohibition on a case of general average and maritime insurance.[42] Insurance was not less serious a loss than affreightment. And it was not only a loss to the civilians. One may look again over Pepys' shoulder, In 1663 he attended the trial of an insurance case before Hyde C. J. and a jury at the Guildhall. "It was pleasant," he wrote in his Diary,[43] "to see what mad sort of testimonys the seamen did give, and could not be got to speak in order, and then their terms such as the judge could not understand; and to hear how sillily the counsel and judge would speak as to the terms necessary in the matter, would make one laugh."

But it was no laughing matter for the unfortunate litigants. We know that in the course of time the common lawyers did at length evolve a body of commercial law based on received mercantile custom, but that involved making a new beginning. It was more than a switch of venue; it involved jettison of the old Admiralty law, the throwing overboard of the old law and creating anew a fresh body of substative law. In the long run and with benefit of hindsight, it is arguable the results could be viewed as not unsatisfactory, but it is not easy to view with indulgence the means employed at the time or to avoid the judgment that too many people suffered too much hardship in the process.

The critical period was the two decades after the Restoration. At the beginning of the 1660s the libel files still show a wide variety of business and somewhere between fifty and one hundred suits litigated in the course of a year. In terms of actual resort to Admiralty process a better index is afforded by the warrant books, which though they do not readily reveal the variety of causes do indicate how much resort was made to the Court for its process, and of course many a claim was satisfied by force of an arrest without the need for further steps in litigation.

There was a steady shrinkage. Going back to the year 1575 some 260 warrants were issued in the first half of the year. Fifty years later, and taking the first half of 1625, a little under 200 warrants were taken out. Taking another fifty year jump to 1675, the half year total is under 140, and by the end of the century a half year count shows approximately 100 warrants. Sampling in the eighteenth century indicates a fairly steady state of issue of about 50 warrants in a half year. It may be mentioned in passing that whereas the great majority of sixteenth century warrants were directed *in personam* rather then *in rem*, the position is reversed by the eighteenth century. But even at the lowest jurisdictional ebb in personam warrants continued to be issued. Even in the eighteenth century owners and masters, as well as their ships, were arrested, usually on wage claims, and the arrests in rem were not invariably of ship and tackle. Cargo was at all times a fairly common object of arrest.

But much more serious than the diminution in volume was the diminution in variety and range. As far as quantity went, the civilians might not like the shrinkage, but it seems unlikely it hit them very hard financially. The later seventeenth century and the eighteenth century was the heyday of prize litigation, and in times of peace (which were in fact never of prolonged duration) they had other jurisdictions within their sphere of control. The loss in quality was, however, more serious and amounted to a capture by the common law, principally during the latter part of the seventeenth century, of practically all the mercantile and general commercial litigation which had previously entered the Admiralty.

The common law reports of the period tell us a good deal of the tactical side of the story with reference to prohibitions (there are, it is hardly necessary to say, no Admiralty reports on the instance side). The law reports also reveal something of the more positive tactics, especially the fictional use of venue in transitory actions. But in the nature of things though the reports may relate the reasons given by the judges, they reveal little in express terms of judicial motives. One would like to know more of the thinking as opposed to the language and behaviour of the judges, particularly those in an influential position. There are scant evidences of their attitudes outside the pages of the reports. Thus Sir Orlando Bridgman, as C.J.C.B., took a part in drafting the civilians' bill in 1662. Fortunately there is one exception to this dearth of information. Hale was Chief Baron of the Exchequer till 1671 and Chief Justice of the King's Bench till 1676. Hale delivered some judgments affecting Admiralty jurisdiction, but it is not in his capacity as a judge, but as an author, that he supplies us with some of the needed information.

Hale was much interested in problems of maritime jurisdiction, and some of his researches are known in published form in his *De Jure Maris*.[44] But he also turned his attention specifically to the Admiralty jurisdiction and composed a lengthy treatise on the subject.[45] He wrote it apparently for his private use; it is a late work,[46] written during the final phase of his career, as Chief Justice, and it is not disturbed by any conscious bias on the topic. It certainly lacks the controversial tone of the published writings (some of which I referred to earlier) and he expressly disclaimed any intention to pursue "any solemn or industrious refutation of any man's discourses." The one author for whom he has a rude word is Prynne, whom he thoroughly disliked, despite their common concern with getting at the primary sources. Hale wrote almost entirely from his extensive collection of transcripts of records and other such sources, and denied himself the pleasure of what he called "pendantique reflections". He was even prepared to find merit in the civil law, remarking that "that law is best that is best for the people whose law it is, as the shell of an oyster is better for an oyster than the shell of a periwinkle or scallop, though this look finer and be fitter for that fish whose shell it is".

The work is not solely concerned with Admiralty jurisdiction (though so entitled), for of the fifteen chapters only the last five are specially so devoted. The earlier chapters are concerned generally with questions of extra-territorial jurisdiction, as exercised by a variety of judicial agencies, Chancery, common law courts, judicial commissions, and so forth. And the general theme is the problem of concurrence of jurisdictions. Hale was also greatly interested in the problem of the criminal jurisdiction of the Admiralty, statutory and otherwise; this he analysed with great care and wrote upon at great length. Here reference to that may be omitted and attention may be given rather to the problem of maritime jurisdiction generally.

Hale divided the area of conflict into three parts. 1. Contracts or injuries made or done entirely on the high sea and outside the body of an English county. This jurisdiction was admitted to belong to the Admiralty, e.g. a salvage service rendered at sea, but the common lawyers had qualified the admission by requiring such contracts or injuries to be essentially concerned with shipping, navigation or maritime affairs. They also claimed a concurrent jurisdiction, so that the plaintiff had a choice of forum.

2. Things done or contracts made beyond the sea. Here the civilians questioned the jurisdiction of the common law courts as well as questioning their ability to deal with such cases effectively. The common lawyers, on the other hand, were disposed to deny the Admiralty jurisdiction and further claimed common law jurisdiction where the cause of action was not purely local but only transitory.

3. Hale's third category concerned those cases where the Admiralty claimed jurisdiction but did not deny a concurrent jurisdiction to the common law. Such were wages, charterparties made at land and broken either in relation to freight on behalf of the owner or master or the performance of the voyage on behalf of the merchant, claims by English shipbuilders and suppliers, and some other minor categories. The common lawyers were not disposed to quarrel much over mariners' wages apparently because their contract was executory upon the high sea, but they were disposed to deny the other cases, and indeed prohibitions, as we have seen, were used.

With regard to the first category, Hale made no difficulty in accepting the validity of Admiralty jurisdiction, but his study of the common law sources led him to assert concurrency of jurisdiction, at least where the contract was made or the injury was done at sea, and the cause of action being transitory could be laid in an English county. But supposing such a contract to be pleaded at common law, what if a plea raised an issue as to performance or breach upon the high sea, or possibly beyond the sea? The question might arise on evidence given on trial of a general plea or it might be raised directly by special pleading. Either way Hale came to the conclusion that a common law court could try the matter so raised. In the latter way, where a pleading expressly put in issue a matter arising upon or beyond the sea, he was certainly in some difficulty over the medieval authorities, but the later cases, from the time of Elizabeth onwards,[47] enabled him to reach a conclusion favourable to the common law and its competence to try such an issue. For instance, he wrote,[48] "in trespass for goods taken, the defendant pleads a special plea that he took the goods at the high sea of the King's enemies. Or if in an action of debt upon a bond, the condition be for payment of 20 florins in Paris . . . or in an action of covenant upon a charter party [or] in an action upon the case upon a policy of assurance, there be a plea pleaded that the ship was arrested in the river of Seine, . . . or the like foreign matter, in this and the like cases the court may proceed to the trial and determination of this issue in that place and county where the original action was laid". Hale indeed was fully convinced of the reasonableness of this position. Suppose, he argued, a bond made or a trespass committed actually and in fact in England, but then the pleading raises incidentally an issue arising on the high sea, e.g. as to the condition of the bond or the justification of the trespass. Here the plaintiff must proceed and begin at common law; clearly he has no option or election. It would be unreasonable to halt the common law action and throw the question into Admiralty,[49] as unreasonable as stopping a civil law court from deciding a suit because incidentally some question arose which raised a question which of itself would normally be a question for decision at common law. Whether this was good logic is perhaps questionable. Certainly it depends on the assumption that a venue based and raised on a fictional averment is as good as one raised on genuine facts, but granting that, one may admit that it is force in Hale's argument.

In relation to transmarine or ultra-marine contracts or torts, Hale was was knowledgeable enough as a historian to detect the untenable character of Coke's assertions about the overseas jurisdiction of the Constable and the Marshal. That jurisdiction was clearly confined to matters of a military nature, hiring of soldiery, supply of weapons and provisions for an army, and the like. Otherwise and putting aside the military jurisdiction of the civil law as irrelevant, Hale divided foreign contracts into two categories, those relating to maritime affairs and those which did not. The Admiralty, he considered, had never claimed jurisdiction over contracts which were unconnected with maritime matters, e.g. buying and selling a horse in Paris. Here he was primarily concerned to establish the validity of common law jurisdiction over foreign contracts as such and whatever their nature. In the treatise the question is indeed discussed in the fullest detail, the question of venue, the technical aspects of jury trial, and the proof and the application of the proper law, whether the law of a particular foreign country or the general customs of merchants. The vital question was whether concurrency was to be admitted for those contracts made abroad but executory upon the high sea and of a maritime nature. On this Hale was disposed to take the position formerly adopted by Coke and Hobart, and he regarded the Admiralty as liable to prohibition. But the general emphasis of his discussion is not so much negatively on the disability of the Admiralty as positively on the ability of the common law courts to deal satisfactorily with such matters. The jury need not be local where justice and convenience otherwise required, and when the traditional rules about the extraction of the jury were not strictly applied, he considered that even so trial by a foreign jury (that is, "foreign" to the locality) "hath all the advantages that the civil law hath in order to trial of causes and many more. The civil law examines the witnesses secretly before commissioners, and then the examinations are published, and the judge of the court determines the cause upon the proof as his judgment leads him. At the trial at the common law the witnesses are examined as well as in the other way, and withal there are the advantages of examination viva voce, and the suffrage of the judge and jury to assist." The principal end of law, *suum cuique tribuere*, was therefore, he argued, "attained with very great advantage and much more than the civil law can reasonably pretend to in their trials".[50]

Even in those cases where the course of pleading could not accommodate, by concealing, a foreign element, he denied there was any difficulty in trying "an incident issue arising wholly out of the realm . . . as whether a ship stayed five months in Spain, whether a ship made a deviation from the voyage, whether the ship were taken by pirates at sea whereby it could not perform its voyage, and many such issues arising at suits at common law upon charter parties. In all those cases the issues shall be tried where the action is brought, though arising wholly at sea, or beyond sea. And the reason is because, although the course to try matters at issue where they arise, is and must be observed where it may, yet where it cannot be so done, to avoid failure of justice, the common law allows a latitude, to try the issue where it may be tried. And this is not only in case of charter parties, and bills of adventure made upon the land, but also in cases of policies of assurance made at land, which till 43 Eliz. c. 12 were wholly determinable by actions of the case at common law. And though the statute of 43 Eliz. hath for convenience erected another judicature, yet it hath not excluded the jurisdiction of the common law, but the party assured may have his action upon the case at common law. And frequently such actions have been brought since the statute. And yet necessarily issues must arise in those actions that are either upon or beyond the seas, which yet notwithstanding may be tried where the action is brought."[51]

And in discussing substantive law Hale made it plain that he saw little difficulty in proving or applying foreign law or indeed general maritime law, e.g. the right of the pledgee to sue on the hypothecation of a ship. All this, and much more, is cogently argued against the background of extensive research. We may acquit Hale, it seems to me, of a conscious bias but it is not unfair to impute a measure of unconscious bias. It is not

H

possible now to examine how far he conflated what appear to later lawyers, two separate ideas, that of jurisdiction, and that of venue. Not that I charge him with a confusion, because the older lawyers habitually discussed questions of jurisdiction with reference to venue; *whether* a case could be tried and *where* it could be tried are questions that can easily be taken together, and they usually were. Nor do I wish to charge him with too easy an optimism over the ability of the common law courts to apply rules not part of the familiar course of the court. Large scale receptions were later achieved but for the seventeenth century it is arguable that he indicated a greater flexibility than in fact existed in the system. Where he is to be criticised, as it seems to me, is an insufficient awareness of some of the practicalities of the question. Leaving aside more general questions let us look, in conclusion, at the interconnected interests of the various parties to a maritime commercial venture, the interest of the mariner in his wages, the interest of the owner or master in his freight, the interest of the merchant in his cargo.

1. Suppose a crew be hired, as was the normal custom, at a monthly rate, and the ship freighted also at a monthly rate, but then after some months of voyage the ship and cargo lost before delivery of the cargo. Here the Admiralty rule was that no wages and no freight was payable. All parties took their own losses, the mariners lost their wages, the master lost his freight, and the merchant lost his profit. In terms of capital interest, the cargo was gone, the ship was gone, and all too often the seaman's life was gone. But for the accrued months the common law of the seventeenth century would, I think, have given the wages and the freight, and non-delivery of the cargo by reason of accidental casualty or disaster at sea would have been no good plea against claims for pay or freight money. The Admiralty rule seems harsh but it was a well entrenched principle of maritime law, designed not only to provide an incentive for the crew but to protect the interest of the merchant on whose financial security seaborn trade depended. If he derived no benefit from the voyage, then he incurred no obligation or burden.

2. Suppose a monthly hiring of crew and ship, and during the voyage the ship were held in a foreign port by reason of an embargo, a not uncommon event. The Admiralty rule was that no wages and no freight was payable for the period of detention or restraint. Again, as I understand it, the common law position of the seventeenth century was that this was no discharge of the obligation to pay wages and freight for that period. In this and in the earlier example we must not suppose that the seventeenth century common law courts would have anticipated the future or applied readily rules of Admiral law.

3. Suppose cargo damaged by carelessness or ill stowage by the crew. In Admiralty the merchant was allowed deductions from the freight payable, and the master or owner could deduct also from the mariners' wages. There was no question of requiring cross actions.

4. Suppose pilfering or stealing from cargo in transit. Here the crew were collectively responsible in Admiralty. The Admiralty justified this joint responsibility on the ground, they said, that "every ship is a little commonwealth", and without such a rule the merchant could not be sufficiently protected. The common law of course did not envisage collective or vicarious responsibility of this sort. This liability was naturally in Admiralty enforced by deductions.

5. Another maritime rule protecting the merchant and to a lesser extent the shipowner was that of general average contribution. This mechanism of apportioning loss was not part of common law thinking.

6. Take the case of desertion in a foreign port. In Admiralty this worked a forfeiture of accrued wages, an obvious disciplinary provision, protecting both the owner and the merchant. But it seems to me doubtful if in the seventeenth century a breach of that sort could be pleaded at common law to bar a claim for accrued wages.

These and other cases of deductions seem harsh on the crew, but where ship and cargo were assets of great value and the crew persons who had little or no money in their pockets, such a system was the only effective way to maintain their responsibility. A right of action against a mariner at common law was a valueless remedy. But the Admiralty enabled such losses to be distributed in a single proceeding. The ship returns with cargo lost or damaged. The mariners can claim their wages in Admiralty, if necessary by securing the arrest of the ship; and if that is all that the court can do, then the result seems unfortunate. The crew with their money disappear again to sea (or more probably spend it before they disappear to sea). If the owner and the merchant are left to litigate at common law on issues of freight and damage, the owner has lost his recourse against the crew, and further there is the difficulty of evidence. The owner is bound to pay for damage caused by fault in ship or crew, but the witnesses are dispersed and gone. By contrast in Admiralty when the mariners proceed against the owner for their wages, either in rem or in personam or both, the owner calls in the merchant for the freight and the merchant can then allege his loss or damage. The evidence is available, because the mariners can be examined before the hearing (and not kept for examination at the trial), and the whole question of wages, freight and damage is settled at one and the same time. The freight payable would normally exceed greatly the claim for damage, so the owner would usually be in a position to pay the crew and let them go, or send them and the ship out on a new voyage. The owner is put in funds or secured for his freight money, and is thus enabled not only to pay the crew but to finance the further use of the ship, a vital point since there was no surer way of immobilising a ship than the non-payment of freight.

Now the security afforded to all parties by such a method was simply not attainable where different claims had to be litigated in different courts and at different times. Among the many blows the common lawyers dealt at the Admiralty I am not sure that the hardest was not the blow at contracts of affreightment.

Let me conclude shortly by offering a contrast between the legal controversy and the practical considerations of the whole debate. In that debate the common lawyers had a strong case, judged by such materials as fill Hale's treatise, statutes, reports, plea rolls and the rest. In practical terms the Admiralty case judged with reference to the interest of the litigants and the efficacy of procedure, seems to me by far the stronger. Since the attempts to invoke the lay voice of Parliament failed, the contest was fought out between lawyers, and naturally enough it was the first set of considerations which prevailed, backed as it was by the writ of prohibition. In the nineteenth century the Admiralty jurisdiction did belatedly achieve a statutory settlement. But by then the object of the contest, the commercial law of England, had long been in the hands of the common lawyers, and time had ratified the conquest.

NOTES

1 Συνηγορος Θαλασσης, *A View of the Admiral Jurisdiction* . . .; London, 1661; second edition. corrected etc., London, 1685. Some extracts from the laws of Oleron are added.

2 Diary, for 17 March 1663: Everyman edition i.349.

3 See Arthur Bryant, *Samuel Pepys, the Man in the Making* (Cambridge, 1933) 190–91.

4 *The Jurisdiction of the Admiralty of England asserted against Sr E. Coke's Articuli Admiralitatis in the xxii. chapter of his jurisdiction of courts*, London, 1663; republished in 1686 at pp. 79–130 of Malynes' *Lex Mercatoria*. For a biographical account see HEL v.17 ff.

5 The work was republished in the eighteenth century: HEL xii.626–7.

6 For Prynne's career, see William M. Lamont, *Marginal Prynne* (London and Toronto, 1963). His *Brief Animadversions on . . . the Fourth Part of the Institutes* (London, 1669) was inspired not only by the publication of the Fourth Institute but by his own researches as counsel in one of the principal prohibition cases of the 1640s.

7 13 Ric.2, St.1, c.5; 15 Ric.2, c.3, reinforced by the penal statute of 1400, 2 Hen.4, c.11.

8 The patent for Richmond in 1525 (Pat. 17 H.8, pt 2, m.15; printed Rymer, *Foedera* xiv.42 (reprint, vi, pt ii, 19) set the pattern. For a medieval patent see Bedford's in 1426 (Pat. 4 H.4, pt 2, m.11, printed in Prynne, *Animadversions* 85). The medieval patents contained non-obstante clauses.

9 4 Inst. 135; Prynne, *Animadversions* 128–33.

10 The principal legal discussions took place before the Lords Commissioners of the Admiralty, and the minutes of the conference are in SP 16/231/114. The judges signed an agreement on 4 February 1633 (SP 16/232/12), and this was amended before the Privy Council (SP 16/232/136, 144, 146). Some printed versions are of the text of 4 February (Zouch, *Jurisdiction*, Assertion VII; Browne, *Compendious View of the Civil Law and of the Law of the Admiralty* (second edition, London, 1802) ii.78–9, from the first edition of Croke's Reports, p.216), but the final and published form of 18 February is to be found in Prynne, *Animadversions* 100–101 and Exton, *Dicæologie* 262–3.

11 C. H. Firth and R. S. Rait, *Acts and Ordinances of the Interregnum* (London, 1911) i.1120; LJ x.186–7. For the Commonwealth, Firth and Rait ii.510, 712, 902.

12 Sir Robert Wiseman, *The Law of Laws; or the excellency of the civil law* . . . (London, 1657) 148.

13 Thomas Bedford's Common Place Book (Admiralty Registry MS.), fo. 210b. This collection was transcribed for Pepys and is now in the Pepys Library (Magdalene College, Cambridge), MS. 2872.

14 Bedford's CPB fo.211.

15 LJ xi.375b, 377a, 415b.
16 D. E. C. Yale, *Lord Nottingham's Chancery Cases* ii (1961–2/1961) 79 SS 940–52.
17 Finch was gratified "that his Royal Highness doth in no degree concern himself in this bill": 79 SS 951–2.
18 Book IV, §38 ff. (Oxford edition, 1888, i.404 ff.).
19 Bedford's CPB fo.204.
20 *Ibid.* fo.200; HCA 30/3.
21 William Wynne, *Life of Sir L. Jenkins* (London, 1724) i, pp. lxxvi–lxxxv.
22 Bedford's CPB fo.156.
23 *Ibid.* fo.208.
24 *Sandy* v. *East India Company*, Skinner 91, 93.
25 Above, n.13.
26 An argument for legislative settlement published in 1690 and attributed to Sir Charles Hedges is in the Harleian Miscellany (1744–56) viii.359, (1810) ix.465.
27 Trinity Hall MS. Admiralty VI, fo.67.
28 Their reason for this emphasis was that they argued that prohibition was justifiable against a jurisdiction which was not the King's, e.g. the pre-Reformation church courts, but that it was not proper for one royal jurisdiction to inhibit another.
29 G. I. O. Duncan, *The High Court of Delegates* (Cambridge, 1971) 178–83.
30 The writs addressed to the High Court of Admiralty are preserved among the Court's miscellanea, HCA 30. It is noteworthy that none are printed in the Register, F.N.B., or even in Coke's Book of Entries. The earliest printed collection seems to be those in Rastell's Entries, fo.23–5.
31 Wynne, *Jenkins* i, p.lxxxii. The one important concession by the common law judges was that they would not award a prohibition after sentence unless the jurisdictional defect was apparent in the written proceedings of the Admiralty suit. Even Coke affirmed this rule, e.g. *Tourson* v. *Tourson* (1614) 1 Rolle 80.
32 *Delabroche* v. *Barney*, 3 Leonard 232.
33 There is no evidence of any such practice before the 1590s. The right of the Common Pleas to issue prohibition in any case other than those of which they were already seised by original writ was only settled in *Langdale's Case* (1608) 12 Co.Rep. 58, and the subsequent judicial conference in 1612: 4 Inst. 99, 12 Co.Rep. 109.
34 *Anon.*, 2 Brownl. & Golds. 10, 11.
35 *Palmer* v. *Pope*, Hobart 79, 212, 2 Brownl. & Golds. 16. Kiralfy, *Source Book* 372–3, prints the HCA libel.
36 *Bridgeman's Case*, Hobart 11, Moore 918.
37 *Tucker* v. *Cappes*, 2 Rolle 492, 497.
38 *Furnes* v. *Smith*, 1 Rolle Abr. 530 (C) pl.3.
39 E.g. *Ball* v. *Trelawny* (1641) Cro. Car. 603; the principal contest was in Johns v. Hooper, described by Prynne, *Animadversions* 123–5.
40 1 Ventris 32, 1 Levinz 267, 2 Keble 511, 610, 1 Sid. 418.
41 E.g. *Wier's Case* (1607) 1 Rolle Abr. 530 (B) pl.12.
42 *Gold* v. *Goodwin*, 2 Keble 678.
43 Diary, for 1 December 1663: Everyman edition i.434.
44 Published by Francis Hargrave in his *Collection of Tracts* (Dublin, 1787).
45 The complete text survives in transcripts in two MSS., BM Hargrave 93 and 137. The former has been here used. There is no doubt that these MSS. are derived from Hale's autograph noted by Burnet in his *The Life and Death of Sir Matthew Hale* (London, 1682), p.114, no.19. The text has been edited by Mr M. J. Prichard and myself.
46 The dating depends on internal evidence. E.g. at fo.45r he refers to a pleading in the year book of 15 Ed.4 "which is now above 200 years since". This indicates that Hale was writing in the last or the penultimate year of his life.
47 E.g. *Gynne* v. *Constantine* (1586), cited in *Dowdale's Case* 6 Co.Rep. 48a.
48 Cap.6, fo.36r.
49 "Desinit in piscem, Mulier formosa superne," he adds at this point, quoting Horace, *Ars Poetica* 4.
50 Cap.8, fo.48r.
51 Cap.8, fo.51r–51v.

The Forty-Shilling Jurisdictional Limit in Medieval English Personal Actions*

John S. Beckerman

THE forty-shilling limit is usually said to have had its origin in chapter eight of the Statute of Gloucester (1278):

> Purveu est ensement, qe Viscuntes pleident en Cuntez les plesz de trespas auxi com il soloient estre pledez. E qe nul eit desoremes bref de trespas devaunt Justices se il na fie par fei, qe les biens enportez vaillent quarante souz al meins. E si il se plaint de Baterie afie par fei qe sa pleint est veritable.[1]

The chapter made two provisions—that thereafter sheriffs were to hold pleas of trespass in county courts, as had been accustomed; and that persons were not to have returnable writs of trespass unless they swore that the *bona asportata* were worth at least 40*s.*, or, if the plaint were battery, that it was true. According to Professor Milsom, the forty-shilling provision was understood to apply generally to personal actions, in order to prevent the royal courts from being flooded with personal actions for trivial sums.[2]

It is frequently asserted, however, that the construction placed on the statute limited the civil jurisdiction of local courts in personal pleas to claims for amounts of less than 40*s.*[3] This is indeed curious, for, if true, it indicates the adoption of a policy at odds with the original purpose of the statute. A limit to the civil jurisdiction of local courts, far from preventing congestion in the royal courts, would have abetted it. It is not amiss, then, to inquire further into the matter.

The only contemporary sources to limit the jurisdiction of local courts to claims of less than 40*s.* in *trespass* are the Statute of Wales (1284) and *Britton* (c. 1290). The purpose of the Statute of Wales was to impose a new and artificial jurisdictional system in Wales after the Edwardian conquest, and it cannot be taken as a guide to English practice. Moreover, as will be argued shortly, *Britton*'s statement is probably erroneous. Aside from *Britton*, no contemporary source of which I am aware places any restriction on the jurisdiction of either a seignorial or county court in England in terms of the amount which could be claimed in a plea of trespass.[4] In fact, the only restrictions concerning trespass relate to allegations which turn the plea into a plea of the crown:

Et notandum est quod omnia brevia transgressionis cuiuscunque generis fuerint possunt placitari in comitatu mutatis mutandis in ordine eorundem exceptis illis brevibus in quibus fit mencio de uulneribus et imprisonamento et de vi et armis, quia huiusmodi breuia habent terminari coram rege uel capitali iusticiario vel coram iusticiariis de banco et non in comitatu eo quod tangunt specialiter coronam domini regis[5] [1293—c. 1300].

Roughly contemporary with this note is a summary description of pleas which can be heard in seignorial and county courts, printed below as an appendix. As can easily be seen, it does not restrict the amount of the claim in trespass, either.

In the summary description, the only restrictions regarding amounts which can be claimed in personal actions have specifically to do with debt-detinue. In seignorial courts, pleas *de debitis non attingentibus summam quadraginta solidorum* can be heard, while in the county court one can bring a plea *de debito sine brevi ut predictum est* [i.e. for less than 40s.] *et per breve de qualibet summa pecunie et catallorum reddenda*. Thus, debts of under 40s. could be sought without writ, but a viscontiel writ was necessary for debts in excess of that amount. This is confirmed by a pleading manual written in the late 1290's, which contains an exception against the jurisdiction of a local court:

Ore a la iurisdiction, sicome dire "la court nad mie poer de trier tiele chose, pur ceo qe chose touche la coroune," *ou* "pur ceo qe la dette demaunde amounte xl souz, dount parmy pleynte en counte ne en hundred ne en court de baroun ne peot home pleder saunz bref de dette demaunde a la summe auantdite."[6]

The evidence of the local court rolls shows that the forty-shilling jurisdictional limit in debt-detinue was generally enforced. In the county court of Bedfordshire-Buckinghamshire, in 1333, for example, Richard Warner of Sharnbrook sued John son of Walter Smith in two pleas of debt for 39s. 11d. and 9s., respectively.[7] In the manor court of Wakefield, Yorks., in 1342, John Clerk of Sandal sued the executors of Hugh of Sandal for detaining 39s. 11d. from him.[8] In the borough court of Lostwithiel, Cornw., in 1399, Joyce Tailor sought 39s. 11d. from Hugh Whippisdene in a plea of debt.[9] In 1331, in the same court, Nicholas Mark craved judgment against Peter Spaignol in a plea of debt because Peter was suing him for 100s. without a writ.[10] Moreover, Helen Cam, reporting her researches on the rolls of hundred courts, wrote of debt claims of 39s. 11½d. recurring there "with monotonous regularity".[11]

In debt-detinue, however, forty shillings had been a significant divider for a very long time. In the "Irish" register of writs of c. 1227, it is stated that a *justicies* for debt-detinue for an amount under 40s. could be had *sine dono*, but that for greater amounts the writ only issued when the plaintiff gave sureties for giving "one-third of the first pennies of the proceeds" to the king's use.[12] It appears probable that no significant financial advantage could accrue to the crown from the sale of *justicies* writs for small amounts. For large sums, however, of 40*s*. or more, it was profitable to exact part of the proceeds in return for the aid of the court in recovering the debt. The rule that a writ was necessary for pleas claiming debts of 40*s*. or more was almost certainly related to this practice. It was probably intended to reserve to the king this source of income in the days when a *justicies* for debts in excess of 40*s*. was not a writ "of course", and it is thus considerably older than the Statute of Gloucester.[13]

A levy of one-third of the first pennies of the proceeds would have had another effect as noteworthy as supplementing the royal income. It is not certain whether a third of the first pennies would have amounted to a consistent proportion of the proceeds—that would have depended on the meaning of "first pennies". It may well have been that the king's share was determined by the size of the first instalment of the payment, a reflection of the efficiency of the sheriff's justice. Professor van Caenegem has determined that in the great majority of cases the cost of writs of *justicies* in the late twelfth century was normally from one-quarter to one-third of the debt recovered.[14] In any case, as can be seen from the accompanying table, it is not likely to have been profitable to sue by *justicies* for amounts of 40*s*. or slightly more, since after the king's share had been subtracted, the plaintiff would have kept less than if he had sued for less than 40*s*., obtaining his writ *sine dono* (if he obtained a writ at all). Plaintiffs would have kept their claims within the forty-shilling amount in local courts or, having agreed to pay a substantial part of their recovery for the writ, would have gone significantly over it.

TABLE

THE AMOUNT KEPT BY THE PLAINTIFF AFTER PAYING FOR HIS WRIT OF *JUSTICIES*

$$R - K = U, \text{ where:}$$

R = amount recovered by plaintiff
K = king's share for writ of *justicies*
U = amount ultimately kept by plaintiff

when $K = \frac{1}{4}(R)$

R	K	U
up to 40s.	0	up to 40s.
40	10	30
48	12	36
52	13	39
56	14	42

$$\text{when } K = \tfrac{1}{3}(R)$$
$$R - K = U$$

up to 40s.	0	up to 40s.
42	14	28
45	15	30
48	16	32
51	17	34
54	18	36
57	19	38
60	20	40

But what about the forty-shilling limit enacted in chapter eight of the Statute of Gloucester? Plucknett wrote generally writs of *justicies*,

> The old view that these writs of *justicies* were an attempt to revive the county so as to relieve congestion at Westminster is no longer tenable, for it is now known that our earliest registers of writs contain many such writs, and that the more familiar forms returnable at Westminster are a much later development.[15]

If this is true of *justicies*, it nevertheless cannot apply to the viscontiel writ of trespass. Mr Hall has recently queried whether viscontiel trespass was not first given by the Statute of Gloucester, since the oldest example which he has found of a viscontiel writ of trespass dates from 1280.[16] If viscontiel writs of trespass did exist before the Statute of Gloucester it is more than a little strange that no examples have been found.

It would appear, then, that around 1280 congestion in the courts at Westminster was enough of a problem to warrant the introduction of a jurisdictional limitation. The purpose of the forty-shilling limit in chapter eight of the Statute of Gloucester was to deter people from bringing trivial claims to the royal courts. It had to do with returnable, not viscontiel writs, unlike the older, "customary" forty-shilling limit in debt-detinue. It did not require the purchase of a writ in trespass claims of over 40s., as it easily could have, for this had nothing to do with the purpose of the statute, to keep claims of less than 40s. out of the royal courts. This, again, was in contrast to the purpose of the rule in debt-detinue which required a writ for claims of 40s. or more, for, as we have seen, its purpose was to protect a profitable royal perquisite—specifically, the crown's jurisdiction over large debts.

Thus, chapter eight of the Statute of Gloucester did not limit the jurisdictions of local courts to claims of under 40s. in pleas of trespass, and if the plea rolls are to be believed, no one in the late thirteenth or fourteenth centuries interpreted the statute as having done so.[17] Damage claims of 39s. are occasionally encountered, as at Wakefield in 1335 in a case of assault; in 1336 in a case of broken agreement; and in 1338, again in assault.[18] The same court, however, frequently entertained trespass pleas in which more than 40s. were claimed. The present writer has not encountered any claims for 39s. 11d. except in debt-detinue.

Claims of damages in trespass of 40s. and more are not at all unusual in local court records. At Wakefield, in 1334, a man claimed damages of 40s. in a case of assault;[19] at Mapledurham, Hants., in 1283, 40s. damages were claimed in a case of cutting down boundary markers.[20] In the Clare honour court, in 1314, damages of 100s. were claimed in a plea of the taking of animals (one horse and two cows) and committing other "enormities".[21] At Fordington, Dors., in 1349, damages of 100s. were claimed by a father against his son in a plea of seducing his wife (presumably not the son's mother), giving her bad counsel, and receiving a variety of his chattels from her, mostly jewelry and clothing.[22] At Chilton, Suff., in 1359, damages of 100s. were claimed in a plea of depasturing and cutting down trees.[23] At Cheylesmore, Warws., a manor belonging to the Black Prince, in 1365, damages of 100s. were claimed in a plea of breaking an agreement to build a house.[24] At Mapledurham, Hants., in 1368, damages of 100s. were claimed in a lawsuit involving the burning down of a house.[25] At Tottenham, Mdx., in 1394, damages of £10 were claimed in a plea of illegal entry into a tenement and destruction of grass and fruit growing there.[26] In addition, the court rolls of Highworth Hundred absolutely abound with damage claims in trespass in excess of 40s.[27] Thus, local courts apparently did not observe a jurisdictional limit of 40s. in damage claims in trespass, in contrast to practice in debt-detinue, in which claims for debts of 40s. or more were not supposed to be heard without a writ.

It may be useful to summarize briefly the jurisdictional provisions concerning personal pleas embodied in the Statute of Wales. Writs of debt, returnable before the justice of Wales, were not to issue for sums of less than 40s. Sums of less than 40s. could be sought in commotes or in county courts with or without a writ of *justicies*.[28] Pleas of trespass in which the damages claimed did not exceed the sum of 40s. were to be pleaded in the county court without a writ. When the damages claimed amounted to more than 40s., trespasses were to be pleaded before the justice of Wales. Before a plaintiff would be heard by the justice, he was required to swear that his *accio* exceeded 40s.[29] This much resembles the *bona asportata* requirement of chapter eight of the Statute of Gloucester, quoted above at the beginning. It can easily be seen, however, that the Statute of Wales imposed an upper limit of 40s. to the jurisdiction of local courts in trespass, a limit which the Statute of Gloucester had not imposed in England.

It only remains to examine *Britton*'s assertion of a forty-shilling upper limit to the jurisdiction of local courts in trespass pleas. Significantly, it occurs in book I, chapter XXIX, "De Dette":

En countez ausi par devaunt nos viscountes et les sutiers, et en hundrez et en courtz des frauncs hommes poent estre pledez sauntz nos brefs par gage et pleges simplement pletz de trespas et de dettes, issi qe les biens enportez en les trespas, ne les dettes demaundez ne passent mie xl. *s.*, save trespas de maheign et des playes et de enprisounement et de bateries fetes encountre nostre pes, dount nous ne voloms qe nul ne eyt la conisaunce ne poer de teles quereles pleder, ne autres trespas des biens enportez outre la value de xl. *s.* ne de dettes passantz mesme la summe, sauntz nos brefs; les queus brefs nous voloms acune foiz qe soint pledez en Countez et en fraunchises, si il ne soint de illucs remuez par nos comaundementz, et acune foiz aylours par devaunt nos Justices. Et les grauntz trespas volom nous qe soint pledez devaunt nous mesmes.[30]

Britton was correct in speaking of the forty-shilling upper limit to local jurisdictions in pleas of debt without writ. It is possible, although it cannot be known for certain, that the treatise writer depended, for his statement about trespass, on the Statute of Wales, since both impose an upper limit of 40*s.* to the jurisdiction of local courts in trespass. It may simply have been the case that the writer of the treatise, in an effort to comprehend as much law as possible under a single rule, succumbed to the temptation of conflating two entirely unrelated English jurisdictional limitations: the upper limit in local courts in pleas of debt-detinue without writ, and the lower limit in the royal courts in pleas of trespass provided by the Statute of Gloucester—because of the coincidence that both limits involved the amount of 40*s.* In view of the lack of any corroborating evidence for *Britton*'s statement that it was necessary to have a writ for trespasses in which 40*s.* or more were claimed, and the presence of much evidence to the contrary, credence can no longer be given to the view that the interpretation of the Statute of Gloucester had, by 1300, limited the jurisdiction of English local courts to pleas involving amounts of less than 40*s.*

APPENDIX: THE JURISDICTIONS OF MANOR AND COUNTY COURTS

THE following summary description of the jurisdictions of manorial courts (exclusive of royal franchises) and county courts is from Arundel MS. 310 in the British Museum. The manuscript, the "Book of Evidences" of St Augustine's, Canterbury, is a miscellany from c. 1300 which includes many items of legal and ecclesiastical interest.

[f. 87r:] *In curiis dominorum qui habent sectam tenencium suorum de tribus septimanis in tres septimanas possunt placitari placita:*

De debitis non attingentibus summam quadraginta solidorum.

De simplicibus contractibus et convencionibus factis infra potestatem dominorum.

De animalibus vulneratis et hujusmodi.

De dampnis factis per animales in blado vel pastura alicujus.

De injuria facta alicui absque sanguinis effusione.

De transgressionibus ut de arboribus prostratis et hujusmodi ubi pax domini Regis non apponitur.

De placito terre per breve domini Regis de recto de tenementis quibus de ipso[31] tenentur usque ad positionem in magnam assisam domini Regis.

[f. 87v:] *In comitatu possunt* (*ista placita placitari:*)[32]

De debito sine brevi ut predictum est et per breve de qualibet summa pecunie et catallorum reddenda.

De convencione facta infra comitatum per breve et sine brevi.

De stagno vel ponte reparando per breve.

De medio per breve tantum.

De dampno reddendo per breve.

De consuetudinibus et serviciis per breve.

De cartis sive scriptis reddendis per breve.

De blado molendo sine multura per breve.

De custodia terre et heredis alicui reddenda per breve.

De racionabili compoto reddendo per breve.

De namio injuste capto et injuste detento contra vadium etc. [f. 88r:] per breve vel sine.

De admensuracione dotis et pasture per breve.

De secta facienda ad molendinum alicujus per breve.

De racionabili auxilio habendo per breve.

De libero tauro sive apro habendo per breve.

De grege adaquando per breve.

De communa pasture per breve.

De racionabili estoverio habendo in bosco alicujus per breve.

De ovili vel porta vel gurgite vel muro vel domo injuste levato ad nocumentum liberi tenementi alicujus per breve.

De arboribus alicujus prostratis.

De blado alicujus vel feno asportato per breve et sine.

De verberibus et insultu facto per breve vel sine.

De placito terre per breve de recto cum in curia domini rite probata fuerit [defalta recti].[33]

NOTES

* While this paper is substantially the same as that delivered to the conference in Wales, a number of errors have been corrected and references expanded. I am particularly grateful to Mr G. D. G. Hall for his helpful suggestions.

[1] 6 Ed.1, c.8; SR i.48.

[2] *Foundations* 407.

[3] PM i.553; Holdsworth, HEL i.72; Plucknett, *Concise History* 93.

[4] *Contemporary* is used here to refer to the thirteenth and fourteenth centuries; see n.17 below.

[5] B.M. Harl. MS. 748, f.53r, printed by G. J. Turner, *Brevia Placitata*, 66 SS lxiv n; S. F. C. Milsom, "Trespass from Henry III to Edward III", (1958) 74 LQR 576.

[6] Harvard Law School MS. 162, f.176r–v. The rule is also expressed in *Fleta*, bk II, c.61 (72 SS 205): "Conceditur eciam quod in hundredis, wapentakiis, tritingis et aliis minutis curiis regis et baronum possunt placita debiti summam xl solidorum non excedentis sine breui discuti et terminari." The rule in debt-detinue refers to the principal sum or the value of the chattels, *not* to the damages.

7 *Rolls from the Office of the Sheriff of Beds. and Bucks, 1332–1334* (ed. G. H. Fowler), (1929) 3 *Quarto Memoirs of the Bedfordshire Historical Record Society* 71, nos. 35 and 36. Although different dates for repayment are specified, the two pleas may well have arisen from the same debt; that is, they may have been a dodge to get around the forty-shilling limit in pleas of debt without writ. In 1293 the court of Appletree hundred, Derbyshire, affirmed that ". . . mos et consuetudo hundredi talis est quod liceat unicuique petendo debita sua aporcionare si voluerit . . .": PRO, DL 30/43/482 m.ld. I owe this reference to the kindness of Mr Paul Brand. This sort of evasion was discouraged: see YB 20 Ed.3, Trin. pl.68 (RS ii.146–9) for a reversal on error of a judgment in the court of Chester in which the plaintiff had split the same debt into two plaints, each claiming 39s.11¼d.

8 Yorkshire Archaeological Society (Leeds) MS. MD 225 (1342) m.6.

9 PRO SC2/161/7 m.3.

10 SC2/161/5. Presumably, if the defendant did not take the exception, there would be nothing to stop the court from hearing the plea.

11 *The Hundred and the Hundred Rolls* (London, 1930; re-issue, 1963) 182. She nevertheless asserts that under c.8 of the Statute of Gloucester only sums below 40s. could be claimed in local courts, failing to distinguish between debt-detinue and trespass.

12 *Early Registers*, 87 SS xxix, 13. A *justicies* for acquittance of pledge for more than 40s. was a writ "of grace", *non sine dono, pro precio* (*ibid.* xxix, 14). According to Professor van Caenegem, *Royal Writs in England from the Conquest to Glanvill* (1958–9/1959) 77 SS 256, the *justicies* for debt began to be used late in Henry II's reign, as shown by payments *pro justiciando* entered on the Pipe Rolls; Lady Stenton shared this view: *Pleas before the King or his Justices* i (1948/1953) 67 SS 17. Van Caenegem also asserts that the *justicies* for debt was originally an executive, extra-judicial, remedy: *Royal Writs* 256. When it became a warrant for a sheriff to hear a plea of debt in the county court he does not say.

13 *Pace* Maitland, *Select Pleas in Manorial and other Seignorial Courts* (1888/1889) 2 SS lvii n.l. In the Bodleian register recently edited for the Selden Society, Rawlinson MS. C292 (c.1318–20), the *supersedeas* writs which could issue on pleas of debt-detinue when amounts of 40s. or more were claimed in local courts without writ make no reference to the Statute of Gloucester, but to "the law and custom of our realm": "Cum placita de catallis et debitis que summam quadraginta solidorum attingunt vel eam excedunt secundum legem et consuetudinem regni nostri sine breui nostro placitari non debeant . . ." (*Early Registers* 223, no.488; also nos.487, 489, 490).

14 *Royal Writs* 260.

15 Plucknett, *Concise History* 92.

16 *Early Registers* cxxxii. I understand from Mr Alan Harding that one of the early-fourteenth-century statute collections in the National Library of Wales has the reading *brefs* for *plesz* in c.8 of the Statute of Gloucester ("that sheriffs shall hear *writs* of trespass . . ."); see p. 71 n.28 above. Subsequent research has shown this reading to have been surprisingly frequent. Cf. Bodleian Library, Oxford, Douce MS. 17, f.70v; Add.MS. A.107, f.30v; Hatton MS. 10, f.57r; Hatton MS. 28, f.20v; Bodl. MS. 940, f.165v; Bodl. MS. 985, f.64r. It is probable that research in other repositories would turn up further examples.

17 A diligent search has not uncovered any writs of prohibition addressed to local courts because damages of 40s. or more were claimed in a plea of trespass. In the sixteenth century, Fitzherbert wrote in his *Natura Brevium* (f.46, 46A) that prohibitions could be had in just such cases. That this may have been thought unusual even then may be inferred from Brooke's citation of it in his *Abridgement*, f. 52v. Cf. YB 19 H.6, Hil. pl.17, f.54.

18 Yorkshire Archaeological Society MS. 759 (1335) 32, 55, (1338) 25.

19 *Ibid.* (1334) 10.

20 BM Additional Roll 28031.

21 SC2/212/49 m.8d.

22 SC2/169/28 m.8d.

23 SC2/203/30 m.2d.

24 SC2/307/18 m.7d.

25 BM Additional Roll 28047.

26 *Court Rolls of the Manors of Bruces, Dawbeneys, Pembrokes* (trans. R. Oram; Borough of Tottenham, 1961) 254.

27 *The Rolls of Highworth Hundred 1275–1287* (ed. Brenda Farr), (1966) 21 *Wiltshire Record Society*, (1968) 22 *Wilts. RS. passim.*

28 Cc. 6, 9: SR i.61, 65; Ivor Bowen, *The Statutes of Wales* (London, 1908) 13, 21.

29 C.11: SR i.66; Bowen 23.

30 *Britton* (ed. F. M. Nichols; Oxford, 1865) i. 155–6.

31 I.e. the lord, not the king.

32 Continued across top of f.88r.

33 Supplied, MS. omits.

The Equity Jurisdiction of the Exchequer

W. H. Bryson

THE equity jurisdiction of the Exchequer has been so overshadowed by the equity jurisdiction of the Chancery and that of other courts that there is today only a foggy awareness that it ever existed. Therefore it is the purpose of this communication to locate this court within the course of English legal history and to say a word or two about its development.

In the fifteenth century and earlier, the royal Exchequer was coextensive with the royal Treasury; it was the primary financial institution of the kingdom of England. It was divided into two divisions: the upper Exchequer or "Exchequer of account" and the lower Exchequer or "Exchequer of receipt," which physically handled the cash. The upper Exchequer was divided into several departments or offices. By 1500, three of these offices had generated so many legal disputes that the Exchequer had become in part a permanent court of law.

The Office of Pleas handled the common law litigation between private parties and determined which of them should pay the money due to the king. The Lord Treasurer's Remembrancer's Office and the King's Remembrancer's Office settled revenue lawsuits between the crown and a private party; these two offices administered the so-called revenue jurisdiction of the Exchequer. In the latter part of the reign of Henry VIII, certainly by the accession of Edward VI in 1547, the equity jurisdiction of the Exchequer had arisen within the King's Remembrancer's Office. This happened, no doubt, in order to supplement the common law remedies of the other Exchequer courts.

Remnants from the pleadings of at least three equity Exchequer cases have been found from the reign of Henry VIII, and there may have been a dozen other cases before 1547. There were at least five cases from the time of Edward VI. The shorter reign of Queen Mary I produced thirteen. The proper archives of the court have been preserved from the accession of Elizabeth I in 1558. They show a continuous increase in the number of bills filed until the 1580's when there was a huge rise. From 1587 to the end of the reign there was an annual average of 334 bills filed. This figure grew steadily (with the exception of the reign of Charles I, which reflects the disruption of the civil wars) until the peak of 739, which was reached in the period of William III and Mary II.

It is most interesting to note how the Exchequer equity jurisdiction arose. No part of the Exchequer in the sixteenth century was a court of general jurisdiction. The many cases that were heard there were allowed only as exceptions to the general prohibitions to the Exchequer to determine suits. The so-called Statute of Rhuddlan of 1284[1] denied the power of the Exchequer to settle litigation except where the crown or one of the officers of the Exchequer was involved. The *Articuli super Cartas*[2] repeated the prohibition in 1300 but allowed no exceptions. However, in 1311 it was confirmed by Parliament[3] that the Exchequer could hear the suits of its officers and of their servants. The purpose of these exceptions was to increase the efficiency of revenue collection by protecting the Exchequer officials from the duty of attending on the other courts.

In the period in which the equity side of the Exchequer evolved, there were three classes of persons who were privileged to sue in the court of the Exchequer: officials of the Exchequer, royal accountants, and debtors to the crown.[4] The officers were specifically allowed to sue in their own court by the above-mentioned ordinances. This same privilege had become customary in the other high courts for their own officers.

The accountants were the officers of the crown who received money on behalf of the crown for which they had the duty to account in the Exchequer. Since the account was to be made in Westminster in person, at least in theory, the accountant must be free from the process of the other courts. Once the account had been settled, it became a simple debt, and the accountant lost his status as such and became a mere debtor to the crown.

Debtors to the king had only a general privilege; they were privileged to sue in the Exchequer, but they could not have a case against them removed into the Exchequer from another high court. This privilege was quite broad, and anyone who owed any money to the king for any reason could avail himself of it. This was the same as the common law privilege based on the *quo minus* allegation on the plea side of the court. In the sixteenth century this privilege was partially fictitious: the allegation that the reason the plaintiff could not pay his debt to the crown was that the defendant was withholding money due to him was not traversable; however, there must have been a genuine debtor-creditor relationship between the plaintiff and the crown.

Until 1649 the Exchequer court rigorously insisted that each case must have some genuine royal interest as a basis of jurisdiction; if it was found wanting, the case was dismissed. However, from the beginning of the Commonwealth, the court opened its doors to all comers. All that was required of plaintiffs was that they insert in their bills of complaint at the beginning after their names the following set phrase: ". . . . debtor and accountant to the Commonwealth (later "His Majesty") as by the records of this honourable court and otherwise it doth and may appear . . ." The court disallowed all traverses of this allegation, and thus the Exchequer became a court of general jurisdiction.

There does not appear to have been any opposition to this move. The most likely source of resistance would have been the court and the clerks of Chancery, the primary court of equity. At this time, however, the Chancery in general and its clerks in particular were themselves under-going a bitter onslaught and were in no position to be aggressive towards the Exchequer. Moreover, there was an increased need for another general court of equity because several courts of equity had been suppressed or had fallen into desuetude during the preceding decade; these were the courts of Star Chamber, Requests, Wards and Liveries, and the councils of the North and of the Marches of Wales. The radical reformers of the civil war and interregnum periods seem to have ignored the court of Exchequer.

By the time of the Restoration in 1660, the Exchequer was firmly estab-lished in its general equity jurisdiction. It had been accepted by the legal profession, and there do not appear to have been any moves to take it away. Since it had not been established by any legislative or executive act, there was no problem with the invalidity of the ordinances of Oliver Cromwell and his parliaments.

In the last quarter of the seventeenth century, the Treasury developed financial departments independent of the Exchequer, and these new offices took over most of the revenue administration of the realm. This left the Exchequer free to continue its tendency to develop into a general court of law. By the eighteenth century the equity side of the Exchequer and the Chancery had grown in similar directions because each court cited as precedents the cases of the other indiscriminately with its own. The result was that in the eighteenth century the Exchequer and the Chancery were following the same procedures and granting the same remedies.

This situation continued until 1841. In that year the equity jurisdiction of the Exchequer was suppressed; the pending cases were transferred to the court of Chancery.[5] This occurred at the beginning of the period of the rationalization of the English legal jurisdictions in the nineteenth century. However, the reasons for it appear to have been not intellectual and theor-etical but more practical. It was a great nuisance to the legal profession to have two separate courts of equity. The jurisdiction was abolished because of the physical conveniences of being able to confine one's legal practice to a single court. Since the Chancery was and always had been the most important court of equity, the equity side of the Exchequer was discarded. There was little comment and no regret.

NOTES

1 SR i.70. This statute must be distinguished from the Statute of Wales of the same year, often called the Statute of Rhuddlan.
2 SR i.138
3 SR i.163
4 *Clapham* v. *Lenthall* (1664), Hardres 365.
5 The Court of Chancery Act, 1841 (5 Vic. c.5).

J

The Early-Tudor Star Chamber

J. A. Guy

THE history of the Tudor court of Star Chamber remains as yet substantially unwritten.[1] Moreover, the excellent work that has been done for the reign of the first Tudor king is, necessarily, part of the much wider study of the king's Council. In Henry VII's years, to quote the most recent commentator, "the king's Council was simply the king's Council; there was no Court of Star Chamber, even though councillors continued to exercise jurisdiction in the *Camera Stellata* as they had for generations before".[2] Henry VII fashioned to his own use with inventiveness and flexibility the existing embryonic conciliar structure at the centre of which lay the Council in the Star Chamber.[3] Many private litigants and even a Lord Chancellor regarded the judicial activity of the lords of the Council as constituting a court.[4] But the king's Council remained the king's Council. Institutionally, the court of Star Chamber did not exist, as the study of the surviving proceedings confirms.[5] However, the nature and quantity of proceedings for the reign of Henry VIII indicates that the "true" court's development was well-nigh complete by 1530. Final recognition and organisation came with the making of the Privy Council in the 1530s.[6] The surviving evidence, however, points clearly to the emergence of the court of Star Chamber during the years of Wolsey's ascendancy. In these years, business rapidly increased, certain areas of jurisdiction became better defined, and procedure formalised. The court continued to develop throughout its life, growing more rigid and experiencing definition and technical complication of its procedure, which involved deceleration in the pace at which litigation passed through the court and increased costs.[7] Nevertheless, the court of Star Chamber was for the most part fashioned during Wolsey's Chancellorship.

The increase in business was dramatic. For the 24 years of the reign of Henry VII, C. G. Bayne's analysis detected 194 Star Chamber cases between party and party.[8] Litigation continued at a similar rate during the early years of the reign of Henry VIII when William Warham remained in office. However, the number of cases between party and party extant in the Star Chamber Proceedings which can be dated precisely into the 14 years of Wolsey's Chancellorship (December 1515–October 1529) stands at 821, and when those cases are added which belonged in all probability to this period, the figure rises to the region of 1,400.[9] This possible total yields, by simple arithmetic, a yearly figure of 100 suits for the 14 years. The 100 average can, however, be tested. For the regnal year 17 Henry VIII, a surviving cause-list prepared at the beginning of the Hilary term detailed 25 suits depending.[10] Minutes taken during the Trinity term refer to 41 different suits in progress.[11] And those surviving proceedings which can be dated to the year add a further 32 cases not previously cited. Although evidence for the longevity of litigation is haphazard and ignoring for this purpose the court's sad record in terms of finality of decrees in civil suits, it can be estimated from the proceedings that the majority of lawsuits required an average of one year to pass through all the formal stages from bill of complaint to final decree.[12] It is therefore reasonable to suppose that the total of 98 cases is a possible minimum figure for this year. For the regnal year 20 Henry VIII, the datable proceedings alone provide a yield of 92 cases. All these figures may be prejudiced by haphazard survival, and are highly conservative in consequence. It is quite impossible to guess at the correct figures, not simply because of the unknown rate of survival but also because many pleadings lack any form of date.[13] However, for comparative purposes, an analysis based on the extant proceedings is adequate. Although it is true that the cases of the late 1520s are in a rather better state of preservation than those of the reign of Henry VII, no different archival methods were applied to the later proceedings and this higher rate of survival is not much more than marginal. The proceedings of the later 1530s and the 1540s are the most satisfactory. For the 17 years of the reign of Henry VIII subsequent to the fall of Wolsey, some 3,500 Star Chamber cases between party and party survive. This almost realistic figure undoubtedly reflects the final organisation of the court in the 1530s, and indicates that in Star Chamber, unlike Chancery, the number of suits did not fall away in the decade after Wolsey.

The jurisdiction exercised by the young court of Star Chamber was both criminal and civil.[14] Limitations were negatively defined by a number of medieval statutes which declared *inter alia* that the Council should not determine matters of freehold, or try matters touching life and limb.[15] The former limitation was difficult to respect in the late fifteenth and early sixteenth centuries. These were years rich in litigation about land: political and social change, accompanied by numerous doubtful claims and the selling of pretended titles, ensured a ready supply of litigants.[16] Prevailing conditions at common law rendered the conciliar courts particularly vulnerable to the complaints of men who were trying their luck. The second limitation was generally adhered to. The court avoided treason and felony.[17] Although the Star Chamber occasionally dealt with felons, these cases seem only to have reached the court because of some difficult technicality which needed to be settled before a case at common law could begin.[18] Limitations apart, the business of the court, at any rate as alleged in plaintiffs' bills of complaint, came to fall into three areas. The first and by far the largest category consisted of riot, unlawful assembly, forcible entry, assault, trespass and related offences. The second category took in maintenance, embracery, perjury, abuse of legal procedure and all offences prejudicial to law enforcement. The third comprised cases of the corruption of royal and franchisal officers. Traditionally the Council's ears were sensitive to allegations of actual or potential violence, and as a result plaintiffs alleged major riots, forcible entries and other breaches of the peace in order to attract the court's attention to their complaints. By virtue of this fiction, a remarkable range of civil matters was brought before the early-Tudor Star Chamber.[19] The real issues at stake were usually revealed in later pleadings, generally in defendants' answers and examinations or in the depositions of witnesses.

Real issues in the second and third areas of business often resembled the alleged issues; for the first category it is clear, when it is possible to get at pleadings other than bills of complaint, that title is doubly more frequent as the real issue in question than all the alleged crimes of violence put together. Five hundred and seventy-two of the 821 definite Wolsey cases in the Star Chamber Proceedings allege riot, unlawful assembly, forcible entry, assault or trespass. However, these 572 cases on analysis break down into 92 real crimes, 184 cases of disputed title, and 296 cases where the real issue cannot now be determined because of insufficiency of evidence. That the early-Tudor Star Chamber regularly entertained civil litigation on title is apparent enough.[20] A few plaintiffs were undoubtedly remitted to the common law.[21] In other cases, the court might hear the riot but leave the title.[22] The weight of the evidence, however, is positive.[23] When determination in Star Chamber was decided upon, the accepted form was the reference of the question of title or committal of the case to the judges. Judicial opinion or certificate was then incorporated into subsequent orders and decrees for possession and execution.[24] If this procedure was generally observed, the common lawyers cannot have found a great deal to object to. Sir Thomas More, when Chancellor, certainly favoured the arrangement.[25] It was, however, impossible to consult legal opinion in those cases where equity was reserved but there are not many of these in Star Chamber. When in reality the business was criminal, cases were decided on the facts in the context of existing English criminal law. The court's emphasis lay on law enforcement rather than the construction of new rules. The strength of Star Chamber's contribution was mainly due to early flexibility and procedural advantages, particularly the sworn examination of defendants, which enabled the court to get at the truth. The "new law" of the Star Chamber derives its meaning from Wolsey's stated intention to enforce law and order with appropriate vigour, and the exalted stature of Star Chamber.[26] The most frequent offences were riot and forcible entry. The position in law on these matters was rehearsed, when necessary, by one of the senior judges present at the Council board.[27] Punishment was by fine or imprisonment.[28] The large majority of suits were between party and party, although official conciliar activity was directed against procurers of riots who, it seemed, might be likely to escape punishment.[29] Official prosecution was, however, more frequent in the second area of business, namely cases of maintenance, embracery, perjury and the like.[30] Proceedings were initiated by the attorney-general who placed an information before the court. The subsequent written pleadings ensued, and the attorney-general enjoyed no procedural advantages. If, however, the accused could be persuaded to file a sworn confession, the court might proceed *ore tenus*. Punishment was by imprisonment, or pillory and wearing of papers.[31] Henry VII's conciliar committees did not survive the advent of Wolsey, and it is clear from the evidence that the Council's law-enforcement function was reabsorbed into Star Chamber under Wolsey's guidance.[32] Star Chamber was, nevertheless, far from being primarily a criminal court by 1529. Further development was to come in Sir Thomas Audley's Chancellorship.

The increase in business was naturally accompanied by procedural developments.[33] The existing written pleadings grew in length and complexity. The examinations of defendants and witnesses became formalised; previously they were taken in court and tended to be informal or *viva voce*. Under Wolsey, they were often taken out of court by the examiner, who would be either the clerk or a lesser councillor. Also it became usual to supply the examiner in advance with interrogatories ready drawn which were then tendered to the party. With the development of written interrogatories, depositions tended to become longer. In this period, the court came to prefer as its form of original process the *subpoena ad comparendum*, and by 1529 the process of the court issued under the great seal almost without exception. Standard procedure was adopted in the face of contempt: attachment, which might be preceded by a *subpoena* charging the defendant to his allegiance, followed by attachment with proclamation, and commission of rebellion.[34] With increasing numbers of litigants attending on the court, the personal appearance of defendants from day to day throughout the term became the exception.[35] In consequence, the position of the two attornies appointed to serve the court became established.[36] Nevertheless, Wolsey considered the expensive inconvenience of personal appearance to be suitable chastisement in notorious cases.[37] Sir Richard Brereton complained that he had been made to attend on the court for over a year.[38] However, he was co-defendant in an unpleasant case of local corruption and violent death, and if nothing else his presence in London enabled investigations to be carried out locally in Cheshire without his interference.

Closely allied to the increased business was Wolsey's frequent reference of cases to commissioners by *dedimus potestatem* for hearing and final determination. Commissions *ad audiendum et finaliter determinandum* were relatively rare in the reign of Henry VII. Wolsey made them the court's method of delegation in the face of rising pressure of work at the centre.[39] Such commissions may have been remarkably ineffective. Of the 64 examples for Wolsey's Chancellorship in which the outcome is known, in 46 cases the commissioners simply referred matters back to Westminster.[40] The main reason for their failure was the disposition of the litigants themselves rather than the procrastination or incompetence of the commissioners. It frequently happened that one of the parties, perceiving from the evidence his to be the weaker case, refused to co-operate with those appointed to end the suit and demanded remission to London or to the common law.[41] Plaintiffs could be as troublesome as defendants. A certificate from Nicholas West, bishop of Ely, the abbot of Bury, William Elys and Sir Robert Clere reported that several cases committed to them for determination had been duly heard and ended, but that the several bills which were at the suit of one Thomas Codlyng could not be determined. Codlyng had apparently exhibited fulsome contempt in the face of the commissioners, having "no more regard to the said bishop of Ely than he had to the straw under his foot".[42] In most cases, the defendant simply refused to appear.[43] A more ingenious defendant frustrated the commission by successfully obtaining a *supersedeas* out of Chancery on the grounds that the *dedimus potestatem* had been awarded on false information.[44] If both parties did appear at the same time, they often obstinately refused to settle, and the commissioners were unable to come to a final determination.[45] In such circumstances, the case was referred back to Westminster, the commissioners generally giving the parties their day of appearance in the Star Chamber and informing the court of this in their certificate. A better and more efficient method of delegation of cases was to committees of councillors, who in addition to taking answers and examinations went on to publication and final hearing. The clerk would be in attendance, and the appropriate entries were made in the Council Register in the usual way.[46] A third method of delegation was, by consent of the parties, reference to arbitrators. This was a method that tended to be reserved for the great men of the realm or for mercantile cases involving aliens. It should, nevertheless, be emphasised that arbitration was in reality the principle guiding most judgements in the conciliar courts, and it was at the very heart of commissions *ad audiendum et finaliter determinandum* directed to local gentry.

By the mid-1520s, the pace of litigation made necessary administrative measures to secure the efficient working of the court of Star Chamber. Wolsey had only himself to thank for a constant accumulation of work, for there can be no doubt that, with some pomp and greater naivety, he had advertised "justice" in the prerogative courts to all who would seek it.[47] Experienced judges do not, in Sir Thomas Egerton's phrase, "bring water to the mill". Wolsey, however, was not entirely deterred and the position in Star Chamber suggested either the appointment of standing conciliar committees or drastic delegation to the provinces. In the event, both methods were tried.[48] Neither worked. On Wolsey's fall, the court of Star Chamber still required the formal administrative organisation necessary to secure its status as a "true" court of the realm. But it was during the years of Wolsey's Chancellorship that the court was fashioned. Wolsey increased the quantity and range of business taken in the Star Chamber, and concentrated the Council's law enforcement function there. At the same time, the Cardinal's ascendancy in matters of policy and the consequent reduction in discussion of the affairs of state at the Council board left more time at regular meetings for matters of justice. Sir Thomas Smith was substantially correct in his appraisal of the court's origins. Star Chamber, he declared, "took great augmentation and authority at that time that Cardinal Wolsey, Archbishop of York, was Chancellor of England, who of some was thought to have devised the court, because that he after some intermission by negligence of time, augmented the authority of it".[49]

NOTES

1 There are a few excellent specialised studies: C. G. Bayne and W. H. Dunham, *Select Cases in the Council of Henry VII* (1956/1958) 75 SS; G. R. Elton, "Why the History of the Early Tudor Council remains unwritten" (1964) 1 *Annali della Fondazione italiana per la storia amministrativa* 268–96, reprinted in Elton, *Studies in Tudor and Stuart Politics and Government* (Cambridge, 1974) i.308–38; S. B. Chrimes, *Henry VII* (London, 1972) 97–114; Elfreda Skelton, "The Court of Star Chamber in the reign of Elizabeth", unpublished M.A. dissertation, University of London (1931); T. G. Barnes, "Due Process and Slow Process in the late-Elizabethan-early-Stuart Star Chamber", (1962) 6 AJLH 221–49, 315–46; *idem*, "Star Chamber Mythology", (1961) 5 AJLH 1–11; *idem*, "The Archives and archival Problems of the Elizabethan and early Stuart Star Chamber" (1963) 2 *Journal of the Society of Archivists* 345–60.

2 S. B. Chrimes, "The reign of Henry VII", *Fifteenth-century England* (ed. Chrimes, Ross, and Griffiths; Manchester, 1972) 72.

3 G. R. Elton, "Henry VII: Rapacity and Remorse" (1958) 1 HJ 21–39 (reprinted *Studies* i.45–65) and "Henry VII: a Restatement" (1961) 4 HJ 1–29 (*Studies* i.66–99).

4 Bayne and Dunham lxxv–vi; PRO St[ar] Ch[amber Proceedings] 2/31/142.

5 Bayne and Dunham lxxv.

6 G. R. Elton, *The Tudor Revolution in Government* (Cambridge, 1953) 317–52.

7 Barnes, articles cited at n.1 above.

8 Bayne and Dunham lxxiii.

9 All the figures in this paper are based on my own research.

10 StCh 10/4 Pt 2 (bundle).

[11] *Ibid.*

[12] By 1600, two years were required. Henry E. Huntington Library, San Marino, California, El[lesmere MS.] 1756.

[13] Some of these proceedings cannot even be safely assigned to a Chancellor, since Star Chamber bills of complaint were, strictly, to be addressed to the king.

[14] Bayne and Dunham lxxvi.

[15] In particular, 5 Ed. 3, c.9; 25 Ed.3, St.5, c.4; 28 Ed.3, c.3.

[16] On these problems the statute 32 Hen.8, c.9 is instructive.

[17] Such few examples of treason as are found in the Star Chamber Proceedings are not cases of the court, but cases investigated by the Council or, later, Privy Council. The case of Dr Benger (StCh 2/8/77, 2/24/163) is described in G. R. Elton, *Policy and Police* (Cambridge, 1972) 317–21. Benger was actually tried for treason at Kent Assizes.

[18] El 2652, fo.13.

[19] Cf. Milsom, *Foundations* 366–7.

[20] El 2652, fo. 5v; BM Harleian MS. 2143, fo. 69; Bayne and Dunham cxi.

[21] *Toft* v. *Thomas*, StCh 10/4 Pt 2 (bundle); *Alatt* v. *Nowell*, StCh 2/1/67.

[22] *Grey* v. *Compton*, StCh 2/16/295, 2/26/48.

[23] The hearing of titles was, of course, contrary to the mainstream practice of the Elizabethan court: Bayne and Dunham clv; BM Hargrave MS. 216, fo.157; El 2768, fo.29v.

[24] For the reign of Henry VII, *Love* v. *Maidford*, StCh1/1/15, 2/20/9; *Collins* v. *Wagge*, StCh 2/10/136–136A; BM Lansdowne MS. 639, fo.24v; Bayne and Dunham 52. For the reign of Henry VIII, *Hasilwood* v. *Seyton*, StCh 10/4 Pt 2 (bundle), 2/27/81; *Perrot* v. *Earl of Northumberland*, StCh 2/18/332, 2/22/302; *Eland* v. *Savell*, StCh 2/14/45–46, 2/19/130, 360 and El 2652, fo.10; *Dutton* v. *Savage*, StCh 2/13/183–6, 178–81, 2/20/220.

[25] There is some evidence that Wolsey did not always respect the formalities of reference as did More, but the judges were well represented at the Council board in this period and it was perfectly possible for informal consultations to take place on the day of hearing. There is never anything to the effect that Wolsey refused advice or overruled legal opinion, although he might lay himself open to criticism.

[26] PRO State Papers 1/16, fo.16.

[27] E.g. the entry for 24 November 1488, El 2768, fo.3v; Bayne and Dunham 19–20.

[28] El 2652, fo.7v.

[29] El 2768, fo.28. In Henry VII's reign, such cases would most likely have been taken before the ministerial tribunal set up by the famous statute of 1487, 3 Hen.7, c.1. Sir Thomas More's statement is interesting as cited in Bayne and Dunham cxxxi. On Wolsey's activity against retaining, a summary is A. F. Pollard, *Wolsey* (London, 1929; Fontana reprint, 1965) 76.

[30] For an account of one aspect of these matters, the problem of local influence and the trial jury, see Elton, *Policy and Police* 310–16.

[31] El 2652, fo. 6v, 8v, 10v, 13v.

[32] This was first claimed by Pollard, *Wolsey* 72–6.

[33] For the undeveloped procedure, see Bayne and Dunham lxxx–cviii.

[34] *Benger* v. *Mexborne*, StCh 2/4/98–108, 2/23/252.

[35] E.g. Wolsey's important orders in El 2652, fo.3v; BM Lansdowne MS. 639, fo.58.

[36] It is clear that in Henry VII's reign a litigant might appoint any convenient person as his attorney, El 2652, fo.3v; but Wolsey established the two attornies as servants of the Court.

[37] Viz. the respective cases of Necton and Sarisburie, both StCh 10/4 Pt 5 (bundle).

[38] StCh 2/31 loose papers.

[39] E.g. Wolsey to the Council at Ludlow in *Philip* v. *Holford*, StCh 2/20/328; More to George Guildeforde in *Brambill* v. *Barre*, StCh 2/29/64.

[40] The problem here is that there is no way of tracing those cases which may have been determined by commissioners, but with no report sent in to London.

[41] *Jakson* v. *Grymston*, StCh 2/31/170; *Cowley* v. *Eccleston*, StCh 2/10/301–5.

[42] StCh 2/19/351.

[43] *Hampton* v. *Abbot of Abingdon*, StCh 2/23/238.

[44] *Jenyn* v. *Lynche*, StCh 2/23/72.

[45] *Stansby* v. *Wright*, StCh 2/25/26; *Leiche* v. *Savage*, StCh 2/21/242; *Durdant* v. *Holborn*, StCh 2/13/150–54, 156–70.

[46] *Benger* v. *Mexborne*, n.34 above.

[47] E.g. StCh 10/1/41; the caustic remarks in Hall's chronicle were picked up by Sir Thomas Egerton, El 2810; Hall was also quoted by Pollard, *Wolsey* 75; Guistiniani's remarks are also quoted *ibid.* 79; William Hudson in Hargrave, *Collectanea Juridica* ii (1792) 116.

[48] Summaries of the evidence for these expedients are given in BM Lansdowne MS. 639, fo.59; State Papers 1/235 Pt 1; Pollard, *Wolsey* 90–92.

[49] *De Republica Anglorum* (London, 1583; Scolar Press facsimile, 1970) 96; ed. L. Alston (Cambridge, 1906) 118.

Aspects of Alien Status in Medieval English Law, with special reference to Ireland

G. J. Hand

THE communication which follows, when originally delivered, was described by its author as "a cry for help". The cry was generously answered by several of those present at the Conference, but circumstances have prevented advantage being taken of their assistance prior to publication in this form.[1] Nevertheless, it appears to the author that some purpose may be served by publication, especially of the Irish material.

I

The problems of certain kinds of alien in medieval English law can be regarded as governed by special considerations: merchants, the alien priories.[2] So may the position of aliens in actual time of war. If, as will here be done, one makes these sweeping restrictions in scope, one is left, obviously, at most times during the medieval period, with a very small group of people. The status problem which most affected them was that of inheritance; a sub-group of some significance is formed by the wives born without the realm who sought dower in their widowhood.

Traditionally, *Calvin's Case* (*the Case of the Postnati*)[3] has been taken as the watershed in the development of the English law of nationality and alien status.[4] It was not, however, particularly concerned with the disabilities of those who *were* alien and in any event the history offered by Coke, Bacon and Ellesmere has to be treated with caution to-day. For example, it is not easy to credit the argument that aliens could not be allowed to inherit because of their incapacity for jury service and the consequent weakening of the administration of justice if numbers of those otherwise qualified for jury service were excluded as aliens.[5] Much more to the point is the stress on allegiance. An alien could not be permitted to inherit because of the practical certainty in his case of a clash of loyalties and because of the complicated pattern of relationships in society in which inheritance was likely to involve him. The historical origin of the later doctrines is no doubt, as Maitland said, to be found in the loss of

Normandy: "And so too Bracton's 'dilatory exception' becomes perempt-ory: 'You are an alien and your king is at war with our king' becomes 'You are an alien.' "[6] Two centuries later, the impact of the loss of Lancastrian France appears also to have been felt in the law of alienage.[7]

The earliest case we have, *Boistard* v. *Cumbwell* (1243),[8] comes from the transition period implied in Maitland's dictum. The tenant in an assize of novel disseisin had refused to admit the demandant because the demand-ant's elder brother was alive—but had done homage to the bishop of Bayeux, who in turn had done homage to the king of France. But it was a war situation; and in any event we did not know the outcome. Eighty years later, there is the *quo warranto, R.* v. *Philip de Beauvais*.[9] Philip claimed by a charter of Edward I to Simon, his grandfather. Scrope argued that the chain had been broken, as it were, by the fact that Philip's father—the intervening generation—had been an alien. In other words, a franchise could not be transmitted to an alien. Since Philip lost by default, the case is again unsatisfactory. But underlying it is an acceptance that aliens as such had not the ordinary rights of inheritance; we have definitely pro-gressed from the earlier position, because there is here no suggestion of a wartime situation.

It was the succession to the crown which triggered off the next clarifica-tion. The birth in Flanders of two of the children of Edward III, Lionel and John, forced a parliamentary discussion of the territorial basis of nationality in 1343, followed by a statute eight years later.[10] Lionel and John were of course sons of a reigning king of England; early in the next century we get two striking cases involving undoubted aliens by birth, though, as we shall see, there may nevertheless have been royal aspects. In the reign of Henry V two Portuguese widows, both named Beatrice, who had been married to the earl of Arundel and Lord Talbot, encount-ered some difficulty in securing their dower. The Talbot case was the simpler of the two; the king granted to her to be his liege and gave her full rights of bringing actions.[11] This was in 1419. In the Arundel case there were various complications and although in 1416 arrangements were in progress to give her letters of "naturalization" she was obliged to petition in parliament in 1421. She sought to have the same rights in seeking her dower as if she had been born a liege of the king; and the king granted this.[12]

It is possible that the careful attention paid officially to the Arundel case, at least, owed much, not merely to the unwillingness of the Arundel family to allow the widow her dower, but to the realization of the implication for the royal succession of all these matters, just as in 1343. When the cases of the two Portuguese ladies arose, neither Henry V nor his brothers had any children.[13] Next in succession was Rupert of Bavaria, the young son of

Henry's deceased sister; beyond him, if the Beaufort line was to be ignored, the Lancastrian claim went to Philippa, Queen of Portugal, and her issue; beyond her was Catherine, Queen of Castile. (Philippa and Catherine were sisters of Henry IV). On the other hand, dower for an alien wife raised rather different issues from alien succession even in the case of ordinary nobility and the king and his brothers were still young men.

As Holdsworth pointed out, with Littleton we come to a statement of an extended disability of aliens—their incapacity in personal, as well as in real, actions.[14] Almost certainly this was a simple extension of the rule about real actions, though it could not be given the same logical foundations as the latter. The refinements to which the rules could lend themselves are indicated by a case put by KEBLE in 1481/2.[15] If a man leaves two daughters, one alien, one denizen, there will be an escheat as to half, though the denizen daughter will have to sue mortdancestor, if necessary, for the whole.

Some years ago, the fifteenth-century position was examined with much care, though from the standpoint of the merchants, by Dr Beardwood.[16] In particular, she contradicted Holdsworth's view that as early as the fifteenth century there was a clear-cut distinction between the full status of a subject, conferred only by Parliament, and denization, viewed as giving no rights in public law and as without retrospective operation, which might be granted by letters patent.[17] It is possible, however, that Dr Beardwood, in writing that in the fifteenth century "there were seldom as many as half a dozen [grants] in any year"[18], has under-estimated the number of grants made. She herself has stated that not all grants were in fact enrolled.[19] It may be noted that the grant, authorized by parliament, to Jacquetta, Duchess of Bedford, in 1433 was never enrolled.[20] Those acquainted with the analogous Irish material, of generally earlier date, will be aware that considerable numbers of letters of this kind were never enrolled.

II

In fact, grants of entitlement to use English law, which have often been called letters of denization, issued regularly from the Irish chancery and from the English chancery to Irish applicants. The first example known came from Edward, Lord of Ireland, before he became king;[21] the steady flow has been traced down to the reign of Henry VII.[22] It is remarkable that this documentation and the circumstances which gave rise to it have apparently never received attention from writers on specifically English legal history. Of the classical authorities only one appears to refer to the Irish matter:

And hereof many ancient precedents and records may be shewed, that the reason why Ireland is subject to the law of England is not *ipso jure* upon conquest, but grew by a charter of king John; and that extended but to so much as was then in the king's possession; for there are records in the time of king E. I. and II. of divers particular grants to sundry subjects of Ireland and their heirs, that they might use and observe the laws of England.[23]

So Bacon in the *Case of the Postnati.* He may conceivably have obtained his information from his slightly younger contemporary, Sir John Davies, in whose *Discovery of the true causes why Ireland was never entirely subdued,* which appeared a few years later, there is the bald statement that "the meere Irish were reputed Aliens" and an account of "the Charters of Denization, which in all Ages were purchased by them".[24]

The major disabilities of the native Irish may here be summarised in the barest and most unqualified way.[25] In criminal law the death of an Irishman was no felony, though a composition might be paid to his lord or patron. While an Irish defendant in civil matters seems to have had no significant disability, an Irishman was incapable of bringing an action real or personal; Irish widows were not entitled to dower. If an attempt was made by an Irish demandant or plaintiff to bring an action, it could be met by the exception of Irishry, which is first mentioned in 1253.[26] Apart from royal letters of denization, an Irishman could enjoy a letter from an Anglo-Irish lord, which held good against that lord and his heirs.

A group of writers in recent years—Mr H. G. Richardson,[27] Professor Otway-Ruthven,[28] and myself—have treated these disabilities of the native Irish as constituting a status analogous to that of the villein in contemporary England. There are obvious attractions in this view. There is the typical form of the exception of Irishry—*quod non tenetur ei inde respondere, eo quod est hibernicus et non de libero sanguine.*[29] There is the practice by which Irishmen who were, so far as the language can be used of Gaelic society, unquestionably free within their own system, sought to be in the avowry of an Anglo-Irish lord.[30] There is the capacity, already mentioned, of a lord, at least in the early days of the colony, to enfranchise an Irishman as against himself. The Remonstrance to Pope John XXII, a major source for the standpoint of the Gaelic Irish in the early fourteenth century, referring to the testamentary incapacity of the native race, expressly accused the English of "making blood, which from of old was free, unfree".[31]

The possible Welsh analogies have not been closely pursued, except in the matter of avowry, because of a belief that the emphasis on personal, as distinct from territorial, distinctions was much more clear-cut in Ireland.[32] While the anti-Welsh legislation of Henry IV's day does provide some useful points of comparison, it is late in date compared with the Irish material and of course is not common law in nature, like the bulk of the Irish evidence.[33]

Yet, despite the villeinage-based approach of Irish historians, Davies had said that "the meere Irish were reputed Aliens".[34] In an important article in 1967, Professor Bryan Murphy went back to Davies and stressed the way in which the great seventeenth-century authority had laid stress on alien status.[35] It was a salutary shock for those of us who had quarried Davies for references without paying sufficient attention to this major part of his interpretation. Professor Murphy argued that the classic rules of alien status had applied to the Irish. He produced, for example, a telling instance showing the Irish Chancery using the same formula of denization for a Greek and for a native Irishman.[36] Developing points made by him, it can be argued that a distinction between Irishmen "who are in the faith of our lord the king" and those "born in the land of war, enemies of our lord the king",[37] matches, granted that war was endemic on the Irish marches, the distinction of the developed English law between alien friends and alien enemies. The distinction may have been reflected in, and may have derived added importance from, the Ordinance of 1331 which provided that, except in the case of the unfree category known as betaghs, *betagii*, who should be treated as villeins were in England, the Irish and English should enjoy one and the self-same law.[38] While lapse of time appears to have rendered the Ordinance ultimately something of a dead letter, there is significant evidence that its application, when it was, as it apparently was at first, effective, was confined to what might be called "alien friends". Dr Frame has drawn attention to a case on the ordinance in 1333 which was, admittedly, side-stepped by the demandant establishing that he was neither English nor Irish, but Welsh (sufficient, of course, for his purposes, but not for ours) but which bears out this interpretation;[39] and recently better documentation has been used for a frequently-quoted case from the months immediately after the ordinance, giving further support to the same view.[40] Twenty years after the ordinance, the Irish wife of an Anglo-Irishman is found petitioning for the enjoyment of English law *ad totam vitam suam* (obviously with an eye particularly to dower) and her petition is granted, letters patent to be issued *in forma consueta*.[41] Another case of later date is highly instructive. In 1 Richard II, the defence to a charge of having feloniously killed an Irishman was that deceased had not been a liege, but *homo et nativus* of a named Irish lord.[42] Consequently it had been enough to have paid money compensation to the lord; acquittal followed. In 1410 a bill was proposed in the Irish parliament that no Irishman should have letters of denization unless he found surety in chancery not to adhere to any Irish enemy afterwards in any manner, but the Governor refused assent.[43] One can construct a pattern of Irish "friends" and Irish "enemies" which to some extent is helpful to the alien status view of the problem.

But the alienage analogy has also considerable weaknesses. No English king and Lord of Ireland could accept that any other allegiance was to be found in Ireland, in the sense that one might be conceded, in, say, the Empire. The English reply to the Remonstrance to Pope John XXII was a request that the pope should use his authority to compel the Irish to fulfil their political duties towards their Lord and King.[44] I know of no occurrence of such a word as *alienigena* in the context of the status of the native Irish. The Irish might be rebels or they might belong to what might anachronistically be called protectorates and native states, but they were not aliens in the sense the two Portuguese Beatrices were aliens.

Further, the alien status theory presupposes a far more developed English law of alien status in the thirteenth century than seems in fact to have been the case—whereas the English law of villeinage was of course well developed. On the other hand, when Davies came to Ireland in 1603 the Union of Crowns had just occurred and the minds of lawyers were already engaged in the problems discussed at length in *Calvin's Case*. Villein status was obsolescent.[45] It can therefore be suggested with much plausibility that the mind of Sir John Davies was more sensitive, because of his own historical situation, to analogies with alien status than to those with villeinage.

Lastly, the status of the native Irish was in fact *sui generis*, for one important element, relating to homicide, was borrowed neither from villeinage nor from any other doctrine of English law, but from the Brehon law.[46] Nevertheless, the partial analogy with alien status is sufficiently interesting to deserve more attention from students of the history of alienage and nationality in English law than it has hitherto received. And those of us who are concerned with the specifically Irish problem would welcome fuller and more satisfactory learning about the alien in medieval England.

NOTES

1 Valuable lines of investigation, chiefly in unpublished materials, were suggested to me by, in particular, Mr Jacques Beauregard, Professor E. B. Fryde, Dr E. W. Ives, and Mr C. A. F. Meekings, and I am very sorry indeed that time has not allowed me to pursue them properly.

2 It should be noted that the PRO class, Extents of Alien Priories (E.106), contains extents of the possessions of laymen who were of foreign allegiance.

3 Co. Rep. f.1 (77 ER 377); 2 St. Tr. 561; Bacon's argument is also conveniently accessible in *Lord Bacon's Works* vii (ed. J. Spedding, R. L. Ellis and D. D. Heath; London, 1859) 641.

4 HEL ix.72–104, esp. at 79–86. F. Plowden, *A disquisition concerning the law of alienage* (Paris, 1818) has a good deal of value.

5 Co. Rep. f.18b; 2 St. Tr. 640; 77 ER 399.

6 PM i.463, referring to Bracton f.427.

7 In general, see the paper by C. T. Allmand, cited in n.16 below; cf. *Bagot's Case* (1468) YB 7 Ed.4, Hil. pl.17, f.29, and (1469) YB 9 Ed.4, Trin. pl.3. f.6.

8 I. S. Leadam and J. F. Baldwin, *Select Cases before the King's Council* (1918) 35 SS 1, with commentary at xlvii–xlix.

9 Cam, *Eyre of London* i (85 SS) 213–17, and commentary, cxxix–cxxx. There is much of more general interest in the section of the commentary entitled "Aliens in London" (cxxvii–cxxxi).

10 PM i.458–9; HEL ix.75; the 1343 discussion is in *Rot. Parl.* ii.139 and the statute is 25 Edw.3, st. 2.

11 CCR (1419–22) 24–5. In the following year she secured the wardship of her infant daughter's lands and those held in Ireland a further year later; but her daughter's death of course ended these arrangements: CPR (1416–22) 258, 367, 393, 415–16; *Complete Peerage*, xii.619.

12 Thomas, earl of Arundel, had had licence in 1415 to enfeoff feoffees to uses to him and Beatrice his wife. Upon his death there was some official indecision, but Beatrice was eventually, in February 1416, licensed to sue for dower, and letters of denization were authorised. Difficulties followed as to the succession, but Beatrice's problem was resolved by the parliamentary petition: CPR (1413–16) 336, 400, 412, (1416–22) 39, 238–9; CCR (1413–19) 265, 266, 290, 304, 305, 313, 407 466, (1419–22) 172–3; *Rot. Parl.* iv.130; *Complete Peerage* i.246. I am indebted to my friend Mr T. Brynmor Pugh, of the University of Southampton, for help with these questions.

13 The future Henry VI, the first and effectively only child of any son of Henry IV, was not born until December 1421.

14 Littleton, *Tenures*, bk II, c.xi (Co.Litt. f.129); HEL ix.93–4.

15 Thorne, *Readings* 71 SS 153. I have not traced the case which Keble had in mind, but it may perhaps have been (1409) YB 11 H.4, Mich. pl.49, f.26; in the Vulgate text it is not quite identical on the facts, though it certainly expresses the same law.

16 A. Beardwood, "Mercantile antecedents of the English naturalization laws" (1964) 16 *Medievalia et humanistica* 66–76; cf. also her *Alien Merchants in England, 1350 to 1377* (Cambridge, Mass., 1931) cap. iv ("The denization of alien merchants"); but the later work is definitely the more valuable in this connection. Cf. also C. T. Allmand, "A note on denization in fifteenth-century England" (1966) 17 *Medievalia et humanistica* 127–9; R. G. Nicholson, *Scotland: the later Middle Ages* (Edinburgh, 1974) 490.

17 HEL ix.77, esp. at n.3.

18 Beardwood, "Mercantile antecedents" 74, *Alien Merchants* 65 n.2.

19 Beardwood "Mercantile antecedents" 73.

20 H. C. Maxwell-Lyte, *Historical Notes on the Great Seal* (London, 1926) 365.

21 Cambridge University Library, Add. MS. 3104, f.50.

22 By Professor Bryan Murphy: "The Status of the Native Irish after 1331" (1967) 2 IJNS 116–28, at 123.

23 *Bacon's Works* vii.660–61; 2 St. Tr. 592; ct. 7 Co. Rep. f.23a; 2 St. Tr. 648; 77 ER 405.

24 London, 1612 (reprint, Shannon, 1969) 102, 103. The most recent attempt at an assessment of Davies is G. J. Hand, "Sir John Davies" (1971) 64 *Gazette of the Incorporated Law Society of Ireland* 174–7.

25 For a fuller survey see G. J. Hand, *English Law in Ireland 1290–1324* (Cambridge, 1967), cap.x, esp. at 198–205; and cf. other writings mentioned in succeeding footnotes.

26 . . . *excepcione, qua repellantur Ibernenses a vendicacione terrarum aliis . . .*: Close Rolls (1251–3) 458–9.

27 "English institutions in medieval Ireland" (1938–9) 1 IHS 382–93, at 386–91.

28 "The request of the Irish for English law, 1277–80" (1948–9) 6 IHS 261–70; "The native Irish and English law in medieval Ireland" (1950–51) 7 IHS 1–16; cf. also comments by her in reviewing material by the present writer, (1968–9) 16 IHS 104–6.

29 Davies, *Discovery* 105.

30 Hand, *English Law in Ireland* 197; G. Mac Niocaill, "The Origins of the *Betagh*" (1966) 1 IJNS 292–8 is extremely important on the native background.

31 *sanguinem ab antiquo liberum facientes auctoritate propria violenter servilem*: Hand, *English Law in Ireland* 205.

32 Cf. Otway-Ruthven, (1950–51) 7 IHS 5, and Hand, *English Law in Ireland* 187–8.

33 While Mr Beverley Smith has pointed out that "the difficulties . . . were not entirely derived from the legislation of the reign of Henry IV" ("Crown and Community in the Principality of North Wales in the reign of Henry Tudor" (1966) 3 WHR 145–71, at 149), that legislation is apparently the most relevant analogy from an Irish point of view; cf., in addition to the article just cited, S. B. Chrimes, *Henry VII* (London, 1972) 253–4, and R. R. Davies, "The Twilight of Welsh Law, 1484–1536" (1966) 51 *History* 143–64, esp. at 146–8, 151–4.

34 Davies, *Discovery* 102.

35 Murphy, "Status" (as n.22 above).

36 (1967) 2 IJNS 125.

37 *qi sont a la foi nostre seignur le roi; nee en terre de guerre enemy nostre seignur le roi*: PRO S.C.8/261, no. 13006, printed by J. F. Ferguson, "The 'mere English' and 'mere Irish'" (1850–51) 1 RSAI Jnl 508–12 at 510; *Foedera* (Record Commn edn) ii (pt ii) 964; CPR (1334–8) 405. For a similar distinction, see PRO S.C.8/265, no. 13232, a petition from the "scholars of the Irish nation", which probably led to letters of 4 March 1360: *Early Statutes, Ireland: John-Hen.V* (H.M.S.O., 1907) 420–21; *Foedera* (Record Commn edn) iii (pt ii) 605; CCR (1360–64) 163.

38 *Early Statutes, Ireland* 324.

39 R. Frame, "The immediate effect and interpretation of the 1331 Ordinance *Una et eadem lex*: Some evidence" (1972) 7 IJNS 85–90 at 85–6, 89–90.

40 PROI, Betham Abstracts, M.2542, from Justiciary Roll, 6–7 Edw.III, m.18d; for discussion, see G. J. Hand, "English Law in Ireland, 1172–1351" (1972) 23 NILQ 393–422 at 416–17.

41 Cambridge University Library, Add.MS. 3104, f.49d (apparently from Justiciary Roll, 26 Edw.III, m.17).

42 Discussed (1972) 23 NILQ 417.

43 *Early Statutes, Ireland* 527.

44 J. A. Watt, "Negotiations between Edward II and John XXII concerning Ireland" (1956–7) 10 IHS 1–20 at 6, 16.

45 HEL iii.507.

46 The composition derived from the Brehon *éraic*: Hand, *English Law in Ireland* 202.

The Origins of the Later Year Books*

E. W. Ives

THE year books of the common law are the most neglected source for the social and legal history of England from 1400 to 1550. The interest of Maitland and the early pioneers and their disciples has been all in the thirteenth and fourteenth centuries, so that while one year in three from 1300 to 1390 boasts a year book text in a modern edition, only two years of the fifteenth century are covered and none of the sixteenth. And this neglect may appear amply justified; T. F. T. Plucknett wrote, "It is quite impossible to believe that there was any lively interest in the Year Books, or any serious desire to have cases reported, in the latter half of the fifteenth century."[1] But as Plucknett himself pointed out, "It was the Year Books, in this most obscure epoch, which maintained the continuity of English law", and if this were not reason enough to study them, then what they can tell us of late medieval society and late medieval law would be.[2] Nor are these later year books of interest only to students of the fifteenth and sixteenth centuries; if the character of the year books remained constant through the 250 years of their existence, then the fuller documentation of the later legal profession and the issue of year books in print may well throw light on the whole history of the genre; conversely, if the later year books are distinct, then an understanding of this distinction must illuminate the golden age of Chief Justice Bereford.

I

As with many conundrums of late medieval law, the only external evidence on the production of the year books comes from Sir John Fortescue. In Chapter 48 of *De Laudibus Legum Anglie* he wrote:

> Reportantur eciam ea que in curiis regis placitantur, disputantur, et iudicantur, ac in libros ad futurorum erudicionem rediguntur in sermone semper Gallico.[3]

The comment is simple—the purpose of the year books "*ad futurorum erudicionem*", and the method of production "*reportantur ac rediguntur in libros*". Unfortunately this simplicity is deceptive in the first case and uninformative in the second. What did Fortescue mean by *erudicionem*; *reportantur ac rediguntur*, by whom and how?

What Fortescue clearly did not mean by *ad futurorum erudicionem* was any doctrine of precedent. The later year books were not, in the modern sense, authoritative. They were not binding; Chief Justice Thomas Bryan said in 1490,

> if the case in 33 Henry VI were to be judged now, the law would be [as he had stated], for he would never be of the opinion that [was in] the book of 33 Henry VI.[4]

Year books were not the only, or even the principal ground on which to plead; in 5 Henry VII, Serjeant Thomas Kebell said,

> it would seem to me that it would be contrary to reason if . . ., and in 49 Edward III an action was maintained . . .[5]

Year books were not expected to be congruent; Kebell and Bryan had this exchange in common pleas in the early 1490s:

> *Kebell* The distinction in our law is where . . . And so it was in the case of the four men and their wives, Anno 11 Henry IV.
> *Bryan* We will look in our books ready for tomorrow.
> *Kebell* said that he had seen many books, and all the books were as he had said . . .
> *Bryan* And I have seen many books contrary to that . . .[6]

Any translation of *ad futurorum erudicionem* as "for future reference" is misleading.

Rudis, the classical root of *eruditio* implies "in a natural state", and the prefix *ex* an active intervention to perfect this condition; hence the basic meaning is "polishing", "educating" or "training". From this derived a second classical usage, "knowledge", with the resulting ambiguity that *eruditio* may refer both to the process of learning and to what is learned. The original sense, "instruction", certainly survived into medieval Latin, and it would be quite acceptable to render *ad futurorum erudicionem* as "to instruct future generations". This, indeed, has been done, and the hypothesis advanced that the later year books were produced in the course of instructing law students.[7] But tenable though this translation may be, it is not mandatory; there remains the alternative emphasis on "knowledge", and thus the translation "for the information of people later". In fact, this rendering is to be preferred in view of the use of the law-French *erudition* in the year books. This occurs sometimes as a term of art, apparently equalling "doctrine" or "maxim". A barrister in a case dated 1485–95 said:

> Yet the law is not as I understand in this case; for this has been held as a maxim: Where the party . . . [*car ceo ad este tenu pour un erudicion: Ou le party* . . .].[8]

Kebell replied:

> There is neither ground nor maxim [*ceo n'est ground ny erudicion*] for what you say, for in many cases . . .; but this has been a maxim [*mes ceo ad este un erudicion*], that the party shall only have . . . But this maxim of which you speak [*mes celle erudicion de quelle vous parlez*], I have never heard it before.

K

The word also occurs in a more general sense to mean "knowledge", as in a year book report of the early 1490s (twenty years after Fortescue wrote), where Thomas Bryan C. J. refused a plea on the ground that it was contrary *ad nostre comon erudition*.[9] This tradition in law-French of *"erudition"* to mean what was accepted legal doctrine, a tradition contemporary with Fortescue and from the professional ambience to which he belonged, suggests that Sir John is transliterating, and certainly that he would intend *"eruditio"* in this same sense; year books were intended *ad futurorum eruditionem*, that is "as knowledge", even "as maxims for future generations".

II

This construction of Fortescue corresponds precisely with the internal evidence in the year books of their use in litigation. In strict theory it was the rolls which were the record of the court, but they can have been of limited value in deciding how to take a particular line of pleading. Counsel who wanted to know the balance of professional opinion on pleading this or that, had largely to rely upon what the year books would tell him. In an action reported under Easter 1490, Kebell defended his plea by saying, "I believe that this is a common plea in our books".[10] In Trinity 9 Henry VII he claimed, "And in Trinity 4 Henry VI it was adjudged that the juror should have 40*s*. . . ." only to be challenged by Rede saying "The contrary has been judged once or twice since then".[11] In Michaelmas 9 Henry VII, Kebell "prayed that the judges would be advised, and he would produce books where this plea was accepted as sound".[12]

At first sight there may seem to be some contradiction between these attempts by counsel to argue on the basis of year book reports, and the evidence already presented that these reports were not binding; the modern reaction is to ask, "were they precedents or were they not?" Perhaps the most useful guide to the role of the year books in court is to compare the part played by personal memory. Justice John Vavasour could reminisce on his career at the bar, "I was driven by the court, when I was a serjeant, to say . . .", and the chief justice replied, "Certainly, I grant you that, for in that [particular] case . . .".[13] Early in Henry VII's reign, Bryan C. J. went back twenty years and remarked, "It was adjudged in my time that . . .; Illingworth being Chief Baron".[14] William Hussey C. J. said in a king's bench case of 3 Henry VII, "It was so adjudged in the past by the advice of Fortescue", perhaps thirty years earlier.[15] Few lawyers, however, could rival—or challenge—Guy Fairfax J. who said (1487–90), "I will prove this to you by a case in the time of my Master Newton", and Newton had been dead for forty years.[16] Quite clearly these recollections were part of the *eruditio* of the court precisely in the same sense as

the reports in the year books. This is clear from the latter part of a king's
bench report from the period 1485–95:

> *Hussey*   Certes, Anno 2 Henry IV a man prayed a *Capias ad satisfaciendum* . . .
> and he did not have it, because . . .; but I have not yet heard such a doctrine
> [*erudition*] about the *Capias pro fine*. And before Anno 36 Henry VI in Debt or
> Trespass . . . it was current in all books that . . . But there is a new opinion taken,
> as you [Kebell] say, to the effect that . . .; but why such an opinion should be taken
> on this point has not yet been adjudged, although the contrary had been many times
> decided.
>
> *Kebell*   It seems to me that the older opinion should be the better, because the
> party . . .
> *Hussey*   In my own time I have seen a party taken by a *Capias pro fine* . . .
> *Kebell*   Certes, I was of counsel in the same case.
> *Constable*   Certes, the contrary was held Anno 6 or 7 Edward IV.
> *Hussey*   See your books against tomorrow, and then you will have your award in
> this case.[17]

Bench and bar alike move readily from memory to the reports and back
again, without distinction. Comments in other cases make the equation
of books and recollection quite specific; Tremayle J. said,

> We cannot order the law otherwise than it has been in time past; and in all my life,
> nor in all the books that I have seen, have I seen that . . .[18]

The later year books were extensions of the memory of the legal profession.
To see the year books in this way explains the puzzle Plucknett noted,
that the first year books printed were already thirty years old. It was not,
as he concluded, "that recent cases had no particular attraction for
lawyers", but rather that men wanted reports of the most recent cases
which they had been unable to observe personally.[19] To see the year books
as the written memory of the profession also removes the apparent
opposition between citing year books in pleading and having no doctrine
of authority. Memory supplies continuity, so did the year books, as a case
of *formedon* from the early 1490s shows:

> *Kebell*   And it seems to me that one could impose upon a feoffee in fee simple the
> condition that he should not alienate.
> *Bryan* interrupted him, and said that they did not wish to hear him argue this conceit,
> because it is plainly contrary to our common knowledge [*ad nostre comon erudition*],
> and is now, in a sense, a principle [*est or in maner un principal*]; because by this
> argument we would be forced to change all our ancient precedents. Therefore, speak
> no more of this point.[20]

On the other hand, memory is not a dead hand upon reason, and neither
were past reports—*l'opinion* and *les livres* were always in tension:

> And then *Hussey* said he had asked the question of the common pleas [bench] and
> the chief justice [Bryan] is of the same opinion as I am. *Vavasour* said at the start that
> his book is contrary, and he said now that he had seen in his book often, and had
> studied, and he thought that the reason of his book is better than their opinion . . .[21]

K[1]

The whole relationship of memory, report and judicial opinion is summed up in one of the last of the published year books, for 27 Henry VIII. Fitzherbert J. recalled a successful case he had pleaded fifteen years before, announced that the court had then been wrong to decide for his client— the judges had done so simply on their own opinions, without consulting the other bench—and when he was told that the case had been reported, asserted: "Put this case out of your books, for without doubt it is not law".[22]

<h1 style="text-align:center">III</h1>

Fortescue's other comment upon the year books, *reportantur et rediguntur in libros*, raises the question "how were these books produced, and by whom?" Again there is no external evidence and the answer must lie in the books themselves. What makes studying the later year books different from work on the fourteenth century ones is the relative importance of manuscript and printed texts. Maitland's rejection of the printed year books as a "hopeless mass of corruption" is well known, but for the Yorkist and Tudor period it is the black-letter editions which are primary.[23] Manuscripts are few in number and may easily turn out to be dependent on the printed text, not *vice versa*. Study of the later year books is study of the early printed book.

Analysis of the published year books for the reign of Henry VII shows that lawyers and historians have uniformly underestimated the ill-usage which the books have received. They are substantially the creation of editorial activity. Texts for the reign of Richard II may be "united by a surprisingly unanimity on all but the slightest details" and have passed as standard texts into print; when it came to publishing the near-contemporary reports for the reign of Henry VII, there was not yet a standard text to print.[24] The very make-up of the volumes is suspicious. Year 1 is a mixture of reports in Latin and law-French, and so are years 2 and 3. In the first known edition, by Pynson and dated conjecturally 1505, year 1 and 2 are each in two parts, separated by blank pages— perhaps bad casting off at the press, perhaps copy that arrived in four bundles.[25] The report for A° 5 is twice as long as for any other year in the edition, and it is the only one fully divided into terms.[26] In the second place, there is no regularity about year book reporting. Some cases are given in great detail, others in a brief summary; sometimes the outcome of the debate is all that matters, more often the argument; there are even lengths and styles of report which seem characteristic of one year or part of one year.[27] Another cause for misgiving is the appearance of individual lawyers in the year books. In the first sixteen years of Henry VII's reign, 609 year book entries give the names of lawyers, and in 313 of these

Serjeant Thomas Kebell takes part; his nearest rival, John Vavasour, is mentioned half as often, and Kebell appears more frequently than even the busiest judge, Thomas Bryan.[28] Kebell's capacity must be allowed, even his cheek in advancing daring pleas, but it is credulous to suppose that he eclipsed everyone else in the legal profession, and he a man who never became a judge. A final indication that there is a considerable distance between the printed texts and the original court cases is the dating. Kebell, for example, appears in thirty cases in the year after his death, 16 Henry VII, together with such ghosts as William Hussey, five, and Roger Townshend, seven years deceased.[29] Indeed, out of thirty-nine datable cases listed under that year, thirty-seven at least are incorrect.[30] Nor is A° 16 exceptional; Michaelmas A° 15 (1499) begins with "the first case that Thomas Frowyk argued after he was made Chief Justice" (which took place in 1502), and ends with a case involving Choke and Bridges (who died in 1483).[31] Out of 228 cases between Michaelmas 1495 and Trinity 1501 where lawyers are named, 97 are incorrectly dated; 42 at least belong to Michaelmas 1493 or earlier, with A° 11 having a minimum of 65% of its cases wrongly dated.[32]

IV

The standard year book edition is that published in black letter in 1678–80. For the reign of Henry VII, this is effectively a reprint of the first uniform edition by Richard Tottell in 1555.[33] His title page makes clear the composite nature of his text, part new, part revision, part reprint:

> Anni Regis Henrici Septimi, Quibus accesserunt Annus Primus & secundus de nova & valde bona collatione, Ac etiam Annus decimus, undecimus, decimus tertius, Decimus sextus & Vigesimus, nunquam ante hac aediti.

For A° 10, 11, 13, 16 and 20, this claim is just. The *nova & valde collatione* of 1 and 2 Henry VII was based on the different versions already published by Richard Redman and his mentor Richard Pynson, supplemented with certain new material.[34] Behind the rest of the text lay a variety of previous editions; for A° 3 to A° 8 inclusive there was an existing Redman printing which, in turn, relied on earlier work by Pynson, while 9, 12, 14 and 15 Henry VII had been covered by Pynson and Berthelet. In other words, the standard text is the product of half a century and more of redaction.

To take as an example the relatively simple case of 3 Henry VII. The earliest printing by Richard Pynson has only spasmodic divisions into terms, prints as continuous passages later broken into separate cases, and omits the final part of what is now the Michaelmas term, twenty-eight cases in all, that is 42% of the whole.[35] The uniform appearance of the year books is, indeed, very largely the creation of the printers and supremely of Richard Tottell; it was Tottell who imposed regular divisions into terms, grouped reports into reigns, made proper citation possible by standard foliation and added copious references.

In due course the vicissitudes of the year books at the hands of their various printers will be patiently uncovered, but even when it is possible to be certain about the copy used by the press each time, textual problems will remain. It is highly probable that before Tottell and his predecessors obtained them, many early Tudor year books were already composite documents. The most obvious sign of this is the number of homologues they contain. Thus the earliest Pynson printing, reports the case of *Carew* v. *Ewerby* twice under 3 Henry VII, and once under 5 Henry VII.[36] It is evident that a case could, over the years, give rise to a series of notices, and the record in 5 Henry VII was certainly of proceedings at a late stage in Exchequer Chamber. But the two reports in 3 Henry VII are independent of each other, the shorter is in French and the other, unusually, in Latin. Other signs of editorial activity are the inclusion of cases out of sequence with an explanatory note, and the inclusion of reports at second hard.[37] This last is true of the Exchequer Chamber consideration of *Carew* v. *Ewerby* where the reporter notes that he was not present In consequence the style of that entry is distinctive; it is a précis, consolidating the opinions of the lawyers involved into summaries of the opposing positions, not reported as a succession of individual arguments. It is clear that this uncommon form is the result of borrowing for one or two first-person remarks do survive in traditional style.

Especially suspicious are parts of the five years of Henry VII's reign which Tottell offered the public in 1555 *nunquam ante hac aediti*. Analysis of the dating suggests that the text for A° 20 was taken from a genuine year book manuscript; all but the last three cases (which could well be accretions) must belong to that year or very near it because of the particular lawyers named. The same must be true of the first part of A° 10, but not of the second where one case in four is an anachronism. In the remainder—A° 11, 13 and 16—errors in dating are so egregious as to preclude any belief that they represent genuine year book texts for the years concerned. It seems highly probable that Tottell was using collections of miscellaneous cases which had "acquired" a regnal year number.[38] The character of Harleian MS. 1624, one of the few manuscripts for the reign, is in point here. Folios 1 to 2ᵛ are headed *Anno 4*, without term divisions; *Hilary 5 Henry 7* begins on folio 2ᵛ and the title *5 H 7* runs to folio 9; folio 9ᵛ is headed *Hilary 6 Henry 7*, and so too folio 10, but thereafter the title is simply *6 H 7* to the end of folio 33 when the reign of Henry VIII starts. While in the first ten or so folios, such cases as do have related matter in the printed text occur under the appropriate regnal year, the thirty or so folios repetitively dated *6 H 7* yield material which turns up in Tottell's suspect A° 10, 11, 13 and 16. The inference is clear. Harleian 1624 comes from a source which began as a strictly kept year book, but degenerated into a loose collection of items labelled 6 Henry VII.

Bibliographical work on the early printed year books is in its infancy, but if this brief critique is sound, then it must substantially determine our view of how year books were made. First, the later year books as they now exist are not the result of any organised production; the appearance of organisation is the achievement of the publishers and especially of Richard Tottell. Second, the "Vulgate", as Maitland called the standard black-letter edition, represents only what the publishers could get hold of, edited and amended as it suited them; it is not an accepted text, still less an official or quasi-official one. Third, if the texts which the printers obtained were already composite it must be doubtful whether there was ever any authoritative reporting in late medieval courts of law; we may talk about "a" year book, never "the" year book.[39]

V

Doubt about a system of law reporting may seem unjustified to those who use the black-letter editions of 1678–80 and are familiar with the appearance of *le reporteur*, indicating his presence very often by that title, or the initial "R". In fact, this identification in the year books of Henry VII is a confusion again introduced by editorial activity. Few, and probably none of these initiallings are original, and to complicate matters, editors have used "R" not only for passages they assumed to be the work of the original reporter, but for subsequent additions as well.[40] Nevertheless, even if the signpost "R" is ignored, there are a considerable number of cases where internal evidence does show an individual reporter at work in court, joining in the discussions, noting his own opinions and what other lawyers said to him. Thus, in a chancery case dated Michaelmas 8 Henry VII there is the entry:

> Rede was against [this argument] but he did not argue because the court rose. Therefore query this point and another good point made by Vavasour, for I [did not] hear the case clearly.[41]

In Trinity 15 Henry VII, after the court had quashed the warrant to call a jury on the ground that the sheriff was related to the defendant, the comment is:

> Yet the serjeants, that is to say Constable and Butler, said to me that this was clearly not a *challenge principal*.[42]

The later editors who annotated the frequent *Quod nota* and *Quaere* with the letter "R" made mistakes, but they were trying to identify the work of particular men who were the ultimate source for the text.

That a year book report originated with a reporter does not, however, imply that there was necessarily such a person as "the reporter". The fact that reports freely criticise judicial decisions and include material from out of court argues against any official appointment to such a post. The existence of variant reports of a single case equally shows that no single individual was involved.[43] The position seems to have been that any lawyer might jot down for his own information a report of a case, and that perhaps most did collect reports fairly systematically during part of their career.[44] What is particularly informative here are certain Yorkist and early Tudor law-books whose authorship is known. One such manuscript is British Museum Hargrave MS. 388. A late sixteenth or early seventeenth century copy, it preserves material which can in part be attributed to John Spelman who began as a member of Gray's Inn and became a serjeant-at-law in 1521, justice of the king's bench in 1532 and died 1544. What proportion the manuscript preserves of the reports by Spelman which are known to have circulated, and in what form is not clear, but the significant point is that the first 107 folios are effectively a year book.[45] More evidence is forthcoming from the so-called *Keilwey's Reports*, published by John Croke in 1602. These have been plausibly associated with John Caryll of the Inner Temple, attorney general to the Duchy of Lancaster (1544–1566), and possibly with his father, Serjeant John Caryll who died in 1523.[46] Again the form of part is that of a year book. Harleian 1624, with its long run of cases dated *6 H 7* may also come from the Caryll stable.[47] Here are year books, but year books associated with named individual lawyers.

Fifteenth century evidence confirms this. In a case from Michaelmas 1465, Walter Moyle "alleged three precedents of his own reporting when he was a serjeant in the time of Richard Newton" (1443–9).[48] Robert Townshend kept reports of cases for the years around 1460, perhaps two years before he became a bencher at Lincoln's Inn; he went on to become a justice of the common pleas.[49] Richard Pynson explicitly stated that the year books for 1 and 2 Edward IV which he printed were the work of Townshend. It is only this printing in the canon of year book publications that has prevented these collections having the title *Townshend's Reports*, or to reverse the point, the only reason Spelman and Caryll are not included with Townshend is that they escaped the publisher.

VI

The reports of Spelman and Caryll suggest that Fortescue's *reportantur* refers to the private reporting of cases by individual lawyers. They also explain the heterogeneous state of existing year books and the evidence already discussed of cavalier editing, in other words, what Sir John's *rediguntur in libros* involved.

The section of Hargrave 388 in year book form and associated with Justice Spelman incorporates other material. The largest single source of this was John Pollard of the Middle Temple, created serjeant-at-law in 1547, but the copyist left spaces for additional matter and in some places entries have been inserted under the appropriate regnal year.[50] A second section of this manuscript, parts of which can also be connected with John Spelman, is a mixture of abridgement and commonplace book, so that the account of a stranded whale being towed up the Thames for Henry VIII's inspection is sandwiched between a description of Anne Boleyn's coronation and a report of her trial, all in a section devoted to pleas of the crown.[51] There is gossip from Gray's Inn and the legal profession in general, and a number of references to law-readings, again from Gray's Inn. The latter parts of Hargrave 388—year books for late Henry VIII, Philip and Mary, and Elizabeth—cannot be associated with Spelman but their inclusion tells the same story, of lawyers building up reports piecemeal from a variety of sources. *Keilwey's Reports*, though edited selectively by John Croke, demonstrate this as well. They consist of two runs of year book material for late Henry VII and early Henry VIII respectively, separated by a section *"casus incerti temporis"*, another entitled *"cases in itinere in temps del tresmemorable Roy Edwardi le tierce"*, and a brief run of eight cases headed *"Quo Warranto, Anno sexto Ed. primi"*. The *casus incerti temporis* have been identified as a set of moot cases from the Inner Temple for early Henry VII.[52] The fourteenth century cases are really an anthology, almost an abridgement, on the theme of *Quo Warranto*, to which the Edward I cases act as an appendix. It is hardly material to ask at what date Hargrave 388 reached its present form, or how much *Keilwey's Reports* owe to Croke as editor. It is sufficient that material of such demonstrably varied origins has ultimately ended up together.

The conclusion would seem to be this. The concern of lawyers for *nos livres* is clear, and so too their habit of commonplacing. They would naturally keep notes of important points which came up in court. They certainly borrowed and copied old reports—items in Pollard's collection went back to 14 Henry IV, while another manuscript (for 18 Henry VI) carries the note that John Caryll wrote it out at Lady Day 1485—and presumably they exchanged current material, not only collections of cases but individual reports.[53] They also had available the libraries of the Inns, both the donations of previous generations and the continuing record of readings and readers' cases. Some of this material might be in the classic form of years and terms or might be organised into such a pattern; at other times a subject arrangement might be tried, or the cases could be recorded haphazardly. If a manuscript of this sort passed through the hands of several lawyers it would accumulate various other items, and the result of this whole piecemeal process would be precisely what is found in the first printed year books—substantial discussions of important cases, side by side with briefer notices of interest, the whole interlarded with runs of *nota* and with a few personalia thrown in.

It is the hypothesis of this paper, therefore, that the reports in the later year books were initially collected by lawyers as a natural but haphazard part of their professional practice. They developed into the form we have now in this same organic fashion as lawyers accumulated collections of the *erudition* of the courts. Texts became available for publication quite fortuitously and it is to the printing shop that we owe a good deal of the form we find characteristic of the species. The year books as we have them, and in any form in which we can recover earlier readings are "random" in inception and content.

VII

The hypothesis that the year books had an organic origin will also explain their association with the Inns of Court. That there was an association is clear. For example, material in the year book for 6 Henry VII has links with Gray's Inn. The opening plea of the Easter term includes "but query [this], for in Gray's Inn all thought that . . ."; plea 3 begins, "Note, it was said by Utton of Gray's Inn, when he was at the assize at Cambridge, that . . ."; plea 5 of the Trinity term ends:

> Query and study . . . whether this would be good? I believe "yes", and so held divers in Gray's Inn.[54]

It is, indeed, probable that the link with Gray's Inn accounts also for items in A° 5—"*vide Fairfax le puisne de Grays Inne*" and "*ut apparet in casu Johannis Ernley de Grays Inne*".[55] 7 Henry VII, too, may have Gray's Inn material since Trinity term plea 1 ends, "Enquire more of this matter from Broke", probably Robert Broke of Gray's Inn who became a serjeant in 1510 and a judge ten years later.[56] Failing this, the connection may be with the Middle Temple where John Broke, "Broke of Bristol", also became a serjeant in 1510.

Sometimes an inn may be suspected but not positively identified. Thus plea 4 of Easter 4 Henry VII appears to be a homologue of *Carew* v. *Ewerby*, but it includes the phrase "*et fuit argue par les barresters*", followed by a comment from Kebell and two judicial decisions.[57] The use of *barresters*, at that time a term domestic to the Inns of Court, suggests that the entry represents a case stated at one of the Inns, based on *Carew* v.

Ewerby, with Kebell's opinion and the court rulings incorporated from the actual hearing, or, more probably, a case stated at the Inner Temple with Kebell present and reporting his own views and those of the judges.[58] Variations between reports of the same case also show the influence of the Inns. Men from different houses would naturally report cases in slightly different ways, especially emphasising pleadings by men they knew or admired; gossip at table on the cases of the day would easily slip into the record; even the identity of plaintiffs might be of interest.[59] Thus an Inner Temple contribution to the year books would help to explain the preponderance of the opinions of Thomas Kebell and account for a report of 13 Henry VII degenerating into a discussion, of obvious Inner Temple provenance, in which Kebell reminisced about a former fellow, Edward Grantham.[60] Similarly, the Inner Temple flavour of *Keilwey's Reports* would account for the brevity in recording *Geinsford* v. *Gilford:*

> Note that in the case between George Guldford & Robert Gainsford and other defendants in battery, it was said by Frowike & all his colleagues that where . . .[61]

The printed year book, however, goes into detail, surely a Gray's Inn reporter:

> Robert Geinsford of Greis Inne and others brought an attaint against George Gilford and others . . . And one of the Grand Jury was challenged as having insufficient a freehold . . . and another juror was challenged because he was a fellow of Greis Inne of which R. G. is a fellow . . . And this matter was maintained by Lord Burgeveny and Sir R. Gilford, one on one side and the other on the other. And the jury found on 2 points for R. Geinsford, and on the 3rd against him, and as to that he was fined; as to the other two points, judgement was solemnly given, *sc.* that . . . and that G. Gilford should be arrested.[62]

VIII

Some scholars, indeed, have suggested that the strong association of the year books with the Inns of Court indicates that they were produced in connection with the educational work there. Some support for this might be claimed from the will of Justice William Calowe, formerly of the Middle Temple, which mentions "ij bookes of Briggementes, oon of myne owen labour and thothir of Lincolnesin labour", thus showing that an inn might produce a law book by collaborative effort. It has been suggested, indeed, that Nicholas Statham's *Abridgement* is such an official production from Lincoln's Inn.[63] But at most Calowe can only be taken to mean that some abridgements were collaborative efforts; his own clearly was not. The phrase "of Lincolnesin labour" is equally capable of a much less specific meaning, simply indicating a text in which several individuals from the Inn had taken a hand, possibly over some years. It seems far more likely that Calowe should have obtained a copy of a book circulating at Lincoln's Inn, or even the book itself, than access to a manuscript officially prepared for the society. In any case, abridgements, by their very nature, are more likely to have been formally commissioned, perhaps for educational purposes, than a running series of year books.

As far as the year books are concerned, if the existing text is at all representative of the original reporting, it is hard to see such casual and fragmented entries as the response to any official initiative by an inn. There is also the argument of silence. We have ample evidence of what other activities were commissioned at Lincoln's Inn in the Black Books of that society, evidence very often from the punishment of defaulters. It seems most unlikely that these records should be silent on such a substantial and continuing task as the making of law reports, and incredible that, alone of the duties there, this one should have been accepted with a universal diligence and enthusiasm. Lack of source material, of course, prevents such an argument being applied to the lesser Inns of Chancery where, it has recently been pointed out, there was an educational exercise called a "report".[64] What this was is not known, but it would be quite natural for some basic instruction to be given on what to look for when attending a court hearing. But the internal evidence of the year books connects them with the Inns of Court, not Chancery, and their utility was in pleading, the business of the utter-barristers and benchers of the four greater Inns. All in all, it seems safer to associate the year books with Gray's Inn, Lincoln's Inn and the two Temples, and to explain that association in terms of the individual lawyers who collected the reports, and not of any decision or formal arrangement by the Inns.

Professor A. W. B. Simpson of the University of Kent has, however, suggested recently that there is good evidence in the year books that their purpose was essentially educational.[65] They contain "explanatory and critical notes, queries, apologies, explanations, exhortations to study and fatherly advice", indicating a "teacher of law instructing his pupils".[66] There is nothing intrinsically against the proposition that students as well as practising lawyers sought in the year books for *erudition*. A tutorial system operated in the Inns of Court and remarks such as "query well this pleading my son" could easily stem from it. But such "instructional" comments are few in comparison with the total number of annotations which are most simply explained as asides by the reporter or some later redactor; it is by no means uncommon, today, for a scholar's notes to be peppered with queries and *aides memoires*, while marginalia in books are all too frequent. A few of the year books comment are personal reflections, like the prayer in 1488 for a condemned felon or the lament in 1522 for the Duke of Buckingham.[67] Others throw doubt on the ruling of the court, as Michaelmas 1 Richard III, plea 2, which ends "Note that this was contrary to the opinion of many apprentices".[68] Michaelmas 2 Richard III plea 42 includes the cryptic, "Brown to the contrary, but I was not there", which along with the references such as "See Fairfax the younger of Gray's Inn", can only be a memo to consult the relevant counsel if necessary, an unlikely invitation to extend to students.[69] Many comments give the professional opinion of the reporter. In Trinity 4 Henry VII he noted that he agreed with Kebell; in Hilary 5 Henry VII he recorded his doubts about a king's bench case, "But query, for it seems to me that . . .".[70] Similarly, the many *nota*, *quaere* and *stude bene* are more signposts for the reporter's own guidance than helps to students. To recapitulate, some comments in year books are probably educational in origin, but the majority seem to fit better the suggestion that they were made by lawyers in the course of their professional work. The year books were essentially for practitioners, not pupils.

IX

One final test which has to be met by any hypothesis about the later year books is that it should explain the decline of the year books in the sixteenth century. No published books cover the years from 21 Henry VII to 12 Henry VIII (1506–20), and after a brief revival, the series comes to a final end with the volume for 27 Henry VIII (1535–6). But if year books give the impression of existing as a regularly produced series largely because of the intervention of printers like Tottell, the ending of the series is a matter for the book market, not law reporting. Lawyers continued to produce material in year book form throughout the century, but this simply was not printed. It was worth publishing recent year book texts as late as the 1540s when volumes for 1526, 1534 and 1535 were put on the market, and Tottell produced his discoveries from Henry VII's reign in 1555. But pleading was changing, and lawyers came to prefer a new way of commenting on cases. As S. E. Thorne says,

> What was wanted was something more informative than the argument between judge and counsel leading to the formation of an issue, . . . the future lay with reports in another form.[71]

There was no sudden collapse of an organised system of year book production; no such system existed. There was no sudden decline in reporting, only the style was gradually changed. The year book reporters and the early law reporters were one and the same, practising advocates making notes of such cases as they wished, for their own guidance. "The year books", P. H. Winfield concluded in 1925,

> had ceased on the one hand to answer the requirements of lawyers, and on the other hand they were being replaced by books that could do this.[72]

The epitaph is undramatic but just.

*   *   *

The later year books are unprepossessing to a degree, which goes far to explain their neglect. But if the hypothesis advanced here is well-founded, then their "hopeless corruption" is itself an indication of the busy world from which they came, the world of the court. To adopt the terminology of the literary historian, the later year books represent "the foul papers" of the legal profession.[73]

NOTES

* This paper was the substance of an article "The Purpose and Making of the later Year Books", printed later in (1973) 89 LQR 64–86, and appears here by kind permission of the Editor.

[1] *Early English Legal Literature* (Cambridge, 1958), 111.

[2] *Ibid.* 114.

[3] ed. Chrimes (Cambridge, 1942), 114.

[4] YB (ed. Pynson, *c.* 1505) 5 H.7 [Pasch. pl.1, f.22], (sig. h1ᵛ). The reference has been altered, but sig. g6ʳ clearly gives A° xxxiij.

[5] YB 5 H.7, Pasch. p.7, f.25.

[6] YB 11 H.7, Mich. pl.12, f.4. The date, Michaelmas 1494, is incorrect; the case was prior to Townshend's death in September 1493.

[7] A. W. B. Simpson, "The Source and Function of the later Year Books" (1971) 87 LQR 95–8.

[8] YB 11 H.7, Hil. pl.11, f.15. For the uncertainty in the date, see p. 142, below.

[9] YB 13 H.7, Pasch. pl.9 f.23.

[10] YB 5 H.7, Pasch. pl.1, f.20.

[11] YB 9 H.7, Trin. pl.2, f.1.

[12] YB 9 H.7, Mich. pl.3, f.7.

[13] YB 10 H.7, Trin. pl.5, f.26.

[14] YB 11 H.7, Hil. pl.13, ff.16–17.

[15] YB 3 H.7, Mich. pl.30, f.15.

[16] YB 4 H.7, Mich. pl.1, f.16. Newton became a judge in 1438, by which time Fairfax was already in practice.

[17] YB 11 H.7, Hil. pl.11, f.15

[18] YB 21 H.7, Hil. pl.30, f.19.

[19] *Early Literature* 112. The notion that the year books were "memory", not "precedent", helps to explain the paradox that lawyers owned relatively small numbers of law books [E. W. Ives, "A Lawyer's Library in 1500" (1969) 85 LQR 108] but that texts were highly valued [A. W. B. Simpson, "The Circulation of Yearbooks in the Fifteenth Century" (1957) 73 LQR 492–505].

[20] YB 13 H.7, Pasch. pl.9, f.23.

[21] YB 9 H.7, Mich. pl.1, f.6.

[22] YB 27 H.8, Trin. pl.21, f.23.

[23] W. C. Bolland, *A Manual of Year Book Studies* (Cambridge, 1925), 61. For Henry VII, L. W. Abbott has traced one contemporary manuscript, plus a single year in another: *Law Reporting in England, 1485–1585* (London, 1973), 11, 17, 256.

[24] T. F. T. Plucknett, *Year Book 13 Richard II* (1948) 7 Ames Foundn xiv, xv. Pynson published 1–8 Henry VII conjecturally in 1505, but possibly as early as 1502.

[25] STC 9928.5, Harvard Law Library. The collation is A⁶, a⁶, b⁴ (b⁴ wanting), B⁶ (B⁶ wanting), c⁶ (c⁶ wanting), C⁴, d⁶, D⁶, E⁶, f⁴ (f⁴ wanting), G⁶, g⁶, h⁶, H⁶, i⁶, k⁶, J⁶, K⁸, L⁶, M⁴, N⁴, O⁶, P⁶, but the gatherings are wrongly bound for A°5 and should run G, H, g, h, i, k.

[26] G1—Michaelmas, g5—Easter, H3—Hilary, i5ᵛ—Trinity. A°6 has three terms: J1—Easter, J2ᵛ—Trinity, K4ᵛ—Michaelmas (see below, note 37). L1 is headed Michaelmas 7 Henry VII and O1 Trinity 8 Henry VII.

[27] The most obvious examples are the runs of short *nota.*

[28] Bryan appears 254 times, Vavasour 188 times, but many of these when a justice. In A° 2, 3, and 4, when the careers of Kebell and Vavasour at the bar overlapped, Kebell is noticed 42 times, Vavasour 23 times.

[29] YB 16 H.7: Kebell—Mich. pl. 1–7, 9, 10; Hil. pl. 1, 3; Pasch. pl.1–4, 6, 9–11; Trin. pl.1–5B, 9, 11–13. Hussey—Trin. pl.17. Townshend—Mich. pl.2, 7.

[30] These calculations omit cases (seven) where no names are given.

[31] YB 15 H.7, Mich. pl.1, f.13; pl.13, f.17. The latter case also mentions *Catesby Justice* and must therefore be later than November 1481.

[32] Cases without names (66) are omitted from the count.

[33] STC 9920.

[34] The following is based on J. Nicholson, *Register of Manuscript Year Books*, and some examination of the Pynson edition *c.* 1505 (STC 9928.5) and the Redman edition *c.* 1530 (STC 9929) of A° 1–8 Henry VII, and the Tottell 1555 edition of A° 1–16, 20 & 21. However, the revision of STC now in progress lists many year book editions not in Nicholson, and M. Jacques Beauregard is currently surveying the bibliographical history of the later year books. Hence these conclusions are both provisional and tentative. Abbott, *Law Reporting* 14–19, discusses the relationship of certain year book editions for Henry VII.

35 YB 3 H.7, Mich. pl.4, f.12 to pl.31, f.16.
36 YB 3 H.7, Hil. pl.7, f.2, Pasch. pl.3, f.5 (sig. C2, dl); 5 H.7, Hil. pl.4, f.11 (sig. H4ᵛ).
37 YB 6 H.7, Mich. pl.11, f.12, Hil. pl.1, f.13 (sig. K4ᵛ, K5). The term division is a later insertion. The 1679
   edition follows Pynson for the Easter term (sig. J1 to J2ᵛ), but Trinity and Michaelmas to pl.9, f.11
   appear in Pynson as Trinity term (sig. J3 to K4ᵛ); Michaelmas from pl.10, f.12 to the end of Hilary at
   f.16 appears in Pynson as Michaelmas (sig. K4ᵛ to K8) with no Hilary term at all.
38 Except for Aº 11, the numbering was well established by Tottell's day: Abbot, *Law Reporting* 18.
39 Abbot, *Law Reporting* 14–19, 35, 59–61, also argues for the determining rôle of the printer, especially
   Pynson.
40 Most of these additions are references to other cases, but YB 3 H.7, Mich. pl.2, f.11, "R. Vide P. 5 H.
   7 fo. 25", replaces Pynson sig. d6ᵛ: "*Et postea Mich. Anno vij aduic' q' l' dd' rec' v's labbe &c.*"
41 YB 8 H.7, Mich. pl.4, f.8 (sig. P1ᵛ).
42 YB 15 H.7, Trin. pl.9, f.9.
43 Cf. A. W. B. Simpson, "Keilwey's Reports, Temp. Henry VII and Henry VIII" (1957) 73 LQR 91–2.
44 The frequent offer by lawyers to produce books in support of their plea (see above, p. 138) is congruent
   with this suggestion; that the offer could produce other books in rebuttal again throws doubt on the
   existence of a recognised text.
45 A. W. B. Simpson, "The Reports of John Spelman" (1956) 72 LQR 336–8 includes some discussion of
   the relationship of Hargrave 388 to the original reports of Spelman. Spelman's reporting is currently
   being edited by Dr J. H. Baker for the Selden Society.
46 *Relationes quorundem casuum selectorum ex libris Roberti Keilwey* (ed. J. Croke, London, 1602); this is
   identical with the better known 1688 edition, entitled *Reports d'Ascuns Cases . . . seliges hors des papieres
   de Robert Keilwey*: 73 LQR 95 ff.
47 *Ibid.* 103 n.15; see above, p. 142.
48 YB 5 Ed.4, Mich. pl.6, f.6: "*de son report demesne quant il fuit serjeaunt en temps Richard Newton*".
   Moyle became a serjeant in 1443, Newton died in 1449. It may be significant that Kebell carried with
   him "a boke in French wreten in parchment", 85 LQR 109.
49 87 LQR 114–15. Townshend read for the second time in 1468, hence for the first time *c.* Autumn 1462.
50 Entries frequently conclude with the name *Pollarde* or [f.31] *quod nota Pollarde.* For additions, see e.g.
   f.10ᵛ. As originally copied, cases are normally in the correct order of terms within the year, but in Aº 14
   [ff.23 ff.] the blank spaces have been filled with later entries for that year, but in random order of terms.
   But cf. Simpson, 72 LQR 336, suggesting that the gaps indicate an incomplete manuscript.
51 British Museum Hargrave 388, ff. 131ᵛ–132ᵛ.
52 Thorne, *Readings* 71 SS xlvi–xlvii.
53 Hargrave 388, f.57: *vide bon case . . . en 14 h 4, f.2; 7 E 4, f.19; 21 E 4, f.96 Pollarde;* 73 LQR 496. Abbott
   shows this co-operation existed later, *Law Reporting* 44ff.
54 YB 6 H.7, Pasch. pl.1, f.1 (sometimes incorrectly cited as 5 H.7 Pasch. pl.1, f.41), pl.3, f.2; Trin. pl.5, f.6.
55 YB 5 H.7, Mich. pl.22, f.10, Hil. pl.1, f.10 (sig. H3).
56 YB 7 H.7, Trin. pl.1, f.16 (sig. N4).
57 YB 4 H.7, Pasch. pl.4, f.7 (sig. D6).
58 In the latter case the inn would be the Inner Temple, where Kebell did teach even after becoming a
   serjeant. Thorne, *Readings* 71 SS xlvi–xlviii, and below n.60.
59 It is noticeable that parties named in later year books are often those connected with the legal profession.
60 YB 13 H.7, Hil. pl.6, f.28.
61 *Reports d'Ascuns Cases*, 20 H.7, Mich. pl.4, f.55ᵛ.
62 YB 20 H.7, Mich. pl.10, f.3.
63 G. J. Turner, *Year Book 4 Edward II* (1911) 26 SS xxxi–xxxv.
64 87 LQR 104. "Reporting" was supposed to be performed by memory at Clement's Inn; that this rule
   was passed, banning the use of "book", suggests that a "report" was first written out.
65 87 LQR 94–118; Abbott, *Law Reporting* 32–5, also supposes, but in more general terms, an educational
   element in year book production.
66 87 LQR 111.
67 YB 3 H.7, Pasch. pl.5, f.7; 13 H.8, Pasch. pl.1, f.11.
68 YB 1 R.3, Mich. pl.2, f.4.
69 YB 2 R.3, Mich. pl.42, f.16.
70 YB 5 H.7, Mich. pl.22, f.9.
71 S. E. Thorne, "English Law and the Renaissance", *La Storia de diritto nel quadro delle scienze storiche*
   (Florence, 1966), 444.
72 P. H. Winfield, *The Chief Sources of English Legal History* (Cambridge, Mass., 1925; reprint, New York,
   1972), 171; Holdsworth, HEL v.357–71, argued also for a continuum of year books and reports.
73 Since this paper was read and first published, some of the material has been discussed in the first two
   chapters of Abbott, *Law Reporting.* The author had no opportunity to take account of this paper, nor
   perhaps of the detailed argument in A. W. B. Simpson's article. "The Source and Function of the later
   Year Books" (1971) 87 LQR 94–118, to which the LQR version of this paper is a reply. Abbott surveys
   the publication of the later year books in more detail than is attempted above, but also concludes that
   the vicissitudes and style of these volumes should be attributed to the influence of the printing trade;
   emphasis, however, is put on Richard Pynson rather than Richard Tottell. On the purpose and production of the year books Abbott is mainly in sympathy with Simpson; their intention was "to instruct
   students and junior barristers" (p.60) and he attributes their production to utter-barristers concerned
   with the educational work of the Inns of Court. On the relationship between year books and reports, he
   sees the two existing side by side, the year books produced by younger men for circulation and the reports
   by more senior lawyers responding to the need for private collections of up-to-date judicial decisions.
   Dr Abbott's main concern is with the established reporters from Bendlowes onwards, and his survey of
   300 or so manuscript reports of the sixteenth century makes his book an important one. But I see no
   need to revise the hypothesis presented in this paper.

Bibliographical Abbreviations

The common abbreviations for Law Reports (which can be traced in ER) and other comparable legal works are not included; nor are abbreviations used only within reasonable distance of the full reference given in the same paper.

AALH   Association of American Law Schools, *Select Essays in Anglo-American Legal History*, 3 volumes, Boston, Mass., and Cambridge, 1907–9.

AJLH   *American Journal of Legal History*.

Abbott, *Law Reporting*   L. W. Abbott, *Law Reporting in England 1485–1585*. London, 1973.

BM   British Museum.

BNB   F. W. Maitland (ed.), *Bracton's Note Book*. Cambridge, 1887.

Bayne and Dunham, *Council Cases*   C. G. Bayne and W. H. Dunham, *Select Cases in the Council of Henry VII* (1956/1958) 75 SS.

Bedford's CPB   Thomas Bedford's Common Place Book, Admiralty Registry MS. (see p. 108, n.13).

Bills in Eyre   W. C. Bolland (ed.), *Select Bills in Eyre, 1292–1333* (1914) 30 SS.

Bolland, see *Bills in Eyre, Eyre of Kent*.

Bracton   *Bracton de Legibus et Consuetudinibus Angliæ;* folio references to the *editio princeps* of 1569, Woodbine-Thorne to the edition by G. E. Woodbine (New Haven, 1915–42), re-issued with introduction and translation by S. E. Thorne (Cambridge, Mass., 1968–   ).

Brevia Placitata   G. J. Turner (ed.), *Brevia Placitata* (1947/1951) 66 SS.

CCR   *Calendar of Close Rolls* (HMSO).

CChW   *Calendar of Chancery Warrants* (HMSO).

CLJ   *Cambridge Law Journal*.

CP, see Maitland.

CPR   *Calendar of Patent Rolls* (HMSO).

Cam, *Eyre of London*   Helen M. Cam (ed.), *The Eyre of London 1321* i (1968) 85 SS; ii (1969) 86 SS.

Cam, *Studies*   Helen M. Cam, *Studies in the Hundred Rolls*. Oxford Studies in Legal and Social History, vol. 6, 1921.

Complete Peerage   G[eorge] E[dward] C[okayne], *The Complete Peerage*. 8 volumes, 1887–98. Second edn by Vicary Gibbs and others, 12 vv. London, 1910–59.

Concise History   T. F. T. Plucknett, *A Concise History of the Common Law*. 5th edn, London and Boston, Mass., 1956.

DL   Duchy of Lancaster (PRO).

DNB   *The Dictionary of National Biography*.

Davies, *Discovery* Sir John Davies, *Discovery of the true causes why Ireland was never entirely subdued*. London, 1612; reprint, Shannon, 1969.

Delisle, *Enquêtes* L. Delisle (ed.), *Les Enquêtes Administratives du Règne de Saint Louis.* Recueil des Historiens des Gaules et de la France, tome 24, Paris, 1904.

EHR *English Historical Review.*

EL = El

ER *The English Reports* [reprints of law reports from before the establishment of the semi-official *Law Reports* in 1865]. 178 volumes, Edinburgh and London, 1900–32.

Early Literature T. F. T. Plucknett, *Early English Legal Literature.* Cambridge, 1958.

Early Registers Elsa de Haas and G. D. G. Hall (ed.), *Early Registers of Writs* (1970) 87 SS.

El Ellesmere MS. in the Henry E. Huntington Library, San Marino, California.

Elton, *Studies* G. R. Elton, *Studies in Tudor and Stuart Politics and Government.* 2 volumes, Cambridge, 1974.

Exton, *Dicæologie* John Exton, *The maritime Dicæologie, or sea jurisdiction of England.* London, 1664. Second edn, London, 1755.

Eyre of Kent *Year Book of the Eyre of Kent, 6 & 7 Edward II,* i (1909/1910) 24 SS; ii (1912) 27 SS; iii (1913) 29 SS.

Fifoot, *Sources* C. H. S. Fifoot, *History and Sources of the Common Law, Tort and Contract.* London, 1949.

Fleta Folio references are to the *editio princeps* by John Selden (1647); latest edition (in progress), ed. H. G. Richardson and G. O. Sayles (1953/55) 72 SS, (1972) 89 SS.

HCA High Court of Admiralty (PRO).

HEL W. S. Holdsworth, *A History of English Law.* London, i (7th edn, with an introductory essay and additions by S. B. Chrimes) 1956; ii and iii (3rd edn) 1923; iv–xvi, 1924–66.

HJ *Historical Journal.*

HMSO His/Her Majesty's Stationery Office.

IHS *Irish Historical Studies.*

IJNS *Irish Jurist* (New Series).

JI Justices Itinerant (PRO).

KB King's Bench (PRO).

King's Bench Cases G. O. Sayles (ed.), *Select Cases in the Court of King's Bench,* i (Edward I; 1936) 55 SS; ii (Edward I; 1938) 57 SS; iii (Edward I; 1939) 58 SS; iv (Edward II; 1955/1957) 74 SS; v (Edward III; 1957/1958) 76 SS; vi (Edward III; 1965) 82 SS; vii (Richard II, Henry IV, Henry V; 1971) 88 SS.

Kiralfy, *Source Book* A. K. R. Kiralfy, *A Source Book of English Law.* London, 1957.

LJ *Lords Journals* (for which see Maurice F. Bond, *Guide to the Records of Parliament;* HMSO, 1971).

LQR *Law Quarterly Review.*

Linc RS Lincoln Record Society.

Lond RS London Record Society.

Lot & Fawtier F. Lot and R. Fawtier, *Histoire des institutions françaises au Moyen Age.* Institutions royales, Paris, 1958.

Maitland CP H. A. L. Fisher (ed.), *The Collected Papers of Frederic William Maitland.* 3 volumes, Cambridge, 1911.

Maitland, see also PM, SHE.

Milsom, *Foundations* S. F. C. Milsom, *Historical Foundations of the Common Law*. London, 1969.

NILQ *Northern Ireland Law Quarterly.*

Nicholson, *Register of Year Book Manuscripts* J. Nicholson, *Register of Manuscripts of Year Books extant.* London (Historical Manuscripts Commission for Selden Society) 1956.

OED *Oxford English Dictionary.*

PBA *Proceedings of the British Academy.*

PM F. Pollock and F. W. Maitland, *The History of English Law before the time of Edward I.* 2nd edn, Cambridge, 1898 (several times reprinted, most recently with new introduction and select bibliography by S. F. C. Milsom, 1968).

PRO Public Record Office: references are to classes of documents.

Plucknett, see *Concise History, Early Literature.*

Procedure without Writ H. G. Richardson and G. O. Sayles, *Select Cases of Procedure without Writ under Henry III* (1941) 60 SS.

Procter, *Pesquisa* E. S. Procter, *The Judicial Use of the Pesquisa in León and Castile*, EHR Supplement no. 2.

Prynne, *Animadversions* William Prynne, *Brief Animadversions . . . on the Fourth Part of the Institutes.* London, 1669.

RHS Camden Royal Historical Society Camden Series; Roman numerals after the abbreviation indicate the number of the series.

RS Rolls Series (Year Book editions).

RSAI Jnl *Journal of the Royal Society of Antiquaries of Ireland* (begun as *Transactions of the Kilkenny Archæological Society*).

Richardson and Sayles, *Rotuli* H. G. Richardson and G. O. Sayles, *Rotuli Parliamentorum hactenus inediti* (1935) 51 RHS Camden/III.

Richardson, see also Fleta, *Procedure without Writ.*

Rot. Parl. [England, Parliament], *Rotuli Parliamentorum.* 6 volumes, London, 1767–77.

Royal Writs R. C. van Caenegem, *Royal Writs in England from the Conquest to Glanvill* (1958–9/1959) 77 SS.

Rymer, *Foedera* Thomas Rymer, *Foedera.* London, 1704–32. Reprint, the Hague, 1739–45 (reprinted, Farnborough, 1967). Record Commission edition, 1816–69. For an account of the editions, see Thomas Duffus Hardy, *Syllabus (in English) of the Documents . . . in . . . "Rymer's Fædera"* i (London, 1869) lxxxi–xcviii; David C. Douglas, *English Scholars 1660–1730* (2nd edn, London, 1951) 229–31.

SC Special Collections (PRO).

SHE Helen M. Cam (ed.), *Selected Historical Essays of F. W. Maitland.* Cambridge and Selden Society, 1957.

SP State Paper Office (PRO).

SR *The Statutes of the Realm . . . From Original Records and Authentic Manuscripts.* London, 1810–24; reprint, London, 1963.

SS Selden Society (regular series).

SSSS Selden Society Supplementary Series.

STC A. W. Pollard and G. R. Redgrave, *A short-title catalogue of books . . . 1475–1640.* London, 1926 (reprint, Oxford, 1946).

Sayles, see Fleta, *King's Bench Cases, Procedure without Writ*, Richardson.

Siete Partidas   Los Codigos Españoles: Codigo de las Siete Partidas. Madrid, 1848. A list of the contents of Las Siete Partidas is in E. N. van Kleffens, *Hispanic Law until the end of the Middle Ages* (Edinburgh, 1968) 291–373.

StCh   Star Chamber Proceedings (PRO).

TRHS   *Transactions of the Royal Historical Society;* Roman numerals after the abbreviation indicate the number of the series.

Thorne, *Readings*   S. E. Thorne, *Readings and Moots at the Inns of Court in the fifteenth century*, i (1952/1954) 71 SS.

Tout and Johnstone, *State Trials*   T. F. Tout and Hilda Johnstone, *State Trials of the Reign of Edward I* (1906) 9 RHS Camden/III.

UL   University Library.

WHR   *Welsh History Review.*

Wallace, *Reporters*   J. W. Wallace, *The Reporters*. 4th edn, Boston, Mass., 1882.

Wilts RS   Wiltshire Record Society.

Wynne, *Jenkins*   William Wynne, *Life of Sir L. Jenkins*. London, 1724.